Why All People Suffer

Paul Chaloux, Ph.D.

Why All People Suffer

How a Loving God Uses
Suffering to Perfect Us

SOPHIA INSTITUTE PRESS
Manchester, New Hampshire

Nihil obstat: Reverend Joseph D. Bergida, *Censor Deputatus*
Imprimatur: +Michael F. Burbidge, Bishop of Arlington
February 18, 2021

The *nihil obstat* and *imprimatur* are official declarations that a book or pamphlet is free of doctrinal or moral error. There is no implication that those who have granted the *nihil obstat* and the *imprimatur* agree with the content, opinions, or statements expressed therein.

Sophia Institute Press
Box 5284, Manchester, NH 03108
1-800-888-9344

www.SophiaInstitute.com

Sophia Institute Press® is a registered trademark of Sophia Institute.

paperback ISBN 978-1-64413-421-4

ebook ISBN 978-1-64413-422-1

Library of Congress Control Number: 2020952791

First printing

To all the souls who willingly embrace their
suffering for the redemption of others:
may their joy be complete
in the presence of God.

Contents

Section III
Answering the Call to Share in the Nature of God

Preface

The development of this theology is the culmination of an amazing journey, one that I neither planned nor anticipated, yet felt strangely compelled to take. In fact, I feel like I was being driven to it by circumstances largely outside my control, with numerous people contributing to it, seemingly unwittingly. The journey seemed to begin with a very vivid dream in May 2013, but in retrospect, the seeds had been planted long before that. In May 2013, my oldest daughter Kathy graduated from Cornell University, and I was impressed by one of her professors who had given up a lucrative job in industry to go back to school and teach the next generation.

At the time, I was in a similar situation, having worked for one of the great American corporations for more than thirty years, the last decade of which was spent planning the manufacturing strategy for its most capital-intensive division. I was unhappy in my job, however, for a variety of reasons. The most significant of these reasons was that the company had decided to divest itself of the division that I had spent my whole career building up. In a way, it was not surprising that following that graduation, I had a vivid dream telling me that I, too, should give up my lucrative position and go back to school and teach.

There was a twist, however: it would not be to teach what I had learned in my professional life.

Back in the summer of 2000, I had experienced another overwhelming sequence of events that had begun with a sacramental confession of sins that I no longer remember. What I do remember was the penance: attend a weekday Mass. Although I was a conscientious Sunday communicant, I had never attended a weekday Mass, and for some reason I felt a trepidation to do so. I hesitated for a few days, but I felt compelled to go because I told the priest that I would. I finally went, and it felt profoundly right to me. I continued to go, day after day, until the present. A few months later, when my daughter Kathy was about to enter the fourth grade, the parish put out a call for catechists. I volunteered.

I had never taught anything before, but teaching came naturally to me. I was astonished, however, by how little I actually knew about the faith, despite having read the Bible daily since the sixth grade, which represented a period of about twenty-five years by that time. I found myself learning from the textbook, just like the students did. I had never even prayed the Rosary. I embarked on a program to correct that deficiency, reading voraciously on Church doctrine and the lives of the saints and even engaging in online apologetics. I became a more effective catechist, and two years later, I took on a second weekly class, in part so that I could also teach my three sons. Some years later Sr. Marie Pappas, who also happened to have a nation-wide cable radio show, took over the school of religion in our parish and began encouraging me to expand my catechetical reach beyond the parish. It was her voice that I heard in the dream telling me to become a teacher of the teachers, but in the field of catechetics.

The dream itself was vivid and strangely compelling, not that I can remember anything about it other than the message to quit my job, get a doctorate in catechetics, and teach the teachers. I talked it over with my wife Sue, and she was very supportive; she had fortuitously taken a job recently which allowed her to work from home, making the journey toward obtaining my doctorate economically feasible if we had to move. I proceeded to investigate what it would take to get the required education and took the college boards, on which I did surprisingly well, despite a thirty-plus-year lag in academic studies. I soon found that there were only three Catholic schools on the East Coast with doctoral degrees in catechetics or religious education: Boston College, Catholic University, and Fordham. I went to Washington, D.C., and had an interview with Sr. Margaret Schreiber, who ran the program at Catholic University, and she graciously explained the basics of what I was getting into. At the very least, I was going to have to earn a master's degree in an allied field even to be considered. I appreciated the information and developed a good rapport with her that I believe made the interviewing process easier for both of us.

Equally gracious was Harold (Bud) Horell, the professor at Fordham who ran the online religious education program. He offered me a slot in his course entitled "Introduction to Moral Development," and he told me that if I did well and wanted to continue, I could enter the online master's program that would take approximately four years to complete. I took the class, found it engaging, and did well enough to be accepted into the program, which I completed in fourteen months. To proceed at that pace, I found it necessary to reduce my work schedule from full-time to two days per week, which fortunately was approved by the management team despite the intensity of the work. By the end of 2014, I had completed my master's work, including a thesis on how to teach morality to youth and young adults, and began to apply to doctoral programs in both catechetics and moral theology to pursue that avenue. I applied to ten programs in total, and I was accepted into one: Catholic University's catechetics program, in which I was the only entering doctoral student in my cohort. It was run by Sr. Margaret Schreiber, the nun whom I had contacted eighteen months earlier.

I was happy to be accepted because Catholic University felt comfortable to me from my first visit. It was also convenient from a family perspective, since I grew up in the area and my mother found herself needing more help since my father died in 2011. In the spring of 2015, I accepted the invitation to study at Catholic; put my New York house on the market; bought a house with my brother Richard in Arlington, Virginia; and notified my employers that I would be retiring at the end of July, for which I had fortunately become eligible just a few months earlier. It was at this point that I was diagnosed with Parkinson's Disease. I was told by my doctors in New York, "It is not a death sentence. You will have five to ten years of reasonable functionality." Having already made a series of commitments, there really was no choice but to push ahead.

This diagnosis was also not my first significant medical event. I was born with a congenital heart defect that left me seriously fatigued after any physical activity, and I had undergone open-heart surgery at Boston Children's Hospital in 1965 at the age of five. It was not without complications (my heart stopped twice on the operating table), nor was it successful in correcting all of the problems. I spent my youth enduring extreme fatigue whenever I exerted myself. This was finally corrected in July of 1977 with a second open-heart surgery at the same hospital, but it too had complications. My left arm was paralyzed during the operation, and I was told that there was nothing that could be done—but I was also told that half the time, people regain use of the limb through natural healing processes. I never doubted that the problem would resolve itself, and after six weeks, it did. I regained feeling, and then use, of the arm the week before I started my senior year in high school, all without any specific medical attention.

I was healthy for the next twenty-five years, or so I thought, until I came home from a family trip to California in 2002 to find sixteen urgent messages from my doctor on the answering machine. I had been diagnosed with Hepatitis C after a routine blood check before taking a statin drug to control a hereditary cholesterol problem. I was told that it could be potentially fatal, but that fortunately there was a new ribavirin-interferon drug protocol that was successful in resolving the virus in a high percentage of cases like mine. It had very harsh side effects, however, so I spent the next six months with severe nausea, headaches, and tremors, but it did resolve the issue.

However, the drug protocol came with its own complications, as well. During the last month of treatment, I lost forty pounds off an already thin frame and found myself in the hospital after passing out. After a week of testing, I was diagnosed with celiac disease, an autoimmune disease in which the body's natural defenses attack the person's small intestines in the presence of gluten, a protein found in wheat. Fortunately, this disease can be controlled by avoiding wheat, which is inconvenient at times but not a significant issue. What was an issue, however, was that the experience left me with was severe and unrelenting nausea that lasted until 2015, despite the efforts of many medical experts. Just as I was about to enter Catholic University, my wife found a book by a doctor in Rye, New York, that suggested that I had small-intestine bacterial imbalances that could be corrected with some supplements that she sold. I tried them, and surprisingly enough, they gave me some relief just at the time I was embarking upon my doctoral journey.

I started at Catholic in August 2015, and I really had no idea as to what was required of me. I was operating under the assumption that my goal was to develop a program on how to teach morality for future catechists. I was a generation older than my fellow students, and even older than most of the professors, but that was never a problem. What *was* a problem was that as an engineering major, I had never experienced the liberal arts training that is fundamental to doctoral studies in theology at a research university like Catholic. Fortunately for me, as the only doctoral candidate in catechetics, I had an independent study class my first semester with Rev. Dr. Emmanuel Magro, a priest from Malta. He took the time to teach me how to research and write an acceptable academic paper. Because I was minoring in moral theology, I was splitting my course load equally between the two disciplines, which was also fortuitous.

Roughly a week or so after starting my doctoral studies, I found a neurologist in the area, Dr. Natalia Kayloe, to help manage my Parkinson's symptoms. I was dumbfounded when in the initial interview, upon learning that I was studying at Catholic University, she asked me why people suffer. I, of course, had never given the question any serious thought, and so I told her I was not prepared to answer that question. She encouraged me to pursue it, explaining that doctors confront this question every day, but have no answer to give. I was non-committal, but the question stuck in my head.

Over the next year, I used the twenty-five-page essays assigned in my doctoral classes to explore the concept more fully, and I became convinced that it was a viable topic for me to pursue if

I were studying moral theology. Since I had taken an equal load of moral theology and catechetics classes, I inquired whether I could have a dual major. The answer came back that I could not, but also that the catechetics program was losing its director, so there was no one left to administer my doctoral program. Instead, based on my course work in moral theology to date, they offered me the opportunity to switch to the program that I had been denied entrance to at every school to which I had applied (and deservedly so, since I had none of the pre-requisites). Furthermore, one of the bright young professors, Dr. Paul Scherz, for whom I had written my initial essay on suffering, made it clear that he was willing to become my advisor on the project, which again was fortuitous because he has since been very effective in compensating for my academic shortcomings. He, along with the other members of my doctoral committee, was invaluable in giving me the necessary insight, critique, and encouragement to complete this work.

From that point on, I have been consumed with the topic of suffering. As my wife will attest, I regularly get inspiration at four in the morning; the bulk of this text has been written when I should be asleep, but I cannot help myself. I have drawn insight from my own struggles and from those around me, particularly my mother, Dolores Chaloux, who has suffered mightily for the last few years following an accident in an assisted living facility that caused third-degree burns. Her ability to overcome extreme pain and bodily degradation has been a true inspiration.

I have also received tremendous encouragement and insight from the students I taught at Catholic during this process, learning as much from them as they did from me. In 2019 I was teaching Freshman Theology as I wrote the doctoral dissertation that provided the background for this book, and the students in the fall and spring sections were highly engaged in the project on their own time, helping me fine-tune the arguments. In the 2020 spring semester, I was assigned to teach three sections of Nursing Bioethics that allowed me to teach this theology as part of the curriculum, and the nursing students collectively taught me how it could be best applied to their vocation, for which I am highly grateful. The greatest encouragement, though, has come from my family, and most specifically my wife, who had to sacrifice her comfortable life in order for me to pursue a dream, which I recognize was a huge leap of faith.

It is unclear where this journey will lead. There seems to be a destiny to it that I do not understand because so many things have broken just the right way to make it reach this point. Every decision, except to cooperate, has seemingly been made for me: the choice of schools; my major; my topic of study; my advisor. I think this situation applies to a lot of people, and one never knows why they are called to do certain things. I am sure that the priest who sent me off to my first weekday Mass had no idea how it would affect me, nor did my doctor anticipate that a simple question would change my academic (and maybe even my life's) trajectory. It is possible that this journey was only for my benefit, but then again, one can never know the extent of one's role in God's plan. As my personal story shows, seemingly small things said or done unwittingly by one person can radically change the life of another. Who knows? Perhaps the entire reason for this journey is to change one person's perspective about God, and maybe that person will influence others. That thought has certainly given my suffering purpose, and I embrace it when I do not feel well, which makes the suffering much more bearable.

Preface

Suffering has a way of turning a person inward, toward where God resides. I know that God takes no delight in human discomfort, but I see now that it is unavoidable when breaking humans of the vices with which they have become comfortable in order to set us firmly on the path of redemption. I also have come to understand that God must truly love us if He puts this much effort into keeping us on the path to joy. This is, after all, the same God Who waits anxiously for the Prodigal Son to return (Luke 15:11-32). I say to all who may happen to read this: God has a plan for you, and even if you cannot see where it is going, trust Him and follow where He leads you. It will be a remarkable journey for you, as well.

Section I

Rethinking Suffering

1

Suffering as a Detector of Evil

"Why do we suffer?" It is a question we all ask at some point in our lives. Sometimes, when seeing all the suffering around us, we ask in a generic, philosophical way: "Why is there suffering in the world?" However, if it affects us directly, the question becomes personal: "Why am I suffering?" It also comes naturally with the more urgent follow-up: "How do I make it stop?"

"Suffering" is the term we use to describe the worst experiences of our lives. Dr. Eric Cassell, writing from a medical perspective in 1991, recognizes that while physical pain is the primary image formed by people when they think of suffering, it is only one of many sources of human suffering.[1] Simply put, suffering is the sense of loss people feel when they are deprived of goods such as health, friends, family, possessions, and ultimately, union with God. It can be felt as pain, sorrow, loneliness, isolation, or a yearning for God, or a combination of these. In fact, whatever the initial source of suffering, whether it be from a physical, psychological, or social loss, there is a growing consensus that true suffering must consist of more than just physical pain but must also cause psychological distress and social isolation.

[1]   Eric J. Cassell, *The Nature of Suffering and the Goals of Medicine*, 2nd ed. (New York: Oxford, 2004), 31-40.

Cassell also argues convincingly that physical pain is not synonymous with suffering. He notes that while it is commonly believed that the greater the pain, the greater the suffering, this is often not the case.[2] He uses childbirth as an example of extreme pain that can be perceived by the mother as uplifting. In his experience, patients can writhe in pain from kidney stones but not experience it as suffering (by their own statements) because "they know what it is." His best example of this phenomenon is that when a person, through great pain or deprivation, is brought closer to a cherished goal, such as completing a marathon, he or she may experience a feeling of enormous triumph rather than suffering.

The fact that people experience suffering physically, psychologically, socially, and spiritually is a clear indication that our existence is threatened by needs beyond the material ones that result in physical pain. All of this can be experienced and discerned by those who suffer. People know when they need food because they feel hungry, when they suffer physical injury because they feel pain, when they are isolated from society because they feel lonely, and when they lack unity with God because they have a longing in the soul that for many is hard to discern but ultimately is the only need that lasts beyond the material world. When any of these losses becomes so great that it threatens our existence and forces changes in us and what we do, we are experiencing suffering.

Suffering threatens our social standing because it inhibits our ability to fulfill our normal social roles, and it can, in certain instances, make us totally dependent on others. True suffering is an intense experience. At the onset of World War II, French

[2] Cassell, *The Nature of Suffering*, 34-35.

philosopher Simone Weil described it as "an uprooting of life, a more or less attenuated equivalent of death, made irresistibly present to the soul by the attack or immediate apprehension of physical pain."[3] Indeed, when we can no longer do what is expected, it can appear as if our old selves are dead to our friends and families. This can lead them to grieve and even to be angry at us for changing, which adds to the burden of our suffering.

As if that were not bad enough, society often assumes that suffering is some kind of cosmic punishment for some unknown sin we committed against God or man. It is natural for us to ask, "What did I do to deserve this?" as we seek to justify ourselves and protect both our place in society and our sense of self-worth. Even more challenging to many people is the feeling that God has abandoned them. After all, how could an all-powerful and benevolent God allow such suffering to exist? If our earthly fathers protect us from harm, should we not expect the same from our Heavenly Father?

This is not a new concern. The Greek philosopher Epicurus identified the dilemma three centuries before the birth of Christ. He started out with the assumption that evil was opposed to God, and that if God did not have the power to stop evil, He would be weak. On the other hand, if He had the power but not the will to stop evil, then God would be envious.[4] Noting that God

---

[3]   Simone Weil, "The Love of God and Affliction" in *The Simone Weil Reader*, ed. George A. Panichas (New York: McKay, 1977), 440.

[4]   Lactantius, *"De Ira Dei,"* trans. William Fletcher. From *Ante-Nicene Fathers*, vol. 7, ed. Alexander Roberts, James Donaldson, and A. Cleveland Coxe (Buffalo, NY: Christian Literature Publishing Co., 1886). Rev. and ed. for New Advent by Kevin Knight, http://www.newadvent.org/fathers/0703.htm.

is neither weak nor envious, Epicurus could not understand how evil could exist. His logical conclusion was that one of his assumptions must be wrong: either God was not good, or was not all powerful, or perhaps God didn't care about His creation, or didn't exist at all. His logic has been appreciated and propagated over the last two millennia by many people who have also been disturbed by the evil around them and by the apparent failure of God to protect them from it.

In reality, Epicurus erred in developing the logic for his dilemma because, while he questioned his assumptions on the nature of God, he did not question his assumptions on the nature of evil and suffering. Had he had stronger faith in the goodness and power of God, Epicurus might have explored the other possibility: that evil and suffering could in some way be used by God to bring about good for mankind. This did not occur to Epicurus because in his theology, the goal of life is to find pleasure and to avoid pain, and these are things that are not compatible with suffering.[5] Yet, we can and should aspire to much higher goals than simply seeking pleasure. In fact, St. Peter tells us in his second epistle that God has promised that we can ultimately share in His divine nature, which leads to the joy of everlasting life with Him.[6]

St. Peter says that, to share in the divine nature, escaping from the corruption of this world, we need to "make every effort to supplement our faith with virtue, virtue with knowledge, knowledge with self-control, self-control with endurance, endurance

---

[5] David Konstan, "Epicurus," *The Stanford Encyclopedia of Philosophy* (2014), http://plato.stanford.edu/archives/sum2014/entries/epicurus/.

[6] 2 Peter 1:4.

with devotion, devotion with mutual affection, mutual affection with love."[7] He concludes that "in this way, entry into the eternal kingdom of our Lord and savior Jesus Christ will be richly provided to you."[8]

It should be made clear at this point that no human can share in the divine nature on his own. When St. Peter starts off his list with faith, it presupposes that we know that faith is a gift from God and that sharing in the divine nature requires us to ratify that faith through the sacraments of the Church (particularly Baptism and the Eucharist). As the *Catechism of the Catholic Church* puts it, "What faith confesses, the sacraments communicate: by the sacraments of rebirth, Christians have become 'children of God' and 'partakers of the divine nature.'"[9] What this means is that through the grace of the sacraments, people are enabled to believe in God, to hope in Him, and to love Him through the theological virtues; are given the power to live and act under the prompting of the Holy Spirit and can grow in goodness through the moral virtues.[10] These are all things beyond the capability of fallen man and require grace and the indwelling of the Holy Spirit. Quoting St. Athanasius, the *Catechism* affirms, "By the participation of the Spirit, we become communicants in the divine nature.... For this reason, those in whom the Spirit dwells are divinized.[11]

In fact, the Holy Spirit transforms us into the kind of people who emulate and follow Jesus, Who always did what was pleasing to the Father and always lived in perfect communion with

[7]   2 Peter 1:5-7.
[8]   2 Peter 1:11.
[9]   CCC 1692.
[10] CCC 1265.
[11] CCC 1988.

Him.[12] As such, the beatitude that leads to eternal life surpasses the understanding and power of man and comes from an entirely free gift of God, a supernatural grace that disposes man to enter into the divine joy.[13] Led by the Spirit to learn to love unconditionally, as God does, can also be described as sharing in the divine nature, for as John says, "God is love."[14]

Those who share in the divine nature will experience joy, one of the fruits of the Holy Spirit that forms in us as a prelude to eternal glory.[15] It is the term we use to describe the best experiences of our lives. The distinguished Dominican theologian Servais Pinckaers defines joy as "the direct effect of an excellent action, like the savor of a long task finally accomplished."[16] Said another way, to be joyful is to experience perfection, to share in the divine nature; in some sense, to become like God. It is God's reward for a job well done when we cooperate with His grace and follow His teachings and the example of Christ.

Most people naturally assume that because joy marks the best experiences in life and because suffering marks the worst, that the two are in opposition. They are not. As Pinckaers notes, becoming joyful is not like experiencing pleasure. Pleasure is a brief and superficial sensation caused by contact with some exterior good. It lasts only as long as that contact lasts. Joy, on the other hand, must be earned, born of trials, of pain endured, of sufferings accepted with courage and with love. It is also as lasting as the excellence that engendered it. Unlike pleasure,

---

[12] CCC 1693.
[13] CCC 1722.
[14] 1 John 1:8.
[15] CCC 1832.
[16] Servais Pinckaers, *Morality: The Catholic View*, trans. Michael Sherwin (South Bend, IN: St. Augustine's Press, 2003), 76.

joy grows by being shared, and repays sacrifices that were freely embraced.[17] Joy is not in opposition to suffering; it is the outcome of successfully meeting its challenges and completing its tasks. It is our reward for loving as God loves.

Joy and suffering can be thought of as co-equal tools of God: a divine carrot-and-stick combination, like that used to motivate horses. Suffering is the stick that is used to guide us to where the Master wants us to go. Joy is the carrot that is our reward when we get there. Everyone loves the carrot but hates the stick, but without the stick to guide us, it is much more difficult to earn the carrot.

The thought that God guides us with a stick might conjure up thoughts of an angry and vengeful God. However, this view must be wrong, because it contradicts the image of God that Jesus presents to us in the famous parable of the Prodigal Son in St. Luke's Gospel.[18] In this parable, Jesus portrays the father as remarkably patient with his son, who demands his inheritance early and strikes out on his own, quickly wasting all of it on prostitutes and a life of dissipation. This son, suffering now from a lack of resources in a foreign land, comes to realize that he would be better off as a slave in his father's house than as a free man on his own. He returns to his father, content to do so as a slave, but the father will have none of it. He loves his son so dearly and is so excited to have him back that he rushes to him, welcoming him with a great celebration and complete forgiveness, not concerned in the least about what the son had or had not done.

If the Father truly is as compassionate, loving, and forgiving as Jesus describes Him, then we need to re-evaluate how we think about suffering. Any true theology of suffering must be

[17] Ibid.
[18] Luke 15:11-32.

consistent with this understanding of the Father's love for all of His children. Suffering cannot be merely a punitive tool. It must be an instrument for God to use to reunite with His wayward progeny. Indeed, in the parable, it is suffering in the form of hunger that brings the young man to his senses and facilitates a return to his father. It also makes the son realize that his father loves him very much and provides everything he needs.[19] This is the ultimate role of suffering: to facilitate our return to our Heavenly Father, Who loves us more than we love ourselves, and in Whose presence we will find joy and fulfillment. It is how He calls us to return home to Him.

There are undoubtedly many objections to God using suffering, which we have just defined as the worst of all human experiences, to call us back to Him. The first of these might be why a loving Father would subject His Beloved Son to suffering for any reason, let alone a seemingly selfish reason: that He wanted His Son to be with Him. The parable can help us discern the answers to these questions and help further our understanding of the nature of suffering in God's plan for us.

The suffering that the Prodigal Son experiences in the parable is hunger. But hunger, like all suffering, is nothing more than a sensation that warns us of the presence of evil in our midst. In fact, hunger did not threaten the son; it warned him that he was starving to death and motivated him to return home to his father, who had what he needed. It is a lot like a smoke alarm in our house. When a fire is present, the alarm goes off in a very loud, piercing way to alert us to the threat. Although the alarm is extremely irritating, we recognize that the alarm itself is not dangerous to us, and that it needs to be unignorable in order to

---

[19] Luke 15:14-19.

alert us to the real threat. It motivates us to take action to save our lives and property. It is there to protect us, not to soothe us.

The same is true of suffering. It needs to be persistent and uncomfortable to warn us of the threat from evil and motivate us to take action to eliminate it. When we are hungry, it is not the feeling of hunger that is dangerous to our well-being; it is the lack of food, which is alleviated by attaining nourishment. Similarly, while breaking a leg is bad, the pain merely tells us that the break happened and motivates us to stay off it, allowing the leg to heal. When we are lonely, it is our need for companionship that is the problem, not the feeling of loneliness. Suffering itself is not evil: it is an evil-detector, put in place by a loving God to protect us from evil in the same way that a smoke detector is designed to protects us from fire.

Suffering is a gift from God, and is therefore a much more sophisticated tool than a smoke detector or a stick. It needs to be because evil is harder to detect than smoke, and it is far more damaging to the person than fire because evil affects the soul. In fact, not only does suffering allow us to detect evil, it protects us from it and perfects us. A few, short examples of everyday life will illustrate this point.

If a man drinks too much alcohol, he will get drunk and suffer a hangover the next day. The man, being chastened by his experience of suffering, deduces that the cause of it was too much drinking the previous night. He therefore does not drink the next night, and thus wakes up the following morning without a hangover. Suffering has taught the man that excess drinking is evil and that controlling his drinking is good because he will no longer suffer hangovers if he is moderate. Suffering initially protected him from further harm by motivating him not to drink in excess again. If the man habituates what he has learned, his moderation will improve him because he is practicing the virtue of temperance and therefore experiencing proper self-love.

This example also provides what many people will find to be a surprising outcome: that a hangover is a good thing for a person because it is both a warning of the evil of excessive drinking and a motivator to drink more temperately in the future. This is the paradox concerning alarms in general and suffering in particular. Suffering itself is a good and useful thing because it provides a warning that protects us from worse things that could happen. But the fact that we had to experience it is a bad thing because it means we have been exposed to an evil that threatens our existence. No one wants a throbbing headache and nausea, to be sure, and yet, following the logic of the value of an alarm, it is undeniably a good. This is true of every form of suffering: it is a warning of the existence of an evil and a motivator to seek the missing good. It is not evil in and of itself, but instead it is a detector of evil and a perfecter of humanity.

Some will undoubtedly object that there is no way that having a hangover can ever be a good thing. Perhaps they will say that there are other ways to teach a person not to drink excessively without causing the person to have a throbbing headache the next day. In fact, they are right. There are other ways to teach a person not to drink excessively; the most obvious way is to witness someone with a hangover. Unfortunately, while a warning like that might dissuade some from excessive drinking, a more forceful reminder is needed for others. Additionally, even if everyone exercised the required restraint after only a verbal warning, there would still need to be one person who experienced those negative effects to provide a witness to all who followed.

Others might say that the warning is too harsh, but the fact is that there are many people for whom even daily hangovers are not enough to keep them from drinking excessively, to the point of addiction and even death. Still others might feel that the warning is worse than the evil it is protecting us from, but this is not true. While the warning is unpleasant, the lack of warning can be deadlier still.

To make this point more clearly, let us consider hunger. When we don't eat enough, we feel hungry. Everyone has felt this sensation at one point or another, and it is not pleasant. When we feel it, we are motivated to eat something so that we no longer feel hungry. If we did not have this sensation of hunger, it would be like driving a car with a broken fuel gauge: it would only be a matter of time before we found ourselves stranded with no fuel in sight. Again, hunger is good because it highlights evil, which is the lack of nourishment. No one wants to be hungry, but it is far better than dying from starvation without warning.

Suffering is our innate ability to sense the presence of evil; or, more accurately, it is the absence of a good that is significant enough to threaten our existence physically, socially, psychologically, or spiritually. As a detector of evil, it is therefore necessary that the sensations it produces are persistent and hard to ignore, in the same manner that human-made alarms operate in order to get a message across in turbulent times. Furthermore, it is necessary that suffering be uncomfortable because that motivates us to move away from the evil that afflicts us in order to attain the good that is lacking. In this way, it is directive, like the stick, but it is not used with malicious intent. It is perhaps a bit ironic that it is discomfort that gives suffering its protecting and perfecting capabilities, but it needs to be that way so as to motivate us to change. If suffering were soothing, it would encourage us to stay in the presence of evil.

One could object that if the father in the parable were an all-powerful God, he could have provided for the needs of the son even in a foreign land so that the son would not starve. After all, in the modern world, a father with abundant resources would be able to extend a line of credit anywhere in the world for the benefit of his beloved son. Why can't an all-powerful God do at least as much?

An all-powerful God could certainly provide for the Prodigal Son, even at a distance. That is not the problem. The problem was created by the son, who severed ties with the father and thus lost access to all that was good for him. The same situation applies to our lives. When we separate ourselves from God, forsaking His wisdom and grace, we too will find that relying only on our own resources will ultimately leave us unfulfilled. As with the Prodigal Son, it is not that God cannot help us: it is that we are refusing God's help.

Suffering is directive, like the stick for a horse, causing us to avoid the things that make us suffer and instead to choose to attain the goods we need to make us whole. If we heed God's directives, delivered through suffering, we move closer to God and, ultimately, to happiness. If we do not heed our suffering, it will persist until we do heed it, or until we die. God encourages and shows us the moves that lead to joy and happiness, but He doesn't force us to make them. He respects our free will.

The next obvious objection might be that a truly loving, all-powerful God would not allow evil to exist at all, so there would be no need to suffer. This, however, is a misunderstanding of evil. In fact, it is established Christian teaching that evil does not exist on its own, and this is consistent with the creation story that begins the Bible. The creation story tells us over and over that everything God made is good.[20] As St. John

[20] Genesis 1.

Paul II explains, "Christianity proclaims the essential good of existence and the good of that which exists, acknowledges the goodness of the Creator and proclaims the goodness of creatures. Man suffers on account of evil, which is a certain lack, limitation, or distortion of an expected good according to a thing's nature.[21] For example, it is an evil thing for a man to be blinded, but the fact that a stone cannot see is not an evil because that is not part of its nature. St. Thomas, echoing St. Augustine, agrees, describing evil in his *Summa Theologica* as the privation of good that is natural to a thing, as darkness is the absence of light.[22]

Evil, then, is not opposed to good at all, as Epicurus assumed. It is instead the lack of good. One might then ask, why would God withhold anything good from a child whom He loves? After all, the father of the Prodigal Son did not hold back his inheritance when he asked for it.[23] While this is true, it is also true that the Prodigal Son did not get every good that the father had. In the parable, the Prodigal Son had to lose everything and hit rock bottom before he would be ready to repent. The wise father understood this and planned for it, having retained the goods that were not part of the son's inheritance for his return. In the same way, God retains goods in Heaven that are not available to us on earth so we have something to come back to when we return to Him after our deaths. It is also true that no person has the capacity to absorb all the good that God could bestow, and so God must withhold good from everyone.

---

[21] John Paul II, *Salvifici doloris* (Vatican City: Libreria Editrice Vaticana, 1984), 7.

[22] Aquinas, *Summa Theologica* (*ST*), I, q. 48, art. 1.

[23] Luke 15:12.

In addition, like any good human father, God would know that at times it is better to let children work for what they need so that they can develop skills and a sense of achievement, and this is something that their spoiled counterparts, who are given everything, may never experience. God is good and gives us what we need, when we need it, just as the father of the Prodigal Son did in the parable.

Some may be under the impression that using suffering to bring people back to God is similar to the coercion of a tyrant to get what he wants. This reflects a flawed view of God, thinking of Him as though He were human. God is all-powerful and has no needs that He cannot fulfill Himself. When He desires us to return to Him, it is for our benefit, not His, because at His Word, we could be replaced instantly by others who could take their places at His side. Instead, God shows His love for each of us by warning us when we get off-track, making it uncomfortable through suffering. We know this because every person suffers in life.

This does not mean, however, that every person who suffers is off-track. It means that everyone is called by God. Indeed, sometimes we are called to suffer for the benefit of others. The most obvious example is that of the sinless Son of God, Jesus Christ, Who suffered a horrible death on the Cross for our benefit. As will be discussed later in greater detail, when we suffer, we should recognize it as a calling from God to help carry out His plan, not as a curse or a condemnation. Even if we are suffering punishment for our sins, it is still a calling to us to return to God. God's purpose is always to rehabilitate us; it is never to destroy us. There is no malice in God, only love. Similarly, when we encounter those who suffer, we should not see them as sinners or complainers, but as instruments of God's mercy and specifically as messengers of what was revealed to them.

The parable of the Prodigal Son also teaches us that it is union with God that makes us happy and fulfilled, which is the goal of all men. Like it did for the Prodigal Son, suffering brings us to the realization that God has all we need, and without Him, we have nothing. St. Thomas Aquinas describes union with God as the Beatific Vision, an experience that we would never wish to end.[24] Imagine that this vision encompasses all that is good and true in the universe: the beauty of mountain vistas and sunsets at the beach, and the warm embrace of the person who loves you best, all wrapped together in a never-ending kaleidoscope of joy. If the human-developed Internet, filled as it is with lies and filth and subject to breakdown, can enthrall us, then we can see Aquinas's point that there is nothing on earth that could compare to what awaits us in the presence of God.

An additional question pertaining to the parable of the Prodigal Son is "How does suffering bring us back to God?" Unlike the son in the parable, we cannot follow the path we used to leave the Father to find our way home. God understands this, of course, and so He sent us His Son to show us the way back. To live with God forever, we must become like God, which is to love unconditionally as Jesus described the father doing in the parable. For us fully to demonstrate unconditional love, we first need the grace of Christ, which is imparted through the sacraments to enable us to follow Christ's example of redemptive suffering and share in His nature; this includes a willingness to suffer for the benefit of others, as Christ did on the Cross on Calvary. As St. Peter describes in his Second Epistle, by following Christ, we can indeed

---

[24] *ST* I-II, q. 3, art. 8.

become like God, so that we can be eternally in His presence and share in His life.[25]

At its deepest level, suffering is a call to conversion by God. As such, its tasks are to break down our faulty assumptions and to give us new perspectives on our purpose and being. At times, we are thrust into situations that give us a new perspective on life that clears up uncertainties and dilemmas and puts us on the road to happiness. These situations that we find ourselves in are not random: they are instances of God working to redirect us toward the kind of life that will lead us to happiness and joy. These situations might be as mundane as reading a book, watching a movie, or talking to a friend who gives us suggestions on how to enhance our lives. They could also be encounters that cause us to suffer the loss of a child; or cause us to suffer the onset of a chronic disease; or to endure the storm that causes financial ruin.

Many people have the misconception that suffering is evil, that God is vengeful or at best inattentive, and that those who suffer are cursed. In fact, suffering is the gift of a loving and generous God, Who actively seeks to lead us to eternal joy in union with Him. He uses suffering to highlight what to avoid and to motivate us to attain the good we need. Far from being cursed, those who suffer are given direct revelation from God to direct their actions toward good. When we suffer, we are also called to be messengers of God, to share our suffering experience with others so that they can learn without experiencing suffering themselves.

Conversion through suffering may seem to be unfair and inappropriate by human standards because our perspective is so limited, especially if we limit ourselves only to what we can detect through our senses. If we are limited to that, then suffering will

---

[25] 2 Peter 1:3-4.

never make sense. God's perspective is infinitely greater than ours, and His plans for us are much greater than simple peace and comfort. He wants us to have eternal joy, but He respects and loves us enough not to force it upon us. He does not leave us to founder, either. The reality is that God loves us so much that He defines a special path in life that corresponds perfectly to our skills and desires, and this path will lead us to develop the faith and virtues need to become like Him so that we can be with Him for eternity. We are kept on this path by suffering, which we experience any time we stray from it.

Suffering is uncomfortable, but it needs to be that way in order to motivate us to change. In our post-Enlightenment society, people understand suffering as something to overcome. This idea completely misses the point of suffering. Suffering is not something to overcome; it is something to be heeded. It is God giving us direction on what to avoid and what to pursue in order for us to attain the joy He has prepared for us. It is a call to action to attain the good we lack; to love and serve others in the role for which each of us was made. Ironically, the worst experiences of our lives often are the ones that God uses to bring us to eternal joy in His presence because they are warnings of the greatest threats to our happiness. Heeding them brings the joy of spiritual achievement. The greater the challenge, the greater the joy in achieving it.

To justify a sinner is no small task. St. Augustine and St. Thomas Aquinas agree that it is a greater task than the creation of the world,[26] so we should expect significant challenges to perfect us, and we should know that suffering will be a constant companion. God will use it to direct us away from vice and toward

---

[26] *ST* I, q. 113, art. 1.

virtue, to orient us toward God, to provide opportunities for us to practice those virtues to fuel our spiritual growth, and ultimately, it will redeem us. It is through these four tasks of suffering that we are called home by God; there we will experience true joy and eternal happiness. They are divinely inspired tasks, so they operate based on our needs and continuously train us to live in accordance with God's will so we can share His life in Heaven. They are brilliant in their design because they systematically attack the faulty assumptions and tendencies that keep us from achieving true happiness, while taking into account the fundamental makeup of the human race. Knowing that this is God's intent, we need to trust Him and follow His lead, heeding the messages and directions He provides through suffering.

2

The First Task: Developing the
Human Virtues and Proper Self-Love

Suffering begins its work of redemption with the simplest of feedback loops, making us feel uncomfortable when we experience something that it not good for us. This feedback process is constantly at work in all humans. It does not require faith or even an acknowledgment of God from the person who suffers. It merely requires people to react naturally to suffering. This means avoiding it or alleviating it as soon as possible, since it is an unpleasant experience by design. Because suffering highlights evil to humans, and evil is the lack of some good (and that lack threatens our existence), suffering motivates all people to seek out the goods that we are missing and to avoid what will potentially harm us. In this way, suffering protects us from greater harm. Once we learn how to avoid suffering, we are highly motivated to continually repeat the process until it becomes ingrained as a habit.

Habits are important to efficient human function because they allow us to react easily, reliably, and repeatedly, based on experience. Simply put, human beings need habits because many decisions that we make do not allow enough lead time for structured reasoning. For instance, if we are accosted on a deserted city street by a gunman who says to us, "Your money or your life?" he will likely not wait for us to create a list of pros and cons before making the decision for us. Instead, we will need to "go with our gut" and make a decision instantly based on past evaluations.

Further, it is not a good use of time and intellectual resources to constantly re-evaluate decisions that are repeated regularly without change, like how best to travel home from work. People naturally form habits without consciously thinking about them by repeating actions that they have previously evaluated, until these actions have become so ingrained that they are repeated without conscious thought. For instance, students pick a seat in the classroom on the first day of class. Typically, they will return to the very same seat, every class of the semester, and never think twice about it unless someone "takes their seat." When that happens, they feel very uncomfortable and angry that "their seat" has been "stolen." The same scenario takes place at countless churches, bars, or any other establishments that people frequent.

Efficient people deliberately create a habit of something they want to accomplish because once it becomes second nature, they do not have to think consciously about doing it. In fact, most habits begin with a conscious decision that becomes ingrained through repetition. Some people, for instance, follow specific bedtime rituals to enhance their sleep. This makes their routine very reliable, but will make the person very uncomfortable, and perhaps cranky, if the routine is broken.

Not all habits are good for us. Vices are habits that are harmful to us in some way. When we begin developing a vice, it is typically because we desire some attribute of the habit that is attached to the elements that cause harm. For instance, people who smoke don't do so because it results in lung cancer. They smoke because it presents an image that they want for themselves, or because they find it relaxing, or because they enjoy the sensation. Habits like these can generally be formed only when they do not initially threaten one's existence, otherwise suffering would result and make continuing to indulge in these activities too uncomfortable to perpetuate.

Once a vice has been formed, be it smoking, drinking alcohol to excess, or any other vice in which people indulge, it is hard to break. This must be true, otherwise habits in general would not provide the benefit of acting without reasoning that makes them valuable. This does not mean they are impossible to break, but it usually takes significant effort and external pressure to do so. This is why suffering has to be harsh and persistent to be effective.

The first task of suffering is to make us virtuous. This occurs in several parts: it detects these vices in us; motivates changes in our behavior that will protect us from the harm that can be done by these vices; and creates in us the virtues that will make us better, more perfect people. The culmination of the first task of suffering is to bring humanity to the highest level of perfection that is possible, and that is the attainment of virtue. This was the goal of the thought leaders in the great pagan societies in Greece and Rome. In fact, in his finest work, *Nicomachean Ethics*, the great Greek philosopher Aristotle identifies happiness, the goal of all men, as a "certain activity of the soul in accord with complete virtue."[27]

While there are numerous virtues, we will focus on the cardinal (or moral) virtues to illustrate the workings of the first task of

---

[27] Aristotle, *Nicomachean Ethics*, trans. Robert C. Bartlett and Susan D. Collins (Chicago: University of Chicago Press, 2011) bk. 1, ch. 13, lines 1-2.

suffering. These have been generally recognized from antiquity as temperance, fortitude, justice, and prudence. They are called the cardinal virtues because all other moral human virtues can be derived from these four. As discussed below, suffering has a crucial role in the development of each of them.

Temperance governs and moderates physical desires, including those for food, drink, and sex. If a person pursues too much, too little, or harmful varieties of any of these, suffering will result. In the example already discussed, if someone drinks too much alcohol, he will suffer from a hangover, which will motivate the person to drink less. If the hangover was distressing enough, the person may drink more moderately on a consistent basis, thus practicing the virtue of temperance. The virtue of temperance is all about moderation and is an important component of self-love, since it involves taking care of the body and practicing chastity, both of which ultimately involve self-respect. By motivating each of us to become temperate, suffering is perfecting us, while at the same time protecting us from harm. This sequence of detecting evil, and then both protecting and perfecting a person, is a hallmark of the first task of suffering.

Not everyone responds virtuously to suffering. In fact, when tested with hunger, some people will respond by asking others for help, but others will simply steal from their neighbors. Those that steal from their neighbors are transferring their suffering to that neighbor. In most cases, this suffering will eventually be transferred back to the thief in some fashion, whether by direct retaliation from the victim, arrest by the police, or by the thief's own conscience when he realizes that his actions have caused another to suffer. If the ramifications are painful enough to stop future thefts, then the thief will have been taught an element of justice through suffering.

There are, of course, easier ways to learn what is just than to suffer for one's own injustices. Justice governs our interactions between ourselves and others. When we fail to give to others what is due to them, it causes them to suffer. When we are confronted with their suffering, it provides the impetus for us to act justly. When suffering ceases, our actions are validated as just. Justice is the cornerstone of all relationships, and it allows us to operate efficiently and effectively with others with a minimum of conflict by balancing the interests of each party through prudence. This balancing through prudence and justice leads to the establishment of the common good of society and is the basis for all good government and for all healthy human relationships.

At the same time, societies have recognized that suffering is required to enforce justice, because without the threat of punishment, some people will simply do as they please without concern for their neighbor's well-being. This is why organizations define penalties for unjust behavior on the part of their members and employ policing functions to ensure compliance. Suffering aids the common good by detecting interactions that are unfair and cause pain or discomfort to one or more of the parties involved. It protects the interests of all the society's members because its members want to avoid the punishment they will receive if they act unjustly. As people act justly toward each other with more consistency, the society and its members become more perfect.

Suffering also is responsible for building the virtue of fortitude within us, which is the ability to persevere in goodness against difficulties and impediments. Suffering does this through its own intensity and persistence. When a person faces difficulties in doing good, suffering is always present to detect what is evil. By making us uncomfortable, suffering motivates us to attain the good that is found to be lacking. This protects us from giving in to disordered choices and ultimately perfects us as we stand diligently against what oppresses us. This is also true of suffering that results from social injustices, like institutional slavery. Evil eventually loses because suffering never stops detecting it, protecting the good, and ultimately perfecting the people, no matter how entrenched the evil in society seems to be.

Ultimately, the first task of suffering leads us to prudence, which is the wisdom to make decisions aligned to God's will for the universe. Prudence governs reason and the ability to make the right decisions. When people make poorly reasoned decisions, it causes suffering, whereas making prudent decisions avoids suffering. This provides both the impetus for prudent decisions and the validation of whether decisions were indeed prudent. With practice, prudence becomes habitual and controls the other moral virtues. As we become increasingly prudent, we are protected from harm that can result from disordered or sinful choices. We are also becoming better people with the perfection of our decision-making processes.

There is a hierarchy in the development of virtue.[28] To do a good deed well and consistently is the definition of virtue, and this requires all of the human moral virtues to work in unison, governed by prudence. For instance, an action is not prudent if it is unjust or intemperate and if it is not carried out with fortitude. Similarly, one cannot act justly without making a prudent decision. One needs prudence to act with temperance and to separate fortitude from foolhardiness. Without prudence, which is alignment with God's intentions, habits are imperfect and do not constitute true virtue.

[28] Aquinas, *ST* I-II, q. 65, art. 1.

Regardless of the religious or philosophical system by which one abides, everyone should be able to relate to the goal of the first task of suffering, which is to engender virtue: to make all men temperate in their consumption, just in their dealings with others, and prudent in their decision-making process, and to act with fortitude in all things. At the same time, there should also exist an agreement that the parameters of what makes a thing just, prudent, or temperate is rendered clearly by whether suffering ensues or is alleviated. In a very real way, suffering helps define the natural law because we all can see the things that make people suffer and what things cause suffering to stop. All of the great civilizations of antiquity highly valued virtue: they developed legal codes and religious and philosophical principles based on it. The Ten Commandments, used by the Hebrews, and Aristotle's *Nicomachean Ethics* are two such examples of texts and laws ordered toward virtue.

3

The Second Task:
Reorienting the Soul to God

The first task of suffering engages us at an instinctual level, teaching us to love ourselves properly and to live in society effectively by making the alternatives persistently uncomfortable. The types of suffering used in the first task do not need a lot of interpretation from ourselves or others because they reflect obvious first-order problems that are generally cause-and-effect in nature. For example, if we eat or drink too much, we will feel sick, and if we do not eat enough, we will be hungry. All the required actions for fulfilling the first task are well within the capability of fallen man, since they promote our self-interests and thus are consistent with human nature.

The remaining tasks of suffering are to make us increasingly God-like, to share in His nature so that we can also share in His life. Because only God can reveal Himself and share His nature, the remaining tasks require His help (or that of the Church He left for that purpose) to discern. The second task of suffering is to re-orient ourselves to God. The re-orienting of people toward God often requires more than re-direction from vice to virtue. It may also require refining a person's understanding of the nature of God, which is obviously required if one is to partake in it.

False images and understandings of God and His nature are very hard to break, and so suffering has a prominent role in doing so.

An example of this is described in the classic biblical text on suffering, the book of Job, in which the righteous Job is systematically deprived of his property, his family, and his health. As St. John Paul II points out, the suffering that Job undergoes in the Old Testament account has the nature of a test to demonstrate Job's righteousness.[29] Job does not understand this and demands a hearing before God to defend his innocence, only to recognize when confronted by God that he himself is in no position to judge God. God, however, recognizes Job's righteousness before Job's friends, who had been actively encouraging Job to admit the sins that caused his suffering, and insists that they will only be forgiven for doubting Job's innocence if Job prays for them, which he does.

Most commentaries explain that the separation of suffering from punishment is the point of the story, but it does more than that. It also teaches the righteous Job about the nature of God, of Whom Job admits, "By hearsay I had heard of you, but now my eye has seen you. Therefore, I disown what I have said and repent in dust and ashes."[30] From this encounter, Job has understood that God is indeed just, but that He has other considerations in carrying out His plans that are beyond Job's comprehension.

In learning something about God, Job has learned something important about himself as well: he needs to trust in God's goodness, and his own perspective is limited. Job's encounter with God was undoubtedly a moment of grace for him, but it also was one for others. Not only did the suffering of Job open him up to

---

[29] John Paul II, *Salvifici doloris*, 11.
[30] Job 42:5-6.

a new and more appropriate understanding of the nature of God, it also did the same for his friends and even today's readers of the text. Eliphaz, Bildad, and Zophar spend most of the book of Job convinced that Job's suffering was the penalty for some unstated or unknown sin against God or man. God uses Job's suffering as an opportunity to correct that misconception for the three men (and the multitude of people who have heard the story since then), giving us a better understanding of His nature.

The problem of an improper image of God still exists today. In fact, the common misunderstanding of suffering as an evil brought upon humanity as punishment for its disobedience and ingratitude to its Creator still exists much as it did in the time of Job. This undermines the Christian understanding of the nature of God as a loving Father, perhaps best exemplified in the parable of the Prodigal Son. Those with this misunderstanding of God and His intentions toward man, when confronted with suffering in their lives that they do not feel they deserve, will think that God is unjust and may either hate Him or deny His existence. Alternatively, they may feel guilty about something they have done and will separate from God for this reason. Either way, it is counterproductive to God's goal of suffering, which is to call all humanity to join Him, to partake of the Beatific Vision with eternal joy and utmost happiness.

Conversely, the correct understanding of suffering can aid in our reconciliation with God. When we come to understand that suffering is not evil but a tool that God gave us to detect evil, protect us from the harm it could do to us, and perfect us so that we can be like God and with God for eternity, it should change the conversation. While the wrong interpretation of suffering can drive us away from God, the correct one should drive us into His arms by making it clear that God has infinite love and forgiveness for us and is waiting for us with open arms, if and when we decide to return to Him.

Suffering is often a catalyst for conversion, particularly when a person is unable to resolve his material suffering through human means, as is the case with chronic illnesses. As the *Catechism* describes:

> Illness can lead to anguish, self-absorption, sometimes even despair and revolt against God. It can also make a person more mature, helping him discern in his life what is not essential so that he can turn toward that which is. Very often illness provokes a search for God and a return to him.[31]

In essence, what happens in these situations is that God uses suffering to gain our attention, to show us that there are things beyond our control, to remind us of our mortality, and to give us time to consider what is important in life. As discussed in the first two pages of this book, true suffering affects every facet of our lives and is impossible to ignore. Some people will resist God in this, but suffering is relentless and will not stop unless the problem is resolved or the person dies. This more direct path to conversion, wherein the person has no other option to resolve his suffering but to turn to God, is explained by perhaps the least expected, and at the same time most powerful, insight from St. John Paul II in *Salvifici doloris*: "In suffering there is concealed a particular power that draws a person interiorly close to Christ, a special grace. To this grace many saints, such as Saint Francis of Assisi, Saint Ignatius of Loyola and others, owe their profound conversion."[32]

---

[31] *Catechism of the Catholic Church* (CCC), 1501.
[32] John Paul II, *Salvifici doloris*, 27.

The pope uses these saints as examples of people who owe their profound conversion to the special grace concealed within suffering, so it is useful to review their stories to understand his insight. St. Bonaventure, in his original biography of Francis, explained that Francis was so engrossed in worldly affairs that God needed to use severe physical pain to get his attention and prepare him to receive the graces of the Holy Spirit.[33] This came when Francis was captured in a battle in a war with a neighboring city and kept in a dank dungeon for more than a year, during which he was constantly ill with a fever.[34] While the account says that it was Francis's body that was changed, the more important change was his perspective. Faced with his own mortality by his suffering and given time during his convalescence to ponder what is important in life, Francis completely re-oriented his life toward emulating Christ.

St. Ignatius of Loyola has a similar story which he recounts in *Reminiscences*, his life's story that he dictated to Goncalves da Camara from 1553 to 1555.[35] He too was a baptized Christian who was distracted from God by the pleasures of life. After living an early life of self-described dissipation and laxity, he was severely injured in battle and suffered much during a long convalescence.[36] During this time, the only thing available for him to read to pass

[33] Bonaventure, *The Life of St. Francis of Assisi*, ed. Cardinal Manning (Rockford, Ill: Tan Books and Publishers, 1988), 13.

[34] Paschal Robinson, "St. Francis of Assisi," *The Catholic Encyclopedia*, vol. 6 (New York: Robert Appleton Company, 1909), http://www.newadvent.org/cathen/06221a.htm.

[35] Ignatius, *Saint Ignatius of Loyola: Personal Writings*, trans. with intro. and notes by Joseph A. Munitiz and Philip Endean (New York: Penguin, 1996), 7.

[36] Ibid., 13, 14.

away the time was *The Lives of Christ and the Saints*, which led to his profound conversion and the founding of the Jesuit Order.

In each of these cases, it was suffering that precipitated their conversions by forcing a change in their environment from battlefield to bed. But it was more than just a change in the environment; it was a realization that what they had been doing was lacking something critical: communion with God. Undoubtedly, they could appreciate Simone Weil's description of affliction as "a marvel of divine technique that introduces into the soul of a finite creature the immensity of force, blind, brutal and cold," by which God reveals Himself to those who are oriented to Him in love.[37] God announced His presence to these two saints with the full force of suffering and, in giving them ample time while convalescing to contemplate its meaning, made clear what was important. St. John Paul II says that "such a conversion involves not only the discovery of the salvific meaning of suffering by the individual but a complete change in the person in which he discovers a new dimension of his or her entire life and vocation."[38]

The ability of illness or injury to redirect people's lives to be in line with God's plan is not unique to the Church's most famous saints; it is lived daily by countless people who are forced to take notice of God when He redirects their lives. At the same time, it does not always have the same result. As discussed above, the Church's own experience as recorded in the *Catechism* admits that "for some, illness can lead to anguish, self-absorption, sometimes even despair and revolt against God while for others it will lead to spiritual maturity and provoke a search for God

---

[37] Weil, "The Love of God," 452.
[38] John Paul II, *Salvifici doloris*, 26.

and a return to him."[39] God is no tyrant. Although He is vigorous and persistent in His call to us through suffering, He does not force us to love Him or to believe in Him. He gives us the grace to do so, but every person has the ability and the choice to reject that grace and remain unconverted, even though it is much to their detriment.

Nor is illness or injury the only means of suffering God uses to re-direct people from the various forms of idolatry that keep their focus away from Him. If monetary greed is the impediment to holiness, the means to conversion might be through utter financial ruin. If the problem is vanity, the means to conversion could be an accident or simply old age that reduces one's attractiveness. If it is fame, there could be a shameful situation that reestablishes the correct end. These forms of suffering are also forms of grace because they highlight what needs to be changed for us to become truly happy and motivate us to take the right actions. As the Book of Wisdom relates, "Chastised a little, they shall be greatly blessed, because God tried them and found them worthy of himself. As gold in the furnace, he proved them."[40]

On the other hand, the conversion of many people is accomplished incrementally through the use of many small, redirecting setbacks rather than through a single conversion experience so debilitating that the person has nowhere else to turn but to God. In these more incremental cases, the person first is led by suffering from vice to moral virtue as discussed in the previous chapter, which is the preparation that precedes the acceptance of grace. In this scenario, the first two tasks of suffering are in a sense hierarchical, with suffering leading a person to proper

[39] CCC 1501.
[40] Wisdom 3:5-6.

self-love which prepares one to accept the grace of faith that re-orients the person toward God. For instance, St. Thomas notes that fortitude removes the inordinate fear that hinders faith, and humility removes pride that keeps a man from submitting himself to the truth of faith. In this way, even the acquired virtues discussed in the previous chapter can lead to beatitude, albeit indirectly.[41]

When St. John Paul II states that within suffering is concealed a special grace which produces profound conversions of heart, many are undoubtedly skeptical. Yet, when viewed from the proper perspective, it makes perfect sense. Others have reached the same conclusion: Simone Weil, Dorothee Söelle, and Eric Cassell, each from different times, places, and specialties, recognize that suffering drives people to change. This is easily explained. Because suffering is uncomfortable, people will change their habits to avoid it. If one also understands that suffering is an experience of evil and that evil is the absence of good, then suffering is an indication of when some good is missing. This means that people are motivated to find the good they are missing, which is God. This, in turn, makes them receptive to grace, which brings forth faith and then the rest of the infused virtues,[42] allowing these people to align their wills with God.

Conversion is actually like breaking a habit. It is hard to do and requires something to motivate the change. This is why suffering is so often the catalyst for conversion. It is possible to convert without suffering. Some people, by the grace of God,

---

[41] *ST* II-II, q. 4, art. 7.

[42] Infused virtues are those given to the soul by God instead of being acquired through human means. They include the theological virtues of faith, hope, and charity as well as perfected forms of the moral virtues.

are spurred on through the preaching and example of others. These situations still have to overcome the barrier to change that is inherent in habits, so they would need to change the person's perspective in a radical way. It might be possible to do this as a strictly intellectual exercise for a few people, but most will require the negative motivation from suffering that results when we stray from the path.

4

The Third Task: Unleashing Love

The development of human virtue is the culmination of natural human capability, which, since the Fall of Man, is based on a philosophy of self-interest. To rise above self-interest and practice true charity, which is self-giving love, is above the natural capability of man and thus requires grace. Having first prepared the way for the grace that transforms human souls, and having provided the grace that orients a person to God, the third task of suffering provides the opportunity and motivation for humans to demonstrate love for each other. Whereas the first response was primarily driven by self-love without the benefit of grace, and the second response focused on love of God as grace was offered and accepted (allowing our will to be ordered to His), this third response concerns the love of one's neighbor. As the infused virtues are put into effect, we begin to act in accord with the divine nature to address the suffering of others. Appropriate for this task, St. John Paul II says that suffering is "present in order to unleash love in the human person, that unselfish gift of one's 'I' on behalf of other people, especially those who suffer."[43]

[43] John Paul II, *Salvifici doloris*, 29.

St. John Paul II uses the famous parable of the Good Samaritan (Luke 10:29-37) as the basis for his discussion on how
suffering leads to human love.[44] In this parable, three travelers
on the road from Jerusalem to Jericho encounter a man who
was robbed, beaten, and left for dead. Two of them, a priest and
a Levite, pass him by without helping. The third, a Samaritan,
shows compassion to him by dressing his wounds and bringing
him to an inn where he arranges for his care. Like the Good
Samaritan, we are called to stop and show loving compassion to
our suffering neighbors; to be "one who brings help in suffering."

Suffering unleashes human love by appealing to a person's
conscience and eliciting compassion when the person comes into
contact with one who suffers. Suffering therefore provides both
the opportunity and the motivation for people to love others.
This parable is particularly interesting because even the imperfect virtue[45] of justice should have been sufficient to motivate
the priest and the Levite to care for their fellow Jew. As leaders
of the community, they would have been expected to help their
injured countryman as a social duty. The Samaritan, however,
had no such expectations, since he was from a country that was
in conflict with the Jews. His actions were truly charitable in that
they demonstrated the desire to unite in love with the injured
man and to serve him with no self-interest in mind. St. John Paul
II describes this as "giving oneself to the other."[46]

---

[44] Ibid., 28.
[45] This refers to the fact that even without the direct infusion of
grace, the human virtue of justice should be sufficiently motivating to get the priest and Levite to act on behalf of their
countryman.
[46] Ibid.

In a very real way, in this third task, we are called to emulate Jesus, Whose entire earthly mission through both His words and actions demonstrates the unconditional giving of oneself. He makes it very clear that His Kingdom is based on love, defining the greatest commandment as "You should love the Lord, your God, with all your heart, with all your soul, and with all your mind, and you should love your neighbor as yourself."[47] In fact, He concludes that "the whole law and the prophets depend on these two commandments."[48]

When the virtues are first infused, the activity is focused on eliminating the vices associated with each virtue. As discussed earlier in chapter 2, suffering can provide the motivation to eliminate the vices that oppose the infused virtues by making them continuously uncomfortable until they are replaced with virtue.

Like faith, charity must be freely exercised. From a practical perspective, this means that when the Holy Spirit infuses grace into our souls to make us charitable, we still must consent to act in love, and we must also have the opportunity to do so. St. John Paul II points out that it is suffering that provides both the opportunity and the challenge to love when he says that "suffering is present in order to unleash love in the human person."[49] He elaborates on this, asserting that the world of human suffering unceasingly calls for the world of human love, and that "in a certain sense, man owes to suffering that unselfish love which stirs in his heart and in his actions."

St. John Paul II describes some of the many ways that people can follow the example of Christ and the Good Samaritan by

---

[47] Matthew 22:37-39.
[48] Matthew 22:40.
[49] John Paul II, *Salvifici doloris*, 29.

showing their love to those who suffer, starting with those who make it their professions. These include medical professionals such as doctors and nurses, whose professions he thinks should actually be considered vocations. He also acknowledges that many show their love for the suffering through volunteer work, both through various social organizations and as individuals, and encourages everyone to do the same.[50]

St. John Paul II notes that at the heart of the Sermon on the Mount there are the eight Beatitudes, which are addressed to people tried by various sufferings in their temporal lives.[51] The *Catechism* adds that these same Beatitudes "depict the counte-nance of Jesus and portray his charity."[52] Said another way, they define ways for us to utilize the infused virtues to love those who suffer. "The Beatitudes are at the heart of Jesus' preaching."[53] They depict His nature and in doing so, provide us with a "blueprint" of how to orient ourselves to God, Who alone can satisfy our desire for happiness.[54] Through the *Catechism*, the Church affirms that "God put us in the world to know, to love, and to serve him and so to come to paradise."[55] To be sharers in the divine nature, the very definition of beatitude, we must understand, accept, and practice the Beatitudes through the infused virtues.

When we are poor in spirit, we are called to help others, re-gardless of the cost to us or the wealth of the sufferer. The Good Samaritan paid the innkeeper to care for the injured man he found beaten and naked by the roadside out of his own funds without

[50] Ibid.
[51] Ibid., 16
[52] CCC 1717
[53] Ibid., 1716
[54] CCC 1718.
[55] CCC 1721.

expecting anything in return.[56] We should be prepared to do the same.

When we encounter someone who is suffering, it is our duty to mourn with him or her. As Dorothee Söelle describes, suffering always involves a sense of isolation, so the first step to aid those who suffer is to let them mourn with you, thus allowing them to normalize their suffering and return to the community.[57] To their credit, the three friends of Job sat silently with him for seven days, mourning his misfortune, which allowed him to speak and ultimately be healed.[58]

The meek put the needs of others before their own. Certainly, the Good Samaritan had other plans the day he encountered the injured man, yet he put them aside and tended to him, while the priest and the Levite passed him by. These incidents should be seen as opportunities for beatitude, not inconveniences that elicit our complaints.

To hunger and thirst for righteousness is to work to remove injustices that cause human suffering. This is a call to action to treat others as we would want to be treated, applying equally to individual cases where people are denied what they are due as to cases of societal sin where whole classes of people are exploited.

We are to be merciful to the suffering, offering both compassion and forgiveness, especially to those suffering punishments for their own sins and offenses. An example of this is to visit the imprisoned, who suffer from both isolation and from guilt.

---

[56] Luke 11:35.
[57] Dorothee Söelle, *Suffering* (Philadelphia: Fortress Press, 1975), 13-16.
[58] Job 2:13.

The clean of heart are in tune with God's will, both in regard to themselves and to those who suffer. They recognize that everyone is a child of God and are willing to both help and be helped by them, thus providing solace for the temporal needs of the other while also being sensitive to their eternal need to provide charity themselves.

Many suffer because of strife and conflict, so we are called to be peacemakers to help resolve their suffering. This can apply to disagreements between individuals as well as wars between nations. If we are part of the conflict, we need to put ourselves in the other's shoes and understand their needs so that we can help meet them, even at a loss to ourselves.

Emulating Jesus, we must be willing to endure persecution for the sake of righteousness. This will be the topic of the next chapter, for giving oneself up for the good of others is sharing in the suffering of Christ, even if it does not end in actual martyrdom, which the Church has always recognized as a sign of beatitude.

Jesus taught about the importance of giving aid to those who suffer not only through His words but through His actions. Indeed, in Matthew's Gospel alone, there are seventeen separate accounts of Jesus' healing, six of which depict mass healings and eleven which document specific incidents involving the healing of lepers, paralytics, the mute, the possessed, and the blind. Jesus even calls attention to what He was doing in His answer to the messengers from John the Baptist, who asked whether He was the Messiah, telling them to observe that "the blind regain their sight, the lame walk, lepers are cleansed, the deaf hear, the dead are raised, and the poor have the good news proclaimed to them."[59]

---

[59] Matthew 11:5.

While many are accustomed to thinking of these miraculous healings as strictly signs of His Messianic role and of the coming Kingdom, they actually also serve to provide credibility to the teaching on suffering in a number of ways. First, and most obviously, they showed that Jesus was the Messiah, which made His teaching authoritative and worthy of emulation. Second, it showed that Jesus and His Father show compassion for the sufferer as an example for those who seek after man's last end, which is union with God. In short, He is teaching us to love those who suffer. This second understanding of the message of the healings of Jesus is an example to us to show compassion to the suffering, and it is well-attested from the teaching of the patriarchs to the current teachings of the Magisterium, which comprises the pope and the bishops.[60] Finally, no teaching is credible if the teacher does not practice what he teaches. That Jesus did this in such spectacular ways made the teaching that much more memorable.

St. John Paul II concludes his discourse on suffering by turning to the Gospel parable of the Last Judgment.[61] In this parable, Jesus separates those to be judged into two groups: the sheep on the right and the goats on the left. To those on His right, He says: "Come, you who are blessed by my Father. Inherit the kingdom prepared for you from the foundation of the world. For I was hungry and you gave me food, I was thirsty and you gave me drink, a stranger and you welcomed me, naked and you clothed me, ill and you cared for me, in prison and you visited me." When the righteous question Him about when these events occurred, Jesus responds: "Amen, I say to you, whatever you did for one of these

---

[60] CCC 1503.
[61] Matthew 25:31-46.

least brothers of mine, you did for me." He then turns to those on His left and condemns them for their failure to do the same.[62]

While he admits that the list of the forms of suffering in the parable could be expanded beyond physical suffering, St. John Paul II says that Christ's words about the Final Judgment unambiguously show how essential it is for the eternal life of every individual to stop and help his suffering neighbors. The pope maintains that "in the Messianic program of Christ, which is at the same time the program of the Kingdom of God, suffering is present in the world in order to release love, in order to give birth to works of love towards neighbor, in order to transform the whole of human civilization into a 'civilization of love.'"[63] This is a profound statement because it asserts that in God's plan, the very purpose of suffering is to release the love that is essential for eternal life. We see this in the story of the Good Samaritan, the one who showed love by giving aid to the sufferer.

St. John Paul II says that Jesus' salvific work liberates humanity from sin and death, and as a result, mankind exists on earth with the hope of eternal life and holiness. He readily admits that this victory over sin and death does not abolish temporal suffering. Instead, it throws a new light upon every suffering: the light of salvation.[64] Indeed, as is becoming more clear, temporal suffering is for the benefit of man, leading us to salvation through its four tasks. If suffering were to be abolished, no one would be saved.

It should be noted again at this point that suffering is a message from God that identifies the evil to be avoided or the good

---

[62] John Paul II, *Salvifici doloris*, 30.
[63] Ibid.
[64] Ibid., 15.

to be attained. We are not to abolish suffering but to heed it, taking the action that is prescribed to protect and perfect us. When this is done, the suffering will be resolved or alleviated.

A question that one might ask in terms of a Good Samaritan is: "What if the person is willing but unable to alleviate the pain that the sufferer is enduring?" In this case, it must be pointed out that charity has two attributes: unity and aid. It is unity that defines love and drives one to seek the good of the other.[65] If the good cannot be gained despite loving efforts, it does not diminish the unity and may actually enhance the love between the parties. In fact, Dorothee Söelle believes it can even relieve the suffering.

Building on the thoughts of Simone Weil, Söelle explains that true suffering begins with physical pain, which leads to psychological distress, and ultimately results in social isolation. In her view, there is no real affliction unless there is social degradation or the fear of it in some form or another.[66] Therefore, she asserts that the way to resolve suffering is basically to "unwind" the process, beginning with socialization. She feels that if the sufferer is given the opportunity to lament and sensitize others to the evil he is experiencing, it begins to normalize the situation and removes the social stigma. From there, the sufferer can develop actions to effect changes that reduce the psychological pressure, leaving only the physical pain, which either disappears or becomes bearable.[67] In reality, suffering highlights the presence of evil or the lack of good, and full resolution cannot be had until the missing good is attained. Suffering can be partially

---

[65] *ST* II-II, q. 27, art. 2.
[66] Söelle, *Suffering*, 14.
[67] Ibid., 70-73.

relieved, however, as Söelle describes, because it also involves social stigmas and psychological uncertainty.

Söelle's observations make it clear that there is great value in a "Good Samaritan" who provides moral support and compassion by being present with the sufferer, even if the good they lack cannot be procured. This is also consistent with the observations of Eric Cassell, who holds that suffering requires a person's existence to be challenged. A show of compassion by another is a recognition of the sufferer's existence and, more importantly, his value and dignity, which according to Cassell will relieve the suffering, if not the pain.[68] Therefore, it seems clear that even unresolvable injuries and illnesses provide opportunities for the release of love toward the sufferer and a path to salvation for those who are present with them. Said simply, coming to the aid of the sufferer has merit for the "Good Samaritan," even without actual healing taking place.

This brings up a final point, and it is the question of whether suffering always unleashes love. It clearly does not, as demonstrated by the parable of the Good Samaritan itself. After all, the priest and the Levite pass the injured man without offering aid before the Samaritan shows him charity. What suffering does offer is the opportunity for people to demonstrate charity — opportunities that are all too often passed by unheeded for countless reasons. Many people are simply so unnerved by suffering that they avoid any contact with it, which isolates the sufferers, adding to their problems. Fallen man is naturally self-centered, so most will not act charitably toward their neighbor even though helping

[68] Cassell, *The Nature of Suffering*, 42-44.

them would bring them spiritual rewards.[69] Giving of oneself and of resources in this way is virtuous. Those infused with grace will take the opportunity to demonstrate the supernatural virtue of charity, while others may not act at all, even for self-centered reasons like public acclaim, which falls short of true virtue.

Suffering, then, plays an important role in God's plan for salvation by providing the opportunities for those infused with faith and charity to demonstrate them, first by being with the afflicted one and then by doing whatever they can to provide the good that the sufferer lacks. In this way, the "Good Samaritan" has the more lasting benefit, receiving eternal salvation while the sufferer gets only temporary solace on earth. In this case, it truly is better to give than to receive love. Yet, those who suffer are also given the opportunity to love in a mystical, redemptive way that is the pinnacle of grace, exceeding that of the Good Samaritan.[70]

---

[69] Matthew 9:13, which references Hosea 6:6. Ironically, many commentators assume that the priest and Levite avoid the injured man because they wanted to retain ritual purity so they could sacrifice in the temple, never considering that God desires mercy, not sacrifice as pronounced in both the Old and New Testaments.

[70] John Paul II, *Salvifici doloris*, 22. The pope calls this final step, where humans share in Christ's sufferings and, in doing so, understand its meaning as the "supreme gift of the Holy Spirit."

5

The Fourth Task: Redeeming the Sufferer

The fourth and final task of suffering in God's providential plan is to lead the sufferer to realize that his suffering is for the good of another and to embrace it for the glory of God, even if it leads to his own physical death. In this way, we completely align with Christ and become sharers in His redemptive suffering, not just spiritually but actually, and those who share in His suffering also share in His glory. Knowing that our suffering is part of God's Providence, His plan for the salvation of others, provides meaning for it and leads to joy. Not surprisingly, St. John Paul II recognizes this type of redemptive suffering as the supreme gift of the Holy Spirit.[71] As such, it is also the final lesson in obtaining the knowledge of good.

The idea of redemptive suffering has played a central role in Christianity since Jesus suffered on the Cross to redeem mankind. Jesus takes on His suffering and death voluntarily, despite His innocence. It is an act of true love, done for the benefit of others. St. John Paul II explains that "although Jesus' suffering has human dimensions, it was of a depth and intensity that only he, the only-begotten Son could endure."[72] He says that Jesus'

[71] Ibid.
[72] Ibid., 18.

prayer to "let this cup pass from me" attests to the truth about His suffering while His qualifying statement, "but not as I will, but as you will" demonstrates His obedience to the Father. Jesus then experiences on the Cross the entire evil of the turning away from God which is contained in sin. Through the divine depth of His filial union with the Father, Jesus perceives in a humanly inexpressible way the suffering of estrangement from God, to Whom He calls, "My God, My God, why have you abandoned me?"[73] St. John Paul II concludes his explanation by saying that "it is precisely through this suffering that (Jesus) accomplishes the Redemption and can say as he breathes his last: 'It is finished.'"[74]

Just as Jesus demonstrates how to love those who suffer, He also demonstrates how to love *through* suffering. This type of love, suffering for the sake of others, is beyond the natural capability of humans in our corrupted state and requires Christ's intercession, and indeed, St. John Paul II asserts that through Jesus' suffering, "human suffering itself has been redeemed."[75] This is the main theme of *Salvifici doloris* which is made obvious from the very first line: "Declaring the power of salvific suffering, the Apostle Paul says, 'In my flesh I complete what is lacking in Christ's afflictions for the sake of his body, that is the Church.'"[76]

St. John Paul II builds on this thought as the document progresses, first making the point that "in the Paschal Mystery, Christ began the union with man in the community of the Church."[77] After noting that the Church is continually being built up spiritually as the Body of Christ through His Sacraments, the pope

---

[73] Mark 15:34.
[74] John Paul II, *Salvifici doloris*, 18.
[75] Ibid., 19.
[76] Ibid., 1, quoting Colossians 1:24.
[77] Ibid., 24.

insists that Christ wishes to be united with every individual in this body, especially those who suffer. He concludes that "in so far as a man becomes a sharer in Christ's sufferings—in any part of the world and at any time in history—to that extent he in his own way completes the suffering through which Christ accomplished the Redemption of the world."[78] He notes that this does not mean that Christ's achievement of Redemption is not complete, "it only means that the Redemption, accomplished through satisfactory love, remains always open to all love expressed in human suffering."[79]

While it is easy for people to see how a person loves someone who is suffering by giving them aid and comfort, it is perhaps more elusive to see how a suffering person can express love toward others. The most obvious way is to emulate Jesus directly in voluntarily suffering for the good of another. St. John Paul II spoke about such a situation in his homily at the Canonization Mass for Maximilian Maria Kolbe on October 10, 1982.[80]

Quoting Jesus from the Last Supper Discourses, "Greater love has no man than this, that a man lay down his life for his friends,"[81] the pope related how Father Kolbe volunteered to take the place of a man he had never met who was arbitrarily chosen to starve to death in the Nazi concentration camp at Auschwitz in July 1941. Kolbe explained that he wanted to do this because the other man had a wife and children depending on him, and

---

[78] Ibid.

[79] Ibid.

[80] John Paul II, "Homily for the Canonization of Saint Maximilian Maria Kolbe," Vatican, October 10, 1982, https://www.pierced-hearts.org/jpii/jpii_homilies/homilies_1982/oct_10_1982_canonization_max_kolbe.htm.

[81] John 15:13.

as a Catholic priest, he did not have a wife or child. He then suffered for two weeks in the starvation chamber before being executed by lethal injection on August 14, 1941. The pope goes on to say, "He bore witness to Christ and to love. For the Apostle John writes: 'By this we know love, that he laid down his life for us. And we ought to lay down our lives for the brethren' (John 3:16). By laying down his life for a brother, he made himself like Christ."

Because he bore witness to Christ to the point of death, Fr. Kolbe was specifically declared a martyr by St. John Paul II.[82] This is important because the *Catechism* describes martyrdom as the supreme witness given to the truth of the faith in which the martyr bears witness to Christ Who died and rose and to Whom he is united in charity.[83] St. Thomas adds that of all virtuous acts, martyrdom is the greatest proof of the perfection of charity and the most perfect of human acts. He argues that "a man's love for a thing is proved to be greatest by what he is willing to give up or suffer for its sake, and there is nothing greater than life to give up and nothing worse to suffer than death, especially when it is accompanied by the pains of bodily torment."[84] While martyrdom is clearly the surest way to beatitude because it entails the largest sacrifice, it is not the only path to redemption through suffering.

It should be pointed out again at this point that self-inflicted suffering is not redemptive. Simone Weil is correct when she says that "it is wrong to desire affliction; it is against nature, and it is a perversion; and moreover, it is the essence of affliction that it

---

[82] John Paul II, "Canonization of Saint Kolbe," 1.
[83] CCC 2473.
[84] *ST* II-II, q. 124, art. 3.

is suffered unwillingly."[85] After all, if Christ's purpose is to free humanity from evil, creating one's own evil cannot be understood as aligning oneself with Jesus.[86] Instead, the point is that suffering, understood properly, is a grace bestowed on people to bring them back into alignment with God, and in doing so, it may help achieve perfect happiness (beatitude). As part of God's providential plan, each person will suffer at the appropriate time and place and with the appropriate intensity for them in order to lead them to their last end: union with God.

Sometimes people are called to suffer for the good of the Gospel or as an example for others. For instance, St. Paul recalls in his Second Letter to the Corinthians that when he complained of a "thorn in the flesh," he was told that "power is made perfect in weakness."[87] Indeed, throughout his ministry he was tested mightily, having by his own count been given thirty-nine lashes five times, beaten by rods three times, stoned once, and shipwrecked three times.[88] Having endured all of that made his message more credible. It is redeeming in cases like this to accept and bear this suffering out of love for God, and the people were convinced by Paul's perseverance. What makes suffering redemptive is its self-sacrificial nature in service of God. It does not need to reach the level of martyrdom to have salvific value, as demonstrated by the non-martyred saints of the Church. Paul sets an example of the attitude needed for redemptive suffering

---

[85] Weil, "The Love of God," 454.

[86] This is not a critique of penitential practices such as fasting or even self-flagellation, which were more popular in the past. These do not rise to the level of suffering and so are beyond the scope of this work.

[87] 2 Corinthians 12:7-9.

[88] 2 Corinthians 11:24-25.

by saying, "I am content with weaknesses, insults, hardships, persecutions, and constraints for the sake of Christ, for when I am weak, then I am strong."[89]

Unlike Paul, most people who enter into redemptive suffering are unaware that it is part of God's plan. In his Gospel, John uses all of chapter 9 to tell the story of the man born blind, its length a testament to its significance. As the account opens, Jesus' disciples ask Him about whether a certain man had been born blind because of his own sins or those of his parents. Jesus assures them that the reason the man was born blind was not due to sin but so that the works of God might be made visible through him. Being the recipient of a miraculous healing is not redemptive, however. It was that he continued to cooperate with God's grace after his healing that redeemed his soul.

After Jesus heals the man, the man becomes a vocal and credible witness to Jesus' ministry before the people of Jerusalem and the leaders of the Pharisees. This willing acceptance of his participation in God's plan through his suffering blindness up to the point of his cure was redemptive in itself. In addition, as the chapter ends, the no-longer-blind man, despite being ejected from the synagogue for his witness, professes his faith in Jesus and worships Him. Unlike scores of other people Jesus had healed, this particular man was willing to incur a second type of suffering, that of social isolation as he was expelled from the community, in order to spread the gospel. This is also redemptive.

Most people will experience at least one of the two forms of suffering that the man born blind did at some point in their lives, and they too will have the opportunity for redemptive

---

[89]   2 Corinthians 12:10.

suffering. Some will be called to witness to the gospel and will be persecuted for the sake of righteousness. For some, this may end in martyrdom, for others, in social isolation. In many parts of the world, this type of suffering is very real and takes great grace and fortitude to endure, but there is no question that this type of suffering can be redemptive because at the end of His earthly ministry, Jesus issued this statement of both warning and promise: "You will be hated by all because of my name but the one who perseveres to the end will be saved."[90]

Not everyone is called to be a martyr in this way, however, and redemptive suffering does not always require death. What makes suffering redemptive is that the sufferer is willing to endure it for the benefit of another, whether they step forward as a substitute like Maximilian Kolbe, or if the suffering is thrust upon them, like the man born blind. Everyone who suffers is providing an opportunity for others to love them in a way that is spiritually beneficial to the "Good Samaritans." To state it plainly, like the man born blind, these sufferers become God's instruments of salvation for those who help them.

This is not to say that the sufferer does not or cannot benefit from his suffering as well. As was previously discussed, suffering identifies a lack of some good in a person's life and motivates the person to correct it. For instance, an alcoholic suffers from various symptoms because of her drinking. When they get bad enough, she will seek help or others will intercede, and, hopefully, she will ultimately stop drinking. Suffering has also been shown to drive conversion by refocusing the sufferer on what is important in life. In both of these previous discussions, the implied assumption is that these types of suffering, once the problem is identified, can

[90] Mark 13:13.

ultimately be resolved. There is a class of problems, however, that will eventually lead to death, whether it be in the short-term or after a prolonged period of suffering. It is in these cases that the grace of God is most needed for us to love others.[91]

As Weil so poignantly writes, such suffering can be felt as "an uprooting of life, a more or less attenuated equivalent of death, made irresistibly present to the soul by the attack or immediate apprehension of physical pain."[92] It requires grace to see the good in such a situation, even more so to undergo suffering willingly for the benefit of another, whom you may not even know, because you love God and want His plan to succeed. As will be discussed in more depth in the next section, this could apply to any suffering situation, from that of a child with a debilitating birth defect, to a young mother with breast cancer, to a severely injured soldier, to an elderly patient with Alzheimer's or Parkinson's disease. If that person can see past his own suffering to grasp that his situation is providing opportunities for others to practice the virtues that are required for salvation, and if he can embrace his suffering for the good of the others and the love of Christ, then the suffering will be redemptive for that person, leading to eternal salvation. At the same time, this recognition of the salvific opportunity that the suffering provides, for both the sufferer and the people who help, will also provide meaning for their suffering. As Cassell and Söelle both note, finding meaning in one's suffering can mitigate or even resolve the feeling of suffering in the agent, giving some level of temporal relief.[93]

---

[91] These issues, briefly mentioned here, will be dealt with in far
       more detail in the next section.
[92] Weil, "The Love of God," 440.
[93] Cassell, *The Nature of Suffering*, 44. Söelle, *Suffering*, 72-74.

The key, of course, is for the sufferer to be both aligned with Christ's will and to act in love accordingly. Even the execution of a criminal can involve redemptive suffering if the criminal confesses his crime with full contrition because it was counter to Christ's will, and then accepts the punishment because he felt justice was being served and that it would deter others from sinning. This was demonstrated by St. Dismas, the "Good Thief" who was crucified along with Jesus. In St. Luke's account, St. Dismas says to the other criminal being crucified, who had been taunting Jesus, "Have you no fear of God, for you are subject to the same condemnation? And indeed, we have been condemned justly, for the sentence we received corresponds to our crimes, but this man has done nothing criminal."[94] Turning to Jesus, he adds, "Jesus remember me when you come into your kingdom."

The way that the sufferer benefits from these scenarios is by recognizing that he is sharing in Christ's redemptive work and embracing it. Weil states it well when she concludes that "the only valid desire is that if affliction should come, that it may be a participation in the Cross of Christ."[95] St. Dismas did, of course, have a participation in a very real way in the Cross of Christ. He embraced it, recognizing that it was justice for his crimes, and he shared in Christ's redemptive work, ministering to the other man in the hopes of saving him from spiritual condemnation.

From a simply human perspective, this gives meaning to the suffering, and as both Cassell and Söelle observe, will help to resolve it, even if the pain remains. In *Spe Salvi*, Pope Benedict XVI wrote about an extension of this concept in terms of "offering

---

[94] Luke 23:39-43.
[95] Weil, "The Love of God," 464.

up" our hardships to Christ.[96] This devotion effectively assumes that our suffering benefits others when we offer it up to Christ as a willing spiritual sacrifice to join with His, thus making us sharers in His suffering. This show of solidarity with Jesus, as Pope Benedict attests, can provide meaning for the sufferer as well as the onlookers who recognize the willingness to love others in the devotion and might themselves be converted.

The spiritual benefits are far more expansive and important, however, as St. John Paul II describes in *Salvifici doloris*. One way this is described is that it is necessary to share in Jesus' suffering to be made worthy of sharing in the Kingdom of God. St. John Paul II says that through their sufferings, in a certain sense they repay the infinite price of the Passion and Cross of Christ. It is also through their sufferings that they become mature enough to enter this Kingdom.[97] As St. Paul explains in his Letter to the Romans, "We rejoice in our sufferings, knowing that suffering produces endurance, endurance produces character, character produces hope, and hope does not disappoint because God's love has been poured into our hearts through the Holy Spirit which has been given to us."[98] St. John Paul II observes that by persevering in suffering, the person recognizes that it will not deprive him or her of human dignity, and through the working of God's love, the meaning of life will become known. The more the person shares in this love, the more he discovers himself in suffering.[99]

---

[96] Benedict XVI, *Spe salvi* (Vatican City: Libreria Editrice Vaticana, 2007), 40.

[97] John Paul II, *Salvifici doloris*, 21.

[98] Romans 5:3-5.

[99] John Paul II, *Salvifici doloris*, 23.

To be able to grasp this final task of redemptive suffering is part of the pilgrimage of faith. St. John Paul II cautions that this learning process happens differently for everyone, often begins and is set in motion with great difficulty, and can take a long time before the truth is interiorly perceived.[100] Gradually, as the individual takes up his cross, spiritually uniting himself to the Cross of Christ, the salvific meaning of the suffering is revealed to him through grace. The pope concludes that it is then that the person finds inner peace and even joy.

This sense of joy is consistent with the observations of Cassell, who found in his medical practice that suffering was resolved when people could attach meaning to their pain.[101]

St. Paul also felt it, telling the Colossians, "I rejoice in my sufferings for your sake."[102] St. John Paul II reiterates the point that the discovery of the salvific meaning of suffering in union with Christ transforms the depressed feeling of the sufferer to the joy of recognizing that he is carrying out the irreplaceable service of serving the salvation of his brothers and sisters.

According to the pope, "Those who share in the sufferings of Christ preserve in their own sufferings a very special particle of the infinite treasure of the world's redemption and can share it with others."[103] This is among God's greatest blessings.

Furthermore, as St. John Paul II points out, "Those who share in the sufferings of Christ are called, through their own sufferings, to share in his glory."[104] The pope shows that this point is well-attested by the Apostles in Sacred Scripture, quoting both

[100] Ibid., 26.
[101] Cassell, *The Nature of Suffering*, 43-44.
[102] Colossians 1:24.
[103] John Paul II, *Salvifici doloris*, 27.
[104] Ibid., 22.

St. Peter and St. Paul.[105] He goes on to say, "Christ's Resurrection has revealed 'the glory of the future age' and at the same time, has confirmed 'the boast of the Cross': the glory that is hidden in the very suffering of Christ and which has been and is often mirrored in human suffering, as an expression of man's spiritual greatness."[106]

---

[105] 1 Peter 4:13: "But rejoice in so far as you share Christ's sufferings, that you may also rejoice and be glad when his glory is revealed." And Romans 8:17-18, "We are … fellow heirs with Christ, provided we suffer with him in order that we might be glorified with him. I consider that the sufferings of this present time are not worth comparing with the glory that is to be revealed in us."

[106] John Paul II, *Salvifici doloris*, 22.

Section II

Suffering in God's Providential Plan

6

Addressing the Problem of Evil

In the first section, suffering was presented as God's way of directing us away from sin and vice and toward faith and virtue, which, with sacramental grace, will make us sharers in the divine nature and ultimately in His eternal life. It also explained that this was accomplished through four tasks of suffering: building virtue, reorienting the soul to God, unleashing our love of neighbor, and ultimately redeeming us. The second section focuses on how these tasks apply to specific suffering situations, caused by natural evil, physical evil, the evil of sin, or the evil of punishment, to support providence, which is God's gracious plan for the salvation of souls. While it is obvious that not every suffering scenario can be discussed, the insights and perspectives covered here should be able to be applied to a wide range of individual cases, allowing people to understand how a loving God uses suffering in His plan to perfect us and lead us to joy.

Perhaps unsurprisingly, suffering and the problem of evil are at the center of current debates on the theology of providence. David Fergusson notes in his 2018 book, *The Providence of God*, that the theology of providence encounters two problems everywhere: suffering and divine action.[107] The concern with suffering is the same that drives the "problem of evil" debate: how to reconcile providence with the existence of evil. The concern with divine action is whether God is attentive to individual needs (particular providence) or whether providence is general, consisting of a high-level plan that is not specific to individuals. Convinced that the problem of evil is intractable, Fergusson advocates separating the task of resolving the problem of evil from the development of the theology of providence.[108] However, because our understanding of the existence and nature of God Himself and how He reacts with humanity is highly influenced by the problem of evil, it is impractical to separate the issues. Indeed, there are several concepts that are critical to understanding providence and God's plan for us, all of which are tied up with the problem of evil.

The most important question that people have when they experience suffering and evil is what is God's goal for mankind in general and for themselves specifically. Scripture and the Tradition of the Church are united and unambiguous in the answer to this: God wants us to become like Him so we can share eternal life with Him. As discussed in the first chapter, Jesus made this very clear in the parable of the Prodigal Son, but to make sure we did not miss such an important teaching, it has been repeated in various formats and forums throughout the ages.

St. Peter was the first to explain that through the promises of Christ, we could come to share in the divine nature.[109] St.

---

[107] David Fergusson, *The Providence of God: A Polyphonic Approach* (New York: Cambridge University Press: 2018), 217.

[108] Ibid., 216-217.

[109] 2 Peter 1:4

Irenaeus, roughly a hundred years later, described the reason for the Incarnation as being that God became man so that man could become God. St. Athanasius and St. Thomas Aquinas used similar terminology in their greatest works as well. The Church captures all of this in its present-day *Catechism*.[110]

The next question people who are exposed to suffering may ask is that if God wants us to be like Him in order to be with Him, why does He allow evil? As St. Catherine of Siena said to those who are scandalized and rebel against what happens to them: "Everything comes from love, all is ordained for the salvation of man, God does nothing without this goal in mind."[111] While St. Catherine tells us that the evil around us is for our salvation, that answer is unlikely to move Epicurus and his followers from their position without addressing their arguments that the existence of evil makes God's existence untenable.

Perhaps the most complete and well-argued positions denying that God and evil can coexist come to us from the philosophical environment in the 1950s, which Michael Peterson describes as particularly hostile to religion and in which most felt the concept of God was meaningless. J. L. Mackie took the lead on this problem with a series of arguments intent on demonstrating that the existence of evil disproves the existence of God.[112] Mackie astutely recognized that the problem of evil exists only if the assumptions are that God is all-good and all-powerful, and that evil is opposed to good. He understands that if God is not all-powerful, then there would be ways for evil to exist, and that if evil is not intrinsically opposed to good or if God is not

---

[110] CCC 460.
[111] CCC 313.
[112] Peterson, *The Problem of Evil*, 3-4.

wholly good, then there would be good reasons for why God allows evil to exist.[113]

Ironically, Mackie unwittingly identified the answer to the problem of evil in 1955 when he noted that if evil is not intrinsically opposed to good, then there would be good reasons why God allows evil to exist. Rather than embrace this possibility, however, he discarded it seemingly out of hand, spending his career trying to discredit theism. Mackie is not alone. The view that evil is opposed to good is widely held and highly insidious because it causes many to lose faith in God when they encounter evil in their lives that disturbs their peace and comfort.

In 1977, Aaron Kushner died at the age of fourteen of progeria, a genetic defect that causes rapid aging. His illness and death caused his father, Harold Kushner, a rabbi of a local congregation in Boston, to question all of his assumptions about suffering, death, and the nature of God. His solution to the resulting dilemma became the basis for his best-selling book, *When Bad Things Happen to Good People*. Like most people, Rabbi Kushner held two standard beliefs prior to this event: that God was all-powerful, and that God is a loving parent who protects us from harm and makes sure we get what we deserve. When his son died, Rabbi Kushner's worldview was shaken.[114] He was convinced that neither he nor his son had committed any sin that would deserve such a severe punishment but, at the same time, he was unwilling to consider that God was unjust or unwilling to help. That led him to conclude that God, the Creator of the Universe, was not powerful enough to cause

---

[113] J. L. Mackie, "Evil and Omnipotence," in *The Problem of Evil: Selected Readings*, 2nd ed. (Notre Dame, IN: University of Notre Dame Press, 2017), 82.

[114] Harold Kushner, *When Bad Things Happen to Good People* (New York: Avon Books, 1981), 1-4.

or cure his son's disease, which he describes as caused by "fate." This gave him peace, because it gave him a way to hold onto his image of a just God while maintaining his own sense of worth.[115]

Kushner wrote the book because these thoughts gave him psychological, social, and spiritual relief, and he wanted to share them with others. He writes in the foreword that his book will be deemed a success or failure based on whether it effectively explains why good people have to suffer.[116] Frankly, it did not do this, but it did give readers what they wanted and needed to hear: that God loved them and that their suffering was not a punishment. As a result, Kushner's book was a resounding success, selling more than four million copies, probably the most popular theodicy in the long history of the problem of evil. However, it came at a high cost, as it distorted people's understanding of the nature of God.

Kushner's solution is not the only theistic attempt to protect the image of a just God by impoverishing God in other ways. Alfred North Whitehead and Charles Hartshorne are advocates of process theodicy, which attempts to work around the problem of evil by restricting the power of God to one of persuasion rather than coercion.[117] Advocates of open theodicy work around the problem by claiming that God cannot see the future so He is not responsible for mistakes that are made when He is "working blind."[118]

---

[115] Ibid., 42-44.

[116] Ibid., 5.

[117] David Ray Griffin, "Divine Persuasion Rather than Coercion," in *The Problem of Evil: Selected Readings*, 2nd ed. (Notre Dame, IN: University of Notre Dame Press, 2017), 288-290.

[118] John Saunders, "God, Evil, and Relational Risk," in *The Problem of Evil*, 339-341.

In each of these cases, including the views of Mackie and Epi-curus, the belief that evil opposes good leads to logical paradoxes that cannot be adequately resolved. To preserve their belief in a just God, the theists are forced to deny that God is all-powerful or all-knowing. This does not make sense if one also believes that God is eternal, living outside of time, and is the Creator of all things. The atheist alternative, which is to deny the existence of God, does not make sense either, since an atheist cannot explain how the universe came to be. The obvious conclusion is that the assumption that evil opposes good is incorrect.

Evil does not oppose good. In fact, evil only exists as the ab-sence of good, like darkness is the absence of light and silence is the absence of sound. As St. John Paul II explains, "Christianity proclaims the essential good of existence and the good of that which exists, acknowledges the goodness of the Creator and proclaims the goodness of creatures. Man suffers on account of evil, which is a certain lack, limitation, or distortion of good."[119] St. Thomas, echoing St. Augustine, agrees, describing evil in his *Summa Theologica* as the privation of good, like darkness is the absence of light.[120]

Understanding evil in this way eliminates Epicurus's dilemma, because there are many reasons that a good God could and should withhold goods from us, starting with the simple fact that an infinitely good God has more good than His creation can hold. A loving God could conceivably withhold goods from us so that we can earn them, gaining skills and a sense of accomplishment in the process. He might also withhold goods until we are ready to use them, saving us from the danger of using them improperly.

[119] John Paul II, *Salvifici doloris*, 7.
[120] *ST* I, q. 48, art. 1.

Considered this way, evil is no longer something that must be vanquished, but instead presents an opportunity to learn and grow.

Mackie understands that this would solve the problem of evil and tries to address it in two ways. His first attempt is to say that withholding goods is cooperating with evil and therefore does not solve the problem.[121] However, as is obvious from the above, there are many reasons that God could withhold goods for our own good and not be cooperating with evil.

Mackie then asserts that the argument that evil is the privation of good is inconsistent with theism because of his assumption that good must oppose evil. In his model, there is balance where a first-order good (happiness) is opposed by a first-order evil (misery) and a second-order good (bravery) is opposed by a second-order evil (threat of injury). Mackie assumes that theists will argue that the benefits of first-order good make it worth accepting the second-order evil in conjunction with the first-order good. He then concludes that there is misery left over in the exchange, which he considers a fatal blow to theism.[122]

The absurdity of this argument is obvious. Mackie's ground rule that good must oppose evil effectively morphs in this exercise to the rule that good must balance evil, which means that evil can never be eradicated. The reality is much different than this accounting model would suggest. Because evil is the privation of good, it can be resolved by attaining the good that is lacking. Humanity, as the steward of creation, has brought about much in the attainment of goods that resolve evils. It has collectively subdued many diseases. Leprosy, the scourge of the ancient world, can be cured with pills. Polio has been largely eradicated. People can now be cool in the

---

[121] Mackie, "Evil and Omnipotence," 83.
[122] Ibid., 88-89.

summer and warm in the winter. This does not mean that suffering is at an end for humanity. Far from it. It will continue to serve God and man until the end of time, highlighting goods to be gained and motivating humans to attain them.

Perhaps recognizing that the previous arguments could be countered, Mackie also takes it upon himself to prepare arguments against what he anticipates will be the theist responses to the problem of evil. The first is "Good cannot exist without evil," or "Evil is necessary as a counterpart to good." He argues that this statement is inconsistent with God because it would show that God is limited in that He cannot create good without evil and cannot eliminate evil.[123] None of this applies to this case. Since evil is the privation of good, God is not limited in His creation, and evil is eliminated when He brings the affected thing to perfection in His own time.

The second argument that Mackie offers is that "Evil is necessary as a means to good." He argues that if this is the case, then the case for theism is destroyed because this would mean God's actions are severely limited.[124] On the contrary, evil is not needed to create good, because evil is the privation of good and will be resolved when the missing good is attained.

The third argument, "The universe is better with some evil in it than it could be if there were no evil," is actually more subtle and complex. Mackie notes two alternate arguments for this. One is an aesthetic analogy, whereby contrasts heighten the beauty of the whole. The second involves the notion of progress, with the idea that an evolving universe where good gradually overcomes evil is a finer thing than the eternal unchallenged supremacy of

[123] Ibid., 84-85.
[124] Ibid., 87.

good. Mackie treats these two cases the same way because he perceives evil as a nature rather than a privation.[125]

The second case defined by Mackie is actually true, but it does not disprove the existence of God. In fact, it confirms it and also helps us understand providence and the role of evil and suffering within it. The Church teaches that "God willed creation as a gift addressed to man, an inheritance destined for and entrusted to him."[126] The Church also teaches that Adam and Eve, our first parents, were constituted in a state called "original justice," in which they were in harmony with themselves, each other, God, and the entirety of creation.[127] As long as man was aligned with the will of God, he lacked nothing, and thus neither suffered nor faced death.[128] However, this does not mean there was no evil in the world because as the *Catechism* states: "The universe was created in a state of journeying toward its ultimate perfection." It also says that "with physical good there also exists physical evil as long as creation has not reached perfection."[129]

This is actually for the benefit of mankind because God deliberately left creation in an unfinished state (that is, with physical evil) to allow humanity the opportunity to participate in perfecting it. This allows mankind to grow and evolve and to share in His providence.[130] Because man still had original justice and was in harmony with creation, there was no need for suffering to highlight the goods that were needed prior to the Fall. Natural evil, the lack of harmony between living creatures, did not exist

---

[125] Ibid.
[126] CCC 299.
[127] CCC 374-375.
[128] CCC 376.
[129] CCC 310.
[130] CCC 307.

prior to the Fall as described in Genesis 1, when man was in harmony with all living creatures and all men and animals ate green plants and no one died.[131]

However, this harmony was broken when man, tempted by the Devil, disobeyed God.[132] The ramifications of this initial sin were and are severe. Having separated himself from his Creator, man lost the inner harmony of his body, leading to sickness and death. The union between man and woman became less harmonious as well, subject to tension, lust, and domination. Even the harmony with creation was lost; the physical world became subject to decay and nature became hostile to man, with both man and beast preying upon each other.[133]

This makes apparent the third critical point in understanding God's providence: the only evil that has lasting negative effect is the evil of sin, which is the loss of union with God. Ironically, the reason given in Genesis for the Original Sin was that Eve wanted to become like God, which we now know was God's goal for humanity as well.[134] Unfortunately, by listening to Satan and not trusting God, the first couple proved themselves unready for eternal life with God. God, Who exists outside of time, knew this with perfect foresight and of course, being all-powerful, could have stopped it.[135] The Church teaches that God permitted this sin because He could draw forth even greater good from it, with the redemptive actions of Jesus on the Cross.[136] The Church also teaches that God did not abandon man after the Fall, but in fact

[131] Genesis 1:29-30.
[132] Ibid., 397.
[133] Ibid., 400.
[134] Genesis 3:6 and 2 Peter 1:4
[135] Luke 15:20.
[136] CCC 411-412.

calls to him.[137] This is consistent with the loving father we see in the parable of the Prodigal Son, who never gives up on his son as he waits by the road for his return.

To facilitate that return, God introduced the evil of punishment, which for the most part was done through the introduction of natural evils like sickness, disability, and death, although physical evils were also intensified.[138] These evils were initiated to deter future sin, to remind men of their mortality, and most of all to bring man from sin to salvation utilizing the four tasks of suffering.

St. Thomas explains that evil is a defect in a creature's operation, a loss of its integrity, or a corruption of its form. The evil that consists of a voluntary defect in a creature's operation has the nature of a fault since it is willed by the creature.[139] God is perfect and thus is never responsible for a defective action, which is the evil of sin. Nor does He will the evil of sin, for it separates man from his Creator. He does permit sin, however. The primary reason is that for man to have legitimate free will, God must allow the possibility that men will at times misuse that freedom by making disordered choices. In essence, God allows moral evil because He wants us to come to Him freely. In addition, the all-powerful God can make good from any evil.[140] As the *Catechism* points out, "From the greatest moral evil ever committed—the rejection and murder of God's only Son, caused by the sins of all men—God, by his grace that abounded all the more, brought the greatest of goods: the glorification of Christ

---

137 Ibid., 410.
138 Genesis 3:14-19.
139 *ST* I, q. 48, art. 5.
140 CCC 311.

and our redemption."[141] This ability of God to bring good out of even moral evil will be explored more thoroughly in chapter 9.

St. Thomas then points out that God is the ultimate cause of the corruption of some things in the physical environment because He designed them in such a way that they are corruptible.[142] The Church agrees with this position, and in fact takes it a bit further, recognizing that God created the world in a state of journeying to its ultimate perfection, and until that is reached, there will be physical good and also physical evil in the form of constructive and destructive forces of nature operating side by side.[143] We were given the responsibility of caring for our physical environment as a means of training us to act according to God's will while participating in perfecting the world around us. If we fail in this task, as was shown in the aftermath of Original Sin, our activities will turn the evil of sin into physical evils. These will cause suffering, which motivates repentance and moral growth. This dynamic will be explored in chapter 7.

Thomas further asserts that the order of the universe requires that there should be some things that can and do sometimes fail, and so God, to bring about the good of the order of the universe, causes the corruption of things.[144] For instance, in a finite universe, for new life to be born and grow requires the consumption of existing life, thus producing the life cycles and food chains that involve all living beings. This process also involves the appearance of certain beings along with the disappearance of others.[145]

---

[141] Ibid., 312.
[142] ST I, q. 49, art. 2.
[143] CCC 310.
[144] ST I, q. 49, art. 1.
[145] CCC 310.

This constant evolution of living matter is consistent with what has been observed by science and is part of divine providence, the dispositions by which God guides His creation toward its ultimate perfection.[146] Thomas states that it is God's will that things are naturally corrupted because that is a requirement of preserving the natural order.[147] God's use of sickness, injury, and disability as a reminder of our mortality and to recall us to Himself will be discussed in detail in chapter 8.

Finally, Thomas notes that the order of justice also belongs to the order of the universe, and that requires that penalties should be dealt out to sinners; therefore, God is also the author of the evil which is penalty.[148] As will be discussed at length in chapter 10, God's punishment is meant to rehabilitate the sinner, not destroy him. God uses secondary causes to execute His plans, and so physical and natural evils can play this role as they did in the case of Original Sin.

In the end, it is important to separate the concept of evil, which is the absence of an expected good, from the concept of malice, which is to cause harm intentionally. Only moral evil, the evil of sin, involves malice. Sin is to put one's self-interest first and thus is the antithesis of love. It is the lack of union with God, and hence is contrary to one's purpose as well as a complete impediment to happiness. Sin is rebellion against God and is therefore the only evil that causes lasting effects. It is also the only evil not attributable to God and can only be perpetrated by creatures with free will. No other evil negatively affects one's salvation.

---

[146] CCC 302.
[147] *ST* I q. 19, art. 9.
[148] *ST* I, q. 49, art. 2.

Why All People Suffer

As Thomas describes above, physical and natural evils belong to the design of the universe and involve no malice or impediments to one's salvation. Although executed by secondary causes, these causes have no free will, and thus the will that is causing them is unmistakably God's. Because these evils result in human suffering, most people identify them as opposing goodness, but this is not the case. They lack goodness. Suffering is our ability to detect that lack, and because it is uncomfortable, it motivates us either to attain the missing good or avoid the situation altogether. As will be discussed in depth in the next four chapters, either one of these alternatives could be God's desired outcome for the person.

Because they are part of the universal design, many people will assume that the effects of physical and natural evils are essentially random. This is selling God short. If God's highest priority is the salvation of every person, it stands to reason that all physical and natural evils are in support of that goal and that each evil in our lives has some salvific purpose. There are no random events with God.

For this to make sense requires one to believe in an infinitely powerful and loving God Who is capable and motivated enough to plan every minute of every person's life. The impoverished God, required for the case where evil opposes good, will not make sense in this environment. Similarly, a solution that compromises the nature of God in a way that implies He does not care about His creation also will not work, and in fact is counter to logic, experience, and Scripture. No rational being would expend the kind of effort it would take to create a universe if he did not care about it, because the very definition of rationality is to do things intentionally and with cause. Our experiences also make it clear that any being that spends considerable effort on something must care about it. Finally, Scripture is clear in that God cares about everything He creates, down to the number of hairs on our heads and the fate of every sparrow.[149] If a person believes with the Church that these things are true, then he will be able to appreciate that when he suffers from an illness or a natural disaster, it is for the salvation of souls, though not necessarily his own.

Providence, God's plan for the universe, reflects the fact that (as Jesus explained with the parable of the Prodigal Son) God desires nothing more than to share His life with His children, and the Church has maintained from its earliest days that "God became man so that man could become God."[150] God designed us for this purpose in His own image and gives us the freedom required to love as He loves, to partake fully of the divine nature. For this reason, He allows sin to exist, knowing with certain foresight that men will abuse their freedom but also knowing that He is all-powerful and can bring good out of any evil. God, knowing that we can never be happy outside of His love, utilizes evil and suffering to put us on the path to joy.

This point makes many people uncomfortable, but it is an artifact of the previously debunked belief that evil is opposed to God and all that is good. Evil is the absence of a good that ought to be there, and, with the exception of moral evil, is a help and not a hindrance to salvation. To deny that God is the author of natural evil, physical evil, and the evil of punishment is inaccurate and misleading in all cases except when they are the result of the evil of sin and fails to give God credit for His rehabilitative efforts.

It is perhaps ironic that what has kept us from solving the problem of evil was not our understanding of the nature of the

---

[149] Matthew 10:29-31.
[150] CCC 460.

unseen but benevolent, all-knowing, and all-powerful God, but the understanding of evil, which we regularly experience through suffering. The solution to the problem of evil, so vexing for so many for so long, can be solved when we recognize that evil is not in opposition to God and all that is good, but is simply the lack of good that we need to attain. It can be thought of not as a curse or a threat, but as an opportunity to grow in faith and virtue, which leads to eternal happiness. Similarly, suffering is not a curse, but it is a grace given by God to detect the good we lack and to motivate us to attain it.

Once we understand that evil is the absence of good and that suffering is God's very powerful way of identifying that we lack some good we need for eternal happiness, then we can start to understand how a loving God can make use of them to lead us to be like Him so that we may live in the eternal joy of His company. With this new perspective that God uses evil and suffering to direct, protect, and perfect us, we can re-evaluate the role of the various types of evil in God's plan. While it is obvious that it is not possible to evaluate every type of evil and every form of suffering, it is possible to show pertinent examples that demonstrate the concept's validity and that can provide a template that can be used to discern the messages of other cases that a person may experience.

7

Physical Evil as an Opportunity for Growth

God gave humanity dominion over the universe and deftly guides it through suffering in its efforts to perfect the earth for its own usage. It is a world of beauty, rich in resources that can provide humans not only with simple pleasures, but also great power, if we can find these resources and discover how to use them. In many cases, the very things that sustain us can also imperil us if not used properly. The sun that warms us can also burn us. We can drown in the water we use to drink and bathe. Nuclear power can run a city and can be used to destroy it as well.

As Pope Francis points out, "our 'dominion' over the universe should be understood more properly in the sense of responsible stewardship."[151] This makes sense because man and his environment are co-dependent: man depends on the material world for his sustenance while the material world depends on man for its care and upkeep. While this is perhaps more obvious in modern times, when man's destructive power from wars and pollution can render an area unproductive and uninhabitable, even in antiquity, over-farming could render the land barren if crops

---

[151] Francis, *Laudato Si': On Care for Our Common Home* (San Francisco, CA: Ignatius Press, 2015), 116.

were not rotated. In fact, as discussed in the last chapter in the Genesis story of the Fall, man and his environment were linked with the land being cursed as a result of human action.[152]

If man does not care for his environment, it will eventually lack the ability to sustain him. Suffering will gradually increase during this process of dissolution, and if not heeded, death and decay for both humans and the environment will eventually follow. As Pope Francis notes, this has been a significant concern for the last half-century, eliciting warnings from St. Paul VI, St. John Paul II, and Pope Benedict XVI, culminating in his own 2015 encyclical, *Laudato Si': On Care for Our Common Home*.[153]

Before the Fall, man was in harmony with the created world, and even though it was still evolving, man lacked nothing and so he did not suffer. When that harmony was lost through Original Sin, divine revelation makes clear that God deliberately placed physical evils in our path to provide us with the challenges we would need to grow. These challenges would also provide us with the opportunity and responsibility to mold our environment to meet our needs.[154] Simply stated, what humans perceive as physical evils are the gaps in the perfection of a still-evolving universe that affect people's well-being, generally by causing them discomfort or to fear for their safety. Often, what we see as physical evils are merely a failure on the part of humans to recognize or utilize their potential for goodness. This explains why the *Catechism* would note the intrinsic linkage between humans and the material world.[155]

---

[152] Genesis 3:17.
[153] Francis, *Laudato Si'*, 4-7.
[154] CCC 307.
[155] CCC 1046.

It may be hard for some people to accept that physical evil — which consists of seismic activity like earthquakes, volcanoes, and tsunamis; weather events like hurricanes, tornados, blizzards, floods, and droughts; and physical dangers like cliffs, undertows, and quicksand, all of which can result in destruction, injury, and death — is for the benefit of humanity. Some will argue that large-scale physical disasters are the works of a punitive God, and others will argue that the people involved are incidental to the bigger picture of the evolving universe. However, when put in the right perspective, one can see how suffering from physical evils brings out greater goods that are important to man's redemption.

The physical universe, then, was created in a way that would provide humans the opportunities to "complete the work of creation, to perfect its harmony for their own good and that of their neighbors."[156] Here, it is important to remember that "man's last end" is union with God in the Beatific Vision, not the perfection of the Earth. It is clear that the omnipotent, omniscient God placed humans in a paradise where there was no suffering, because everything God made was good.[157] But just because everything that was made was good does not mean that everything that would ultimately be needed was made. God left those gaps in the perfection of the physical universe to give humans something to do and provide purpose in their lives. In many cases, people will recognize that their purpose is to correct the gaps experienced by humans as physical evils, impediments to comfort and safety. However, they also present opportunities to grow in virtue. As the *Catechism* notes in quoting Aquinas, God's plan includes

---

[156] CCC 307.
[157] Genesis 1.

physical evil, with both constructive and destructive forces of nature, until creation reaches perfection.[158]

As discussed in the last chapter, there are no accidents in God's plans. The Church states unequivocally that "God has absolute sovereignty over the course of events" and that "God cares for all from the least things to the great events of the world and its history."[159] If someone suffers, it is for a reason and in fact is directed toward the greatest good for someone, but not necessarily the immediate sufferer. Some may consider it unfair that they have to suffer for the benefit of another. However, this is also what Jesus did on the Cross. When we are given the opportunity to suffer for the benefit of another, we have two choices. If we follow Jesus in sacrificing ourselves for another, it will save us. If we think only of ourselves, we will be condemned.[160]

This is true of even the most devastating physical calamities. One such event was the catastrophic earthquake that laid Lisbon to waste on the morning of All Saints' Day 1755. A current guidebook to the city describes the three-fold terror of the event.[161] It began with an estimated 8.5 to 9.0-magnitude earthquake that lasted for three and a half minutes, creating six-foot-wide fissures in the streets, while collapsing many buildings and churches. Forty-five minutes later, a thirty-foot-high tsunami hit the city, toppling buildings and causing widespread flooding. This was followed by five days of devastating fires, many caused by the upended candles from Masses in honor

---

[158] CCC 310.

[159] CCC 303.

[160] Matthew 16:25.

[161] "The Lisbon Earthquake of 1755," LisbonLisboaPortugal.com, https://lisbonlisboaportugal.com/Lisboninformation/1755-lisbon-earthquake.html.

of the saints. In all, more than seventy-five thousand people died, and more than 90 percent of the buildings in the city of Lisbon were destroyed.

Michael Peterson describes the event as a turning point in intellectual history because rationalist religious systems supporting unqualified optimism were discredited.[162] He references Voltaire's poem "The Lisbon Earthquake" as a direct attack on Gottfried Leibniz's view that this is the best of all possible worlds. More importantly, perhaps, was that the well-known poem put to words what many felt: that God had abandoned them for some unknown reason, leaving them without hope. Given that many died in Mass on All Saints' Day as the roofs of the churches collapsed, many lost faith in God altogether. So, along with Voltaire, many ask, "What was gained?"

The physical world presents men with choices, much in the same way that it presented Adam and Eve with a choice. Our first parents could have remained in Paradise indefinitely if they had simply responded according to God's will that they refrain from taking the fruit that they were told would cause death.[163] So too can every human aspire to spend eternity in an even better situation in Heaven if they respond according to God's will when confronted with environmental challenges, or they can choose a path that leads to eternal damnation.

In the specific case of Lisbon in 1755, the population was severely tested, and, like in all crises, some reacted with charity toward their neighbors and others undoubtedly turned to looting. Some people prospered, like the prime minister Sebastiao de

---

[162] Michael L. Peterson, *The Problem of Evil* (Notre Dame, IN: University of Notre Dame Press, 2017), 2.

[163] Genesis 3:1-3.

Melo, known to history as the Marquis of Pombal, who proved adept at dealing with disaster.[164] His simple philosophy of "Bury the dead and heal the living" resonated with the populace, and in just over a month, his chief engineer Manuel de Maia had designed five plans for the rebuilding of Lisbon. Pombal chose the complete redesigns of the neighborhoods of Rossio and Baixa and implemented the first grid system, which was copied the world over. The city was rebuilt, and a statue of the Marquis of Pombal is in a prominent place overlooking it.

The entire point of the Lisbon earthquake was certainly not to improve the career of the prime minister or spread the design ideas of Manuel de Maia. Yet, this might have been some of the point if it led somehow to the salvation of souls. As discussed previously, God is attentive to every one of His creatures, and therefore there is a specific reason for what happens to every individual that was affected by this or any other disaster. Most people's judgment of the event is based on some sort of aggregation of the experiences of each affected person. For instance, on city tours, the discussion is about the thousands who died or were displaced. But doing so is to miss the bigger picture. Ultimately, this is not about an aggregation, but instead is about how it affected each individual. It is not about punishment or indifference on the part of God, either. It is about His reaching out to the elect and calling them to Himself.

Granted, there was incredible suffering and hardship among those in Lisbon and its vicinity that day and in the aftermath: Voltaire catalogs this quite well. But Voltaire, or any other human for that matter, cannot adequately catalog the good that came out of it. Not because it does not exist, but because there

---

[164] "The Lisbon Earthquake of 1755."

is no way for us to quantify how many souls were saved, nor how to value the eternal bliss of a person versus the suffering it took to bring it out. As discussed throughout this book, suffering has four tasks to complete in God's plan for salvation, and disasters like this one offer opportunities for all of them.

While it is true that the lack of institutional control during disasters can encourage some to exploit the defenseless, some people also develop virtuous habits based on proper self-love to mitigate the suffering. While some people's faith in God is shaken, others turn to God when there are no temporal solutions to their problems. Disasters, particularly those of the same scope of the Lisbon earthquake, provide abundant opportunities to aid the suffering as well as many opportunities to share in the suffering of Christ by suffering for the benefit of others, whether through heroic actions to save lives or by simply offering up one's suffering for the spiritual good of those that provide aid. All these things have spiritual value, and in the case of those who share in the suffering of Christ, they also have the promise of sharing in His glory.[165] While it is impossible for humans to measure, a good God must know that the spiritual gain is worth the temporal pain, or else He would not have planned the earthquake to begin with.

The Lisbon earthquake provides an excellent case study on how one's understanding of divine providence effects his attitude toward God and his subsequent actions. Voltaire dismisses the entire concept of divine providence because he deems it incompatible with the suffering involved in the disaster.[166] In answer to Voltaire, Jean-Jacques Rousseau maintained his commitment to providence, choosing to blame humans for the extent of the

---

[165] John Paul II, *Salvifici doloris*, 22, quoting Romans 8:17-18.
[166] Fergusson, *The Providence of God*, 124-125.

disaster, from poor choices in building to the inadequacy of their response. Fergusson rightfully sees Rousseau's response as reflecting only a general rather than a particular oversight by God.[167] He shifts the blame, but does not recognize how it could be part of God's providential plan.

Fergusson offers other theologians' insights as well. John Wesley recognized the disaster as God's judgment on Lisbon, an act of divine retribution that also represented an opportunity for repentance for those involved as well as those who heard about it.[168] This reflects a view of particular interest by God, but most see it as not beneficial to man and thus not providential. This is of course to overlook the spiritual benefits in favor of the temporal costs. Fergusson also notes that some theologians, including St. Thomas Aquinas, see disasters of this type to be governed by God but not as specific divine action. Others blamed natural causes directly; some as the primary cause, others as a secondary cause.[169]

Fergusson maintains that the "somber reflections on the Lisbon disaster cast doubt on a providence that actively wills each event." He feels that this strengthened the position of the Deists, who denied particular providence in mundane matters in favor of a general providence that runs the world through a pre-ordained plan, which is the prevalent view in the world today, as people have become increasingly reliant on technical expertise to explain what they experience.[170]

While Fergusson may be correct in his assessment of the modern view of God's providence, this view is clearly inconsistent

---

[167] Ibid., 126.
[168] Ibid., 127.
[169] Ibid., 128-129.
[170] Ibid., 132.

with the revealed truth held by the Church. First of all, the salvation of individual souls is not mundane to the God represented by the father in the parable of the Prodigal Son. It means everything to Him. If God is not active in our lives, then there would be no reason to pray, yet Jesus admonished us to do so, saying, "Ask and it will be given to you."[171] In fact, every bit of suffering we endure militates against this view, since each incidence is a warning from God that we are somehow lacking something we need. Even many of the evils we perceive are acts of particular providence, leading us to order our lives to the greatest good, which is union with God.

There's another factor to consider as well: God exists out of time. Fergusson seems to understand general providence as God defining a plan and then having it executed with no interference, whereas with particular providence, God will continue to tweak His design. While it *could* happen like that, it doesn't need to for God, Whom we know exists outside of time and can see the whole arc of time at once. God would not need to revisit His plan in this case. He would have seen the various potential outcomes and chosen the one that He felt was optimized. This means that the only potential difference between general and particular providence would be that God would not plan at the individual level if there was only general providence. The Church is adamant that this is not the case, and why would it be? If human parents love and care for all their children, would we not expect the same from an all-powerful God?

The fact that earthquakes are the result of the movement of tectonic plates might make some believe that they are purely natural events, until they stop to consider Who made the plates

---

[171] Matthew 7:7.

the way that they are and Who set them in motion. God always acts through secondary causes, and the physical ones act through a set of physical laws that only God can break, so it is clear that it is God's will that these things happen. If we understand God as all-powerful and all-knowing, while also having the benevolent characteristics of the father of the Prodigal Son, we can recognize that He is capable of setting a plan in place that would arrange for an earthquake at precisely the time needed to provide what was required to optimize the salvation of souls. As St. Catherine of Siena reminds us, God does nothing without our salvation in mind.[172]

Another way of understanding suffering from physical evils, and one perhaps more illustrative of the dichotomies of decision-paths associated with ordering one's life to temporal versus eternal goals, is how people use physical resources to conduct their daily lives. Using the world's resources responsibly alleviates suffering; it helps meet human needs for food, drink, shelter, clothing, medicines, transportation, and the sharing of knowledge. Unfortunately, people are often self-centered, causing them to pursue luxury instead of need and to put their own interests above what is required both for the common good and the good of the environment they are supposed to be maintaining. This will lead to suffering. People have caused suffering by unwisely building on flood plains, fault lines, and in coastal areas that subsequently were destroyed by predictable events, making the impact far worse than it might have been. This was what Rousseau observed in the Lisbon earthquake.[173] In addition, people have poisoned the land, the air, and the seas with pollution from factories and

---

[172] CCC 313.
[173] Fergusson, *The Providence of God*, 126.

automobiles, oil and chemical leaks, and radiation from nuclear events that have made some areas unlivable. People have destroyed forests by clear-cutting, mountains by strip-mining, and fields by over-farming.

God permits humanity to make poor decisions, as is required to maintain a truly free will, but God also admonishes humanity through suffering when we fail in our duty as the stewards of creation. He motivates us to correct the problems we cause through relentless feelings of discomfort and pain, as will be explored in the pages ahead. Unfortunately, as Pope Francis points out in *Laudato Si'*, environmental concerns in the modern age are often caused by those remote from the situation (businessmen, politicians, and the like), and without the witness of those directly affected, there is little to no motivation for these people to stop harming the environment.[174]

The world is beautiful, intricately made to the smallest microscopic detail, which reflects the beauty and intellect of the Creator. But hidden within it are also challenges: steep peaks that are difficult to climb, rivers and oceans that are difficult to cross, ocean currents and undertows that endanger the swimmer, cliffs and falling rocks that endanger the hiker. These things cause suffering when encountered without the right tools and training. Yet, with experience and training, humans have mastered them all, or, at the very least, have learned how to avoid the danger. Steep mountains become ski slopes; high waves become prime surfing locations. What before caused suffering now becomes fun as people learn how to use what God created to their advantage.

God provided the created universe as an environment capable of bringing humanity to its fullest potential, to live as God

---

[174] Francis, *Laudato Si'*, 49.

desires, according to love. What people experience as physical evils, things like hurricanes and earthquakes, but also heat waves and cold rains, are actually opportunities for men to subdue the earth and make the world a more hospitable place. God sets the physical stage in such a way that the gaps in its perfection appear at the very time they are needed to provide mankind the challenges it needs to develop in virtue and the opportunities it needs to share in the perfection of the universe. The suffering associated with those gaps alerts us to the good that is lacking and motivates us to attain it, whether it be ways to subdue the earth or to improve our knowledge of God and His will for us.

Sometimes, these gaps redirect us to other options if the evil is too great for us to bridge. For instance, by destroying a property that was in some way harmful to our soul, God forcefully shows us that there is a better way. For those who are open to the graces it offers, the suffering associated with physical evil is a blessing that leads to union with God and eternal happiness. However, to those who reject God's call and abuse their free will to sin, suffering from all its sources will remain a curse, never to be resolved.

God's ultimate goal in presenting man with an imperfect environment is the perfection of the human race, not the perfection of the physical universe, although that will be a consequence of the former. The *Catechism* provides the linkage between our suffering in the current world and our attaining the next one, when it asserts that by working together in subduing the environment, we develop the virtues that clear the path for grace to enter our hearts. This in turn builds up the Kingdom of God on earth.[175]

The *Catechism* explains that at the end of time, the Kingdom of God will come in its fullness. After the universal judgment,

---

[175] CCC 1042.

the righteous will reign forever with Christ, glorified in body and soul. The universe itself will be renewed.[176] Note that God perfects the universe after perfecting man through suffering to provide the Kingdom a suitable environment, free of the evil that is the source of suffering. This final realization of God's plan is called the "new heavens and the new earth" in Sacred Scripture.[177]

The physical world, then, is a training ground of sorts, provided for humanity to develop the virtues that ultimately lead to beatitude. What men perceive as physical evils are actually opportunities to demonstrate stewardship consistent with the nature of God. It is incumbent on man to care for this world and to maintain it, because to fail to do so would not only deprive man of this "training ground" that is necessary to demonstrate his merits, but it would also not allow man to sustain himself, resulting in temporal death. Even worse, it would mean that man had failed to develop the virtue that leads to the Beatific Vision, which would cause permanent separation from God in Hell.

---

[176] Ibid.
[177] Ibid.

8

Natural Evil in a Contingent World

In this model, natural evil refers to the loss of human function or threats to human existence that are related to nature, the living matter of the universe. These include disability, injury, illness, and death. Each of these is an integral part of the universal design that perfects and elevates man ultimately to share in the life of God and partake of the Beatific Vision and, as such, each will be discussed in turn in this chapter. As the *Catechism* notes, "of all visible creatures, only man is able to know and love his creator. He is the only creature on earth that God willed for its own sake and he alone is called to share, by knowledge and love, in God's own life. It was for this end that he was created, and this is the fundamental reason for his dignity."[178]

In the Thomistic framework, there is a large subset of the evil of pain and punishment called the evil of natural defect. This evil exists because God allows some things to be corrupted as part of the natural design of the universe.[179] As a reminder, St. Thomas holds that

> God brought things into being in order that His goodness might be communicated to creatures and at the same

[178] CCC 356.
[179] *ST* I, q. 19, art. 9.

time, represented by them and because His goodness could not be adequately represented by one creature alone, He produced many and diverse creatures, that what was wanting to one in the representation of the divine goodness might be supplied by another.[180]

He also asserts that the same divine wisdom that causes things to be different for the sake of the perfection of the universe also causes there to be inequality between them.[181] Using the example of a house which uses different materials for the roof and the foundation, St. Thomas demonstrates that inequality is necessary for the perfection of the whole.

Disability

Many people feel that such inequality is unfair and inconsistent with a benevolent God, particularly when confronted with natural or physical evils that are clearly "acts of God."

Perhaps the natural evil that people have the greatest difficulty reconciling with a benevolent God is that innocent children are born with abnormalities, whether it be lack of sensory perception like being blind or deaf; lack of limbs or the use of them; lack of physical size, strength, or control; or lack of mental or psychological capability. St. Thomas answers this concern by reminding the reader that Original Sin deprived humanity of original justice and left human nature on its own and in a disordered state.[182] Not only did this untether reason from God and

---

[180] *ST* I, q. 47, art. 1.
[181] *ST* I, q. 47, art. 2.
[182] *ST* I-II, q. 87, art. 7.

disorder the powers of the soul, but disorder in the body made it subject to corruption.[183]

Consistent with this view, St. Thomas is unapologetic in saying that birth defects and other infirmities from which children suffer are the effects and the punishments of Original Sin. This does not mean, however, that God abandoned humanity in a punitive act of spite. St. John Paul II's insight on God's use of punishment is that He uses it to rebuild goodness in the sinner.[184] The Angelic Doctor seemingly agrees, insisting that "defects and infirmities are directed by Divine providence, to the salvation of men, either of those who suffer, or of others who are admonished by their means—and also to the glory of God."[185] St. Thomas's point is important because it is unambiguous in its assertion that God has a specific salvific reason for every incidence of defect and infirmity, even if the reasons are often unintelligible to those directly or indirectly affected. As previously discussed, God cares about every element of His creation.

Birth defects need to be treated in two broad categories, lethal and non-lethal, because the ramifications are very different. Some defects are so significant that the person will not survive childhood. One example is Tay-Sachs disease, a rare, inherited lipid metabolism disorder which causes too much of a fatty substance to build up in the brain, a process that begins in the womb.[186] Affected children appear to develop normally for their first six months and then experience progressive loss of mental ability,

[183] *ST* I-II, q. 85, art. 5.

[184] John Paul II, *Salvifici doloris*, 12

[185] *ST* I-II, q. 87, art. 7.

[186] NIH, "Tay-Sachs Disease Information Page," https://www.ninds.nih.gov/Disorders/All-Disorders/Tay-Sachs-Disease-Information-Page.

dementia, blindness, deafness, difficulty swallowing, seizures, and even with the best of care, death before their fifth birthday. There is no cure; the best that can be done for the child is to manage his symptoms and show him love and attention for as long as the child lives.

Fatal childhood diseases like Tay-Sachs are very challenging because they involve the suffering of innocents. These children are "martyrs" of sorts, suffering and dying for the spiritual benefit of others, without the benefit of understanding why it is happening to them. Since they live and die in a state of innocence, their path to eternal life, while painful, is fairly clear. Incapable of committing personal sin before the age of reason, baptized children are assumed to be in the state of grace and Heaven-bound. However, the Church also hopes that God will have mercy on the unbaptized children but implores its members to baptize their children as soon as possible since that is what the Lord said was required in John 3:5.[187] In these types of situations, it seems that the children suffer not for themselves but for those around them.

Many people assume that the child is better off dead than to suffer so severely, so they procure an abortion when they are made aware of the situation.[188] Others do so to spare themselves what is undoubtedly a heart-wrenching experience of watching their child suffer without hope of a cure. In fact, Marrick Kukin came to the conclusion that "not taking precautions to prevent a Tay-Sachs tragedy seems to be the cruelest path to follow."[189] However, when people take matters into their own hands, they

---

[187] CCC 1261.

[188] Marrick Kukin, "Tay-Sachs and the Abortion Controversy," *Journal of Religion and Health* 20, no. 3 (Fall 1981): 224.

[189] Ibid., 225.

sell God short. We know that God does everything for a reason, and they overestimate their own knowledge of the situation. Indeed, despite what Kukin calls "suffering of unimaginable dimension, affecting every aspect of a couple's life" in caring for a Tay-Sachs child, those who choose to try to avoid it through abortion may simply be adding to their suffering.[190] For example, Michael Ruse reports that "it seems overwhelmingly clear that couples who have a fetus aborted because it is found to be diseased suffer a great deal." He notes that in an admittedly small study of thirteen couples who had a therapeutic abortion, almost all the men and women suffered severe depression following the abortion, and four of the couples separated.[191]

Looking at it a different way, couples with a lethally disabled child might see that God is teaching them to love profoundly by caring for the suffering child, giving of themselves in a way that most are not called to do. As hard as it is, when they hold their Tay-Sachs child and offer him or her comfort, they are taking on part of the child's suffering. This is suffering carrying out its third task of unleashing love, but it also includes the fourth task, which is that of redeeming the soul of the suffering parent. The parent suffers for the benefit of the child, who is also suffering for the sake of his parents. In this way, the parents and the child are profoundly bound together in redemptive love, a bond that will not be broken when the child ultimately dies and which can extend out to those who witness it. If the suffering is borne well by the parent or caregiver, it can also encourage others in similar situations to look at it differently and perhaps see the value in the

---

[190] Ibid., 226.
[191] Michael Ruse, "Genetics and the Quality of Life," *Social Indicators Research* 7, no. 1/4 (January 1980): 429-430.

love they give to their afflicted child as well as in the wisdom of God. In fact, loving, devout parents of lethally disabled children can be effective catalysts for conversion while unleashing love by the witness and example they give to the community at large.

There are times where the death of a child provokes a response in the parents that can be used to further God's plan. As mentioned earlier, the death of Aaron Kushner as described by his father Harold led him to write *When Bad Things Happen to Good People*. Despite its impoverished view of God, it gave solace to millions of people with its message that suffering was not about punishment, which allowed them to forgive themselves and God.[192] As he wrote his book, Rabbi Kushner could see that Aaron's suffering and death could be for the benefit of others, and that gave him some solace as well.

The concerns of both the child and his family are different if the child's disability is non-lethal but instead limits natural human function in some way. Such birth defects are truly evil in that they are, by definition, the lack of some good, whether it be the lack of a limb or some other body part, or the lack of capability, whether it be sensory, intellectual, psychological, or social. The reality of birth defects of this kind is that they only are disabling relative to specific roles. Indeed, what disables a person for one role can often position him or her for success in another. For instance, being short in stature is a disadvantage for basketball and volleyball players, but it is an advantage for jockeys and gymnasts and has no impact at all on the vast majority of vocational choices. The blind are at a disadvantage in roles where sight is required, but lack of sight has not impeded people from having highly successful careers in music, computer

---

[192] Kushner, *When Bad Things Happen*, 3.

programming, and other vocations in which their limitations are not a factor or can be reasonably accommodated.

As we learn in the Creation story in Genesis, God makes everything perfect for its role in His plan. This is true for all people, even those we perceive as having severe disabilities. God's expectations of us are consistent with the skills and opportunities that He gives us. Jesus Himself says that "much will be required of the person entrusted with much and still more will be demanded of the person entrusted with more."[193] A central tenet of Thomistic theology is that for perfection of the whole, the world needs every kind of good, and that is the reason for both diversity and inequality.[194] Said another way, every person has a role to fill and is built specifically for that role. Even the most limited individuals have a role to play, if only to provide others the opportunity to demonstrate love toward them. Therefore, our expectations should also be aligned with what we are given, and we should not be jealous of those who have not only more skills and opportunities but more obligations. We should instead focus on what God has made us to do.

This is not meant to minimize the challenges that people with disabilities and their families face; in many cases, they can be overwhelming. The point is that every person has some form of limitation that is part of what defines the person. Even the most limited people are part of the human continuum of diversity and were made with a specific purpose in mind. Most do not suffer from their disabilities because non-lethal defects do not threaten their existence, they define their existence. Nevertheless, they can certainly be causes of frustration and irritation.

---

[193] Luke 12:48.
[194] *ST* I, q. 47, art. 2.

Why All People Suffer

An example is the case of Diane DeVries, who was born in 1950 without legs and with above-elbow upper extremity stumps.[195] Her physician saw her birth as such a shocking catastrophe that he passed out during the delivery. While her maternal grandmother rejected her, labeling her as "the devil's daughter" because of her impairment, her parents were loving and supportive, helping her to develop a remarkably positive self-image. Taking a cue from her father, she accepted her unique body as being something that could not be helped and was nobody's fault. She explains that she has always been "really in tune with my body," which she understood to be compact and streamlined; different, yet intact and healthy.

Despite her lack of limbs, DeVries experienced many of the ordinary events for a woman of her age. She was raised at home with her family, went to public school, and graduated from UCLA. She had an active social life, got pregnant, was married, and later divorced. As Nancy Eiesland put it, "She has lived an ordinary life in an unconventional body."[196]

The disability experience of those with mental handicaps is different and, in many ways, worse than that experienced by those with physical handicaps like DeVries.[197] First of all, because they think and communicate less efficiently than other people, some will find them hard to relate to, resulting in a tendency to dehumanize those with mental handicaps. Secondly, they are incapable of advocating for themselves, which leaves them

[195] Nancy L. Eiesland, *The Disabled God: Toward a Liberatory Theology of Disability* (Nashville, TN: Abingdon Press: 1994), 33-34.
[196] Ibid., 39.
[197] Stanley Hauerwas, *Suffering Presence: Theological Reflections on Medicine, the Mentally Handicapped and the Church* (Notre Dame, IN: University of Notre Dame Press, 1986), 176.

vulnerable. Third, their deficiencies cannot be solved by physical accommodations, so in most cases, they require care from others. Fourth, they do not hide their needs, which makes others uncomfortable, leading to alienation. Nevertheless, Stanley Hauerwas, a theologian and an advocate for the mentally disabled, asserts that "there is no reason to think they would on their own come to understand their condition as 'retardation' or that they are in some decisive way suffering."[198] It seems that even without a reasoning impediment, they would not miss what they never had. Further, even if they notice that others can do things faster or better than they can, that doesn't constitute suffering. In fact, everyone is subject to the experience of someone else doing something better than they do.

While it is likely true that those with Down syndrome do not suffer specifically because of their mental limitations, it is also likely that they will be discriminated against because of their disability, which will cause suffering. Hauerwas points out that those born with Down syndrome suffer from inadequate housing, inadequate medical care, inadequate schooling, and a lack of love and care. They will be discriminated against, teased, and bullied.[199]

The situation can be much the same for those with physical defects. As she got older, Diane DeVries was also regularly exposed to hostility and prejudicial treatment by people who interpreted her lack of limbs as monstrous.[200] For instance, a waitress objected to her sitting at the front of a restaurant because "she will make people sick." DeVries even was discriminated against by a charismatic Christian church she belonged to, when the

---

[198] Ibid.
[199] Ibid., 172.
[200] Eiesland, *The Disabled God*, 34-35.

pastor refused to let her join the choir because "it just would not look right." This treatment is not because of anything they do or fail to do; it is simply because they are different. Therefore, this type of suffering is caused by the evil of sin, not natural evil, and will be discussed further in the next chapter.

Although it has been shown that non-lethal birth defects are not directly related to suffering, the question still lingers for the people affected: "Why them?" There are as many reasons as there are people; in fact, there are more than that because God can often make multiple goods out of an evil. One truth is that limits create focus and help people find their true calling. Limitations force a certain level of humility before God and man and can also teach patience and gratitude toward those that help them. As David Elliot put it, "when one door closes in terms of physical capability, another one opens in terms of moral awareness."[201] There can also be spiritual benefits in being disabled. It can provide the time and aptitude for contemplation. To the extent that the disabled recognize and embrace the fact that their condition leads others toward God, their condition can be redemptive. On the other hand, some people with severe mental handicaps remain forever in a state of innocence.

Sometimes the most compelling reason for a person to have disabilities is for the positive effect they can have on other people. As related in the first section, the ninth chapter of the Gospel of John describes such a situation. At the beginning of the chapter, Jesus is asked by His disciples, "Rabbi, who sinned, this man or his parents, that he was born blind?" Jesus answered, "Neither

[201] David Elliot, "Defining the Relationship Between Health and Well-being in Bioethics," *New Bioethics* 22, no. 1 (2016): 14-16.

he nor his parents sinned; it is so that the works of God might be made visible through him."[202] Jesus then heals the man, who proceeds to be an effective witness to the Gospel, both because of his physical healing and because of his credible witness to the event.

There are many other ways that disabled people can influence those around them. Having a child with a disability can teach a family to love for the right reasons: because the child is a child of God entrusted to them for care. Hauerwas observes that the mentally handicapped bring their parents together in greater solidarity, force them to recognize the value of suffering, and teach them to advocate for themselves and to take responsibility for their child, rather than relying on professionals.[203] While a person's disability might cause people to discriminate and sin against her, at the same time it can bring out charitable love in others who take the opportunity to support her. Seeing the disabled person might also make onlookers reflect on life, and in some cases might change their perspective and drive moral growth. It might also motivate the right people to develop accommodations to reduce the impact of the disability.

People born with disabilities are part of the human continuum of diversity with a role to play in society, just like everyone else. Like everyone else, they are worthy of respect and of love. While their limitations can provide challenges both for the disabled people and the people trying to help them, they also offer an opportunity for moral and spiritual growth for everyone involved and in fact can be considered acts of particular providence. Consistent with that concept, Jesus pointed out that it is our

---

[202] John 9:2-3.
[203] Hauerwas, *Suffering Presence*, 215.

treatment of the least of our brothers that is the decisive factor in our final judgment.[204]

Death

As was made obvious in the discussion on disability, the existence of death changes everything regarding natural evils and suffering. Without the threat of death, evil lacks its sting and might be regarded as no more than an irritation or an inconvenience. Granted, one could argue that people are socially or psychologically threatened by loss of relationships, or a loss of a person's source of meaning, or the possibility of being relegated to Hell for an eternity—and these could cause one to suffer even without the threat of death. This is true, but for most people, death represents the most fundamental threat to their existence and thus plays a fundamental role in differentiating suffering from irritation, particularly in the case of natural evils. Death is thus the ultimate punishment for Original Sin, and suffering is the warning given to mankind that it is near.

Before going further, it is important to point out that the institution of death by God was not done out of vengeance or malice for mankind, but out of love. As St. John Paul II states in *Salvifici doloris*, "Punishment has a meaning not only because it serves to repay the objective evil of the transgression with another evil, but first and foremost because it creates the possibility of rebuilding goodness in the subject who suffers."[205] In fact, as will be shown, death plays a large role in the redemption of man, providing him with a second chance to live the life of joy God always intended for him.

---

[204] Matthew 25:31-46.
[205] John Paul II, *Salvifici doloris*, 12.

The *Catechism* teaches that "after his Fall, man was not aban-doned by God. On the contrary, God calls him and in a mysteri-ous way, heralds the coming victory over evil and his restoration from his Fall."[206] God foresaw that man would abuse his freedom as part of the growing process, so He planned accordingly, making use of man's sin to bring about good while providing suffering and punishment to guide him back on track. As discussed throughout this book, suffering is the God-given ability of humans to sense when they are lacking a critical good. Because the sensation is intense and uncomfortable, people are highly motivated to avoid it. In this way, suffering becomes directive. And because suffering highlights the lack of good, it directs us toward attaining the good we are lacking. In effect, when man chose not to listen to God, Who was telling him how to live in joy, God chose to direct man to his final end through various means, including suffering. It is important to note that considered in this way, suffering becomes a tool of divine providence rather than the proof that God is not benevolent or does not exist.

Philosopher Martha Nussbaum asserts that death is needed from a purely secular standpoint because without it, there would eventu-ally be a lack of resources to support the growth in the population.[207] Death is also an important reality in the plan of God's perfect uni-verse because it provides a second chance for man to fulfill his potential by being the gateway to eternal life. It is this reality that creates the opportunity for God to use the suffering associated with natural corruption for the benefit of the individual. Indeed, as will

---

[206] CCC 410.

[207] Martha Nussbaum, *The Therapy of Desire: Theory and Practice in Hellenistic Ethics* (Princeton, NJ: Princeton University Press, 2009), 226-233.

be shown in the remainder of this chapter, there are many ways that God can use natural evils such as injuries, illness, and even death to reorient people to God and beatitude as St. John Paul II envisioned.

God is no tyrant, however, and He does not force men into union with Himself. Rather, He makes use of natural evils and suffering to lead men to understand the choice before them. Natural evils like disability, illness, and injury provide men with a constant and vivid reminder of their finitude and the lack of good in the physical universe that awaits those who choose to stay separated from God. As in the case with physical evil, God uses natural evil to create an environment conducive to redemption and then employs the four tasks of suffering to lead humans to beatitude: to instill virtue, reorient the soul to God, release love in humans, and then redeem them. This was all made possible by the Incarnation, when God became man in the person of Jesus Christ, Who by His self-giving sacrifice demonstrated to man the path to eternal joy.[208]

In the end, however, death looms, not to end everything, but to give the elect a second chance at the life God intended for mankind, united with Him in the glow of the Beatific Vision.

The *Catechism* notes that "bodily death, from which man would have been immune if he had not sinned, is thus the last enemy of man left to be conquered."[209] It is through the four tasks of suffering that this is accomplished in many, but not all, cases. Indeed, as their faith becomes more mature, people can overcome this fear of death to the point that they will willingly

---

[208] CCC 457-460. The *Catechism* lists four reasons for the Incarnation: to reconcile us with God, to know God's love, to be our model of holiness, and to make us partakers of the divine nature.
[209] CCC 1008.

embrace it for the love of God and their suffering neighbors. By sharing in the redemptive suffering of Christ, they overcome death just as Jesus did, rising to new life.

The *Catechism* explains that death is transformed by Christ, Who through His obedience and free submission to His Father's will, "transformed the curse of death into a blessing."[210] It is a blessing because in death, God calls man to Himself.[211] As Paul wrote to Timothy, "This saying is sure: if we have died with him, we will also live with him."[212] Put another way, death is the entrance to eternal life, a reality that is prefigured in the baptismal rites.

Injuries

Natural evils, then, are a key component of God's plan of redemption, because by potentially leading to death, they serve as standing reminders that choices lay before each of us. Injuries are bodily damages that can be caused by any source of evil, and they result in suffering when the injuries are significant enough to threaten one's existence. Injuries from natural sources are generally related to the food chain, either from predators attacking their prey or from potential prey defending themselves. In modern times, most people do not actively hunt for their food, and so injuries from natural evils are now relegated to things like snake bites and the occasional shark attack. They are mentioned here simply for completeness while identifying a few specific cases below.

Suffering due to injury serves as a warning both to others and to the injured to stay away from the situations that caused the

---

[210] CCC 1009.
[211] CCC 1011.
[212] 2 Timothy 2:11.

injury. This can teach prudence, but it also can re-orient people to God as they contemplate their mortality. Suffering injuries from nature can also unleash love to those who aid the injured, and it can even result in redemption as in the case of a person who sacrifices himself to the lion so that his companions may escape unharmed. Although injuries can lead to death, more often in cases of natural disaster and war than from natural evil, more than 90 percent of deaths worldwide are due to illness.[213]

Illness

Contrary to the view of those who seek to shelter God from the charge that He is responsible for evil and suffering, suffering from illness is not random.[214] As previously discussed, God ensures that every illness serves His providential plan for mankind. It has already been shown through both Scripture and Tradition that God is attentive to His creation, so this is just another example. There are three basic types of illness: the first results from a failure to supply

[213] World Health Organization, *Global Health Estimates 2016: Deaths by Cause, Age, Sex, by Country and by Region, 2000-2016* (Geneva: World Health Organization, 2018). While it is true that everyone ultimately dies of injury or illness, in today's world injuries account for less than 9 percent of the total. In the most affluent nations, they account for less than 6 percent of all deaths and if intentional and road deaths are excluded, it is less than 2 percent. In 2016, less than 5 million people died of injury out of a worldwide population of approximately 7.5 billion people. In comparison, more than 52 million died of an illness. http://www.who.int/healthinfo/global_burden_disease/en/

[214] Peter van Inwagen, *The Problem of Evil* (New York: Oxford University Press, 2006), 89.

the body with its basic needs; the second results from the attacks of microorganisms; and the third by a degradation of the body itself.

The first problem that humanity had to face was to feed itself. In the story of the Fall of Man, Adam's primary penalty was that he would have to toil for his food.[215] This was the first way in which man needed to subdue the earth. Genesis tells us that Abraham went as far as Egypt to escape famine and that in the time of Joseph, there was a worldwide famine for seven years that forced the tribe of Israel to travel twice to Egypt to keep from starving.[216]

Spurred on by the suffering that the hungry feel and articulate, humans have developed countless innovations to supply and distribute enough food to meet their collective needs. It is with good reason that the first work of mercy that Jesus acknowledges to the righteous in His story on the Last Judgment is that they fed the hungry.[217] Indeed, every hungry person represents an opportunity for others to practice charity, both as individuals and as a society. Because people have responded to the suffering, sometimes for selfish reasons, other times out of genuine charity, very few people die of starvation in the industrialized world today.[218]

The problem is more acute in the lowest-income economies, but even there, the rate of death from malnutrition has dropped 50 percent in the last sixteen years. Nevertheless, there is still work to be done in these countries since malnutrition causes

---

[215] Genesis 3:17-19.

[216] Genesis 12:10, 42:2, 43:2.

[217] Matthew 25:35.

[218] WHO, *Global Health Estimates 2016*. Eighteen people per million die of starvation annually in the highest-income economies. In the lowest-income economies, the rate has dropped from 448 to 226 per million since 2000.

almost three percent of all deaths, a level that is more than ten times higher than in affluent countries. This is almost entirely a problem of political and economic policies in the affected countries. Those who are aligned to the will of God will be charitable to the least of their brothers, resulting in low starvation rates. Uncharitable regimes will consolidate resources in the hands of the ruling elite, leading to mass suffering. As will be discussed in the following chapter on the evil of sin, structural sins like these also provide opportunities for redemption through suffering.

Suffering from malnutrition, like all forms of suffering, typically takes four steps to lead humans to reach their fullest potential in God's providential plan. The first is to drive humans to attain the physical good that is lacking, which is nutrition in this case. This initial drive is self-centered, but it can cause people to acquire human virtues like temperance, fortitude, prudence, and even justice in dealing with others as they work together to feed themselves. This predisposes people to seek greater goods, leading to the conversion of heart, the second step that allows them to look beyond their own needs to serve God and the greater good. In the third step, suffering provides an opportunity for that service as people minister to those starving around them. To the extent that they give fully of themselves for the poor, this can be redemptive for the "Good Samaritan." The final and ultimate step is for it to become redemptive for the sufferers, who recognize and rejoice in the fact that their suffering is for the benefit of others. This can be accomplished by accepting suffering that is thrust upon oneself, content to be a servant of God; or through active martyrdom, like Maximilian Kolbe, who, as discussed in section 1, allowed himself to be starved to death in place of another in a Nazi death camp.

Infectious diseases like tuberculosis, malaria, chicken pox, pneumonia, leprosy, and COVID-19 comprise the second category. For most of human history, people lived in fear of contagious diseases. Indeed, the book of Leviticus devotes two chapters to the identification and control of leprosy to protect the community.[219] When the Black Death descended upon Europe in the mid-fourteenth century, it killed one-third of the population in less than three years. It continued to reappear in various localities for the next four centuries.[220]

In a very simplistic way, these microorganisms are part of the "recycling process" that is necessary in a contingent, evolving world to create the raw materials for new life. All of them are potentially life-threatening, with some more deadly than others. Most do not have lingering effects. They either kill a person or, after a relatively short illness, the person's immune system recovers and removes the intruders. Because they are contagious, these illnesses have the capability of causing widespread epidemics and can pose a high risk for non-immune people to care for others.

There are specific reasons why some people and not others are infected at a given time, and why some of the infected die while others live as part of God's plan. Most of the time, only a relative few die of infectious diseases, and they usually are the very young with underdeveloped immune systems, or in the case of COVID-19, the elderly whose immune systems are compromised due to age and pre-existing co-morbidities.

---

[219] Leviticus 13-14.

[220] James Hitchcock, *History of the Catholic Church: From the Apostolic Age to the Third Millennium* (San Francisco: Ignatius Press, 2012), 219-220.

As in all cases, the people who contract and succumb do so for a reason, and that reason is to help someone become more God-like so that they can share in His life. In the case of the young, death can be a protective step to save an innocent child from being lost to sin later, as described in the Book of Wisdom.[221] The Scriptural account notes that in His mercy God calls the innocent child to Himself rather than subject him to the wickedness, deceit, and whirl of desire that could corrupt the innocent soul and cause it to be lost for eternity. At the same time, a child's death from contagious diseases can serve to help the parents or other observers in their path to Heaven by allowing them to love and care for their child, and even to share in his suffering, much as the parents of fatally disabled children do. In effect, the child can play the "martyr's" role, serving God and his parents by being the vehicle for the salvation of others and, in the process, being saved himself either by his innocence or by his active acceptance of his role in God's plan.

In the case of the elderly, death could be desirable if they have been suffering, or if they have completed their mission on earth. In the normal cold and flu season, most will view their illness as a relatively minor inconvenience that may have caused them to alter their normal routine and take care of themselves. Some who are naturally more reflective, or are sick for longer or with more intensity, may develop some humility and look to God for meaning that will resolve their suffering, while others may be hardened. Illness, like all suffering, is a test for onlookers, who can either help the sick or turn from them. As Jesus taught, this decision is what distinguishes the saved from the damned.[222]

---

[221] Wisdom 4:7-14.
[222] Matthew 25:31-46.

It is also important for those who suffer from illness to share what they are feeling with others. This has several purposes. It sets expectations for future sufferers, which helps reduce the uncertainty that is intrinsic to true suffering. It also helps to create solidarity with fellow sufferers, which can help both parties realize their own dignity and value, which all people need, as a lack of solidarity causes more suffering. It can help the medical community develop better treatments. It lets caregivers know that the sufferer needs help, and it provides direction on what the sufferer needs. Because suffering elicits compassion in others, it can also spur others to take action on the sufferer's behalf, acting as the Good Samaritan did, which has spiritual merit.

Over the last century and a half following the discovery of the principles of vaccination by Louis Pasteur, man has made impressive progress in fighting infectious diseases. In fact, simple infections that would have killed a person a century ago are now routinely cured with a ten-day regimen of penicillin, costing less than a dollar. There are now effective cures for diseases that were the scourges of the ancient world, including small pox, leprosy, measles, mumps, malaria, and even the bubonic plague. In fact, in the high-income economies, it is now relatively rare for a person to die of an infectious disease.[223] Infectious diseases still kill more than one-third of the people in

---

[223] WHO, *Global Health Estimates 2016*. Summary table. Only about 6 percent of people die from infectious diseases in high-income economies, a level that has remained stable since 2000. In 2000, the rate of death from infectious diseases in low-income economies was fifteen times higher than that, representing more than 50 percent of all deaths. Over the last sixteen years, this rate has improved by 60 percent but is still more than five times higher than in the high-income economies.

under-developed countries, but this has been rapidly improving in the twenty-first century.

In a universe with finite resources, death is required to provide resources for new life and even for existing life to grow. Death is also paradoxically needed for entrance into eternal life. At times, as we have seen in 2020, God sees fit to concentrate death in a way that will make the whole world take notice. Many people will struggle to understand why God subjects us to pandemics like the plague of the Middle Ages or the COVID-19 virus in 2020. This is not surprising and is just another manifestation of the "problem of evil" that has been with us since at least the days of Epicurus. Just as in the case of Epicurus, the struggle is based on a lack of understanding of the nature of God, the nature of evil, and of God's goals for mankind.

Why would a benevolent, all-powerful God allow a worldwide pandemic in 2020, causing widespread fear and unspeakable losses? Perhaps because He is using it to teach the whole world how to live virtuously, and because we are so ingrained in our vices, nothing short of a global pandemic will suffice. Many are undoubtedly angry at God for the imposition of the pandemic on their lives and the failure of God to protect them from evil, never realizing that God has already put the power to solve the problem into our hands and is now working to make us realize that the problem is not the virus, it is in us. Mankind already has the power to address the underlying virus, as it has demonstrated over the last hundred years of subduing contagious diseases. Granted, it may not have the specific vaccine formulated yet, but there is little question that in time it will. What mankind needs is to learn to love and help its most vulnerable neighbors, putting self-interest aside, and that may well be the legacy of the COVID-19 virus.

The world into which the COVID-19 virus was injected was badly fractured, with strong partisan divides within countries and between the nations on earth. By creating a common enemy for the entire human race that requires us to all work together to survive, God has provided the impetus for a radical re-shaping of the way people relate to each other. At the beginning of the crisis, the initial tendency was to isolate ourselves into our homes and blame all those around us for the circumstances. As the crisis grew and intensified, it became increasingly clear that we all needed to work together for the good of the whole. Communities and nations began to share best practices and, later, to share required supplies. Everyone came to realize that there were vulnerable populations that needed to be protected and that doing so would require sacrifices. At the same time, others were spontaneously offering to help their needy neighbors, and most came to recognize that being socially isolated was a bad thing.

All four tasks of suffering are on constant display in times like these, as God provides more opportunities than normal for men and women to grow spiritually. Many will only focus on the material hardship it brings, because this is the extent of their perspective, but others will take note that times of difficulty will bring out the best in those who love, while at the same time bringing out, and making clear to everyone, those who are self-ish. Because a virus infects kings and paupers alike, it teaches an invaluable lesson to humanity about the dignity of all life and also about how inconsequential human wealth and power are in the eyes of God. Saints and sinners are never easier to detect than in times of crisis, and it also causes people to recognize the value and cost of each and to decide which they prefer to be. Unfortunately, in the past, many people have quickly forgotten the lessons of previous crises, thus forcing additional crises to reinforce them. Others, though, are moved to repent and re-orient their focus to the higher goals, which is the reason that God utilizes contagious diseases as part of His providential plan.

Non-communicable diseases, such as those in which the body malfunctions in some way, are literally the final type of illness. If a person does not die of malnutrition, predation, infection, or injury, he will surely die from degradation of the body. This can actually be seen in the World Health Organization's data on death by cause and region.[224] In the most affluent economies, deaths by malnutrition, predation, injury, and even infectious diseases have been greatly reduced to the point that 88 percent of all deaths are due to some form of bodily breakdown, and 65 percent of males and 80 percent of females live at least seventy years. This level has been stable since at least 2000, with very modest changes in longevity. This might suggest that humanity is approaching its medical limits in terms of controlling nature.

On the other hand, in the lowest-income economies, where modern medicines, practices, and resources are not as readily available, only 37 percent die of non-communicable diseases and only 18 percent of males and 24 percent of females live to seventy years.[225] Interestingly, even though people in these undeveloped areas die younger because they are still exposed to non-degradation forms of death, the overall rate of death is the same everywhere: 100 percent. This might be taken as confirmation that although one might be able to delay death, one still cannot deny it.

St. Thomas Aquinas takes the position that this type of illness occurs because, with the loss of original justice in the Fall,

---

[224] WHO, *Global Health Estimates 2016*, HI table.
[225] WHO, *Global Health Estimates 2016*, LI table.

the body is no longer under the control of the soul and becomes disordered.[226] It is not readily apparent that medical science has a better explanation. Granted, there are many different ways by which the body degrades. Sometimes, this can be manifested initially by chronic disorders that limit capability but are not immediately life-threatening. This can include diseases of the eyes which limit vision; diseases that cause deafness; psychiatric disorders; or damaged joints, muscles, and connective tissue that can limit mobility and cause chronic pain. Ultimately, bodily degradation affects life-sustaining organs and processes in ways that will ultimately be terminal. This includes diseases like muscular dystrophy, ALS, and Parkinson's that degrade neuromuscular function; diseases like Alzheimer's that degrade mental function; advanced cancers; and diseases of critical organs. People have made inroads on mitigating human degradation via artificial joints, pacemakers, eye glasses, hearing aids, LASIK eye surgery, and even organ transplants. Ideally, these advancements reduce suffering by enhancing and extending a person's capability to meet his religious and societal responsibilities.

As was discussed above, if man had stayed within the divine intimacy, he would not have had to suffer and die, but with the

---

[226] *ST* I-II, q. 85, art. 5. The sin of our first parent is the cause of death and all such like defects in human nature, in so far as by the sin of our first parent original justice was taken away, whereby not only were the lower powers of the soul held together under the control of reason, without any disorder whatever, but also the whole body was held together in subjection to the soul, without any defect, as stated in I, q. 97, art. 1. Wherefore, original justice being forfeited through the sin of our first parent; just as human nature was stricken in the soul by the disorder among the powers, as stated above (I-II, q. 8, art. 3), so also it became subject to corruption, by reason of disorder in the body.

loss of original justice, man is subject to decay and death.[227] God does not abandon us, however. Since it has already been shown that God is attentive to His creation and that everything He does supports His providential plan, it follows that God initiates the degrading process strategically in the life of every individual, both for their benefit and the benefit of others. Why a person's function is limited in a particular way at a particular time is unclear, due to the complexity of interactions with others and because human perspective is relatively limited. Nevertheless, it is possible to think of reasons that God might have to degrade a person's capabilities for his benefit, and to trust in His love for us, even if we cannot understand the benefits in our specific cases.

The most obvious reason that God limits a person's options is to focus him on the ultimate goal of reorienting the person to God. Both St. Francis of Assisi and St. Ignatius of Loyola had conversion experiences while forced into inactivity by sickness or injury. Limitations can also serve to redirect a person toward a new goal or to facilitate new relationships. At times they can be to remove people from situations or relationships that are detrimental to them. They can make people appreciate what they have and also what they have lost. They can serve to break bad habits and to offer new perspectives and can be the impetus for developing virtues like humility, patience, fortitude, and temperance. The way that a person deals with his degradation can serve as an inspiration or a warning to others. It can be a source of grace and an opportunity to both love and be loved. It is not unusual for people to realize in retrospect that one or more of these benefits applies to a situation they had thought was wholly evil.

[227] CCC 376.

Nancy Mairs is an example of such a person.[228] Her life as a disabled person began at age twenty-nine when she was diagnosed with multiple sclerosis (MS) just after starting graduate school to study creative writing. She did not adjust well, leaving her husband and two young children, having a series of affairs, and ultimately attempting suicide. After a year of depression and roaming, Mairs recognized that her body was degrading slower than anticipated, causing her to take stock of her situation. She realized that she could continue to do many of her normal activities, and she returned to a normal life similar to what she would have led without MS.

Mairs slowly began to have an increased awareness of her body and its unity with her soul.[229] She also began to accept her braces as part of her embodiment and began to write as a "crippled woman." Her descriptions and self-revelations portray disability as part of an ordinary life. She explained unapologetically to her readers that it could happen to them as well, and she urged them to accompany her as she came to realize that she could indeed live in her disabled body.

Something else happened on this journey: Mairs found God and converted to Catholicism.[230] With this conversion came an understanding of her own need for mercy, as well as an acceptance of suffering and a knowledge that ultimately she would die. Mairs admits that while she would certainly take a cure if one became available, she does not actually need it. As author Nancy Eiesland says, "Recognizing and coming to terms with the difficulty that comes with disability, Mairs lives not with the grace of a martyr

---

[228] Eiesland, *The Disabled God*, 40-42.
[229] Ibid., 43-45.
[230] Ibid., 45-46.

but with the resolve of someone who realizes that an ordinary life is filled with blessings and curses and that sometimes it is hard to differentiate between the two."[231]

There is an important commonality between the witnesses of Diane DeVries and Nancy Mairs: they both saw themselves as living normal lives. Despite their hardships and handicaps, they recognized themselves to be within the human continuum of diversity, even though others might attempt to dehumanize them. This speaks to the insight of Simone Weil, who recognized that social isolation is a key component of suffering and suggested that caregivers can relieve suffering by helping people recognize the "ordinary" things they share with the rest of humanity.[232]

Perhaps this is most difficult in cases of dementia, which most people associate with Alzheimer's disease. This disease, which is marked by severe memory loss, affects mostly the very old who have survived everything else. More than 96 percent of those who die of Alzheimer's disease are beyond seventy years old.[233] As medical science has cured other diseases, the percentage of people who die from Alzheimer's has increased, nearly tripling to 7 percent in high-income economies since 2000.

A significant problem of dementia, beyond the memory loss, is that of disturbing clinical behavior. Behaviors seen as problematic include those that may cause harm to the person with dementia or others; those that overly stress or tire out the caregiver; and those that may be regarded as socially unacceptable. Examples include repetitive questioning about the same subject, screaming or yelling for no apparent reason, agitation, wandering,

---

[231] Ibid., 46.

[232] Weil, "The Love of God," 439-441.

[233] WHO, *Global Health Estimates 2016*, HI table.

inappropriate sexual behaviors, destructive or self-destructive behavior, or physical aggression.[234]

Interestingly, there is an active debate involving social scientists and the medical community about whether Alzheimer's should be considered a disease at all or simply what is "normal" for older populations. Jaber Gubrium, an American sociologist, has been describing the extension of the diagnosis of Alzheimer's disease to the elderly as a social construction since 1987.[235] This does not negate the existence of underlying natural processes; rather, it draws attention to the deliberate social processes by which professionals redefined dementia as a pathology and placed it within the biomedical jurisdiction. This has important ramifications concerning how the elderly demented are viewed and cared for, and also in how they see themselves. This also is critical to the question of suffering for those with dementia. Clearly, if there is an expectation in the community that the elderly will naturally lose memory as they age, then the social stigma would disappear or at least be mitigated, since an elderly person having dementia would be considered normal. However, if the person is viewed as diseased, then the view is much different in the community.

If dementia is seen as the normal condition for people at the end of their lives, then our temporal lives can be seen as an arc or a cycle of sorts. When a person is born, he is totally dependent on his parents for everything: food, drink, clothes, shelter, training, love, and protection. The infant presents an opportunity to love that only the worst parents do not fulfill. The infant can offer nothing in return but affection and the potential to love in the

---

[234] Athena McLean, *The Person in Dementia: A study of Nursing Home Care in the US* (Ontario, CA: Broadview Press, 2007), 22.
[235] Ibid., 29.

future. The infant has no means of communicating other than physical demonstrations like crying and hitting. Yet that does not deter the parent from going through a mental checklist of potential needs (is the baby hungry, cold, tired, in need a diaper change, bored, hurt?) to ease the suffering of the infant. Virtually all parents recognize that parenthood has taught them to love in a most profound way, for they realize they have been given the awesome responsibility of caring for a child of God that cannot possibly survive without their attention.

Elders with dementia present a similar opportunity to love for their spouses, children, and grandchildren. Like an infant, a fully demented senior is dependent on others for all his basic needs, and also like an infant, the fully demented elder has no means of communicating other than physical demonstrations like crying and hitting. Unlike an infant, however, the elder does not deserve love because of potential, but because of a legacy of love, and even the most demented individual can recognize kindness and affection toward him and return it.

Athena McLean explains the agitated and occasionally violent behavior exhibited by patients with dementia is actually their attempt to communicate their needs, feelings, and wishes. McLean states that when patients can no longer verbalize their intentions, organize their thoughts, or interpret the caregivers' intentions or directions, they must use their bodies to communicate needs, distaste, or fear. Similarly, the body is used to protest or resist caregiver treatment. McLean goes on to say that the common practice of using drugs to stop the physical behavior serves to eradicate a patient's selfhood and that the proper approach to patients with Alzheimer's is to acknowledge their agency, to recognize that they are doing the best they can within their limitations, and to try to understand what they are communicating. She maintains that there is promising evidence that this approach will profoundly impact the patient's outcome, even in the absence of medical interventions. Family members who care lovingly for their elders know the benefits. In fact, St. Paul, commenting on the fourth commandment, states, "Honor your father and mother" (this is the first commandment with a promise), "that it may go well with you and that you may live long in the land."[236]

This does not mean that families cannot seek out aid in helping their elders any more than parents cannot legitimately seek aid in caring for their infants. Just as children gain from the social and intellectual stimulation of being with their peers in schools taught by professionals, so too can elders gain from the social and intellectual stimulation of being with their peers and from the professional care in appropriately managed senior living environments. For most families, this will be the best and only option once their loved ones lack the mobility to get around and require medical treatment beyond the expertise of family members. This does not mean that the elder can be "warehoused" in senior facilities, never to be visited, any more than a child can be abandoned by his parents in a school or daycare facility. It simply means that they should feel free to get the aid they need for their loved ones, while still demonstrating the love and affection that the elderly need and deserve.

There is a second debate associated with senility, discussed by Michael Banner in *The Ethics of Everyday Life*, that focuses on whether the person still exists after their memory capability is totally lost.[237] Athena McLean asserts that the dominant view is that the

---

[236] Ephesians 6:2-3.

[237] Michael Banner, *The Ethics of Everyday Life: Moral Theology, Social Anthropology and the Imagination of the Human* (New York: Oxford University Press, 2014), 107-134.

self depends on memory, and once memory is lost, so is the self.[238] As an example, Jonathan Franzen described his father's disability trajectory as "death of autonomy, death of memory, death of self-consciousness, death of personality, and finally, death of body."[239] This view leads to descriptions of dementia as being "death before death," "death of the person," and the "loss of self." It caused one doctor to describe treating an Alzheimer's patient as comparable to doing veterinary medicine. Alzheimer's patients are often considered to be shells of their former selves, or simply "husks."[240]

Because caregivers often act as if the actual person is gone, it is easy for them to disregard the statements or actions of an Alzheimer's patient as meaningless.[241] This discounting of their agency, however, tends to lead to agitation, repetitiveness, wandering, hitting, and screaming by the demented patient. In turn, caregivers will typically try to control or eliminate these behaviors, often through medication, or to use them to justify "warehousing" the patient. This is blatantly dehumanizing, and the resulting suffering is not caused by natural evil but by the evil of sin and will be discussed further in the next chapter.

In *Dementia: Living in the Memories of God*, Scottish theologian John Swinton explains that describing dementia as a "loss of self" is most assuredly wrong. Building off the work of Steven Sabat, Swinton describes three aspects of the understanding of self.[242] Self One relates to the person's experience of himself in the present moment and is manifested by references to the

---

[238] Ibid., 130.
[239] Ibid., 126.
[240] Ibid., 125.
[241] Ibid., 131.
[242] John Swinton, *Dementia: Living in the Memories of God* (Grand Rapids, MI: Eerdmans, 2012), 94-95.

first person in language and gestures. It acknowledges the self as a reference point to experiencing the rest of the universe, and Swinton explains that unless a person is terminally unconscious, Self One remains throughout the experience of dementia. Therefore, it is clear that any suggestion that the self is lost is seriously mistaken.

Self Two contains a person's understanding of his physical characteristics and life experiences.[243] It would include things like one's hair color, one's skill level at painting or dancing, one's strengths and weaknesses, and one's view of self-worth. This changes over time with new experiences and interpretations, and Swinton notes that a person's Self Two can be severely damaged when those around the person treat them as non-entities.

Self Three describes the different social personae that a person has: father, son, uncle, teacher, sports enthusiast, spouse, friend, and so on.[244] Swinton argues that when dementia is treated as a malignant social pathology, then a person's positive Self Three cannot be maintained because the only persona now recognized by society is "dementia patient." His conclusion is that "the neurology of dementia does not destroy the self. Any dissolution of the self reflects the dissolution of the community."[245]

Swinton reframes what the medical community assumes are defects associated with dementia, creating a much different understanding of the demented person.[246] First, he notes that dementia involves more than neurological degradation. It also has significant linguistic and relational components, which inhibit

---

[243] Ibid., 95-96.
[244] Ibid., 96-97.
[245] Ibid., 98.
[246] Ibid., 108-109.

communication and socialization. As such, it involves more than just the person's neurological makeup: it belongs to and emerges from some kind of community. It is not, therefore, a loss of the mind, but a change in how a person's thoughts are communicated and understood, both by the demented elder and by those around him. Dementia does not involve a loss of self, even in extreme cases; any loss of self involves a failure of community. Behavioral symptoms such as yelling and hitting, understood properly, can be seen as reasonable responses to difficult, frightening, or frustrating situations, rather than the result of failing neurological processes alone. Swinton points out that if these insights are taken seriously and we give people with dementia the benefit of the doubt, a much different picture of dementia then emerges.

Besides providing patients' families and caregivers with opportunities to love, elder dementia involves a few more dynamics that highlight its benefits versus other means of death. First, it typically takes place gradually, when the elder becomes increasingly dependent on others. This gives both the elder and the caregiver time to adjust to the new circumstances if they both act in charity toward each other. Second, the first thing that is lost is short-term memory, which greatly reduces functionality, but also reduces the ongoing sense of loss by the elder.

Often, the senile remember vividly the epic stories of the past, which they can continue to share long after they can no longer remember what they ate for breakfast. Further, the habits they have formed over a lifetime still remain as reminders of what they deemed important and also the life choices they made. Pia Kontos claims that "selfhood resists the ravages of Alzheimer's disease precisely because it exists in corporeality."[247] In saying

---

[247] Banner, *Ethics of Everyday Life*, 130.

this, she is consistent with Pierre Bourdieu's insight that most human action is autonomous, relying not on rational conscious thought but on internal habits based on a person's experiences and perceptions.[248] She uses examples of Alzheimer's patients being able to groom themselves, weave, and read the Torah long after they lost their memories to bolster her point.[249] Unlike people who die of cancer or organ breakdown, those who die the "natural death" from dementia simply fade away over time, often without the pain of other forms of death. This slow goodbye allows everyone to prepare for the end if it is considered a part of the natural life cycle.

Although there is clearly loss of goodness in dementia, as the elderly lose capability, it does not have to lead to suffering if kept in the right context. If the elderly continue to be respected not only for what they have done in the past but also for what they continue to provide (love and good habits built over a lifetime, among other things), and they are given opportunities for social engagement, they will have purpose in life and social status, which mitigate suffering.

John Swinton gives three examples in *Dementia* that support this view. The first example is that those with dementia, deprived of their memory, live in the moment and can appreciate the love and kindness given them in that moment.[250] The second is that those with dementia do have moments of lucidity when they recognize what others do for them.[251] In each of these cases, people

---

[248] Pierre Bourdieu and Loïc Wacquant, *An Invitation to Reflexive Sociology* (Chicago: University of Chicago Press, 1992), 18-19.

[249] Banner, *Ethics of Everyday Life*, 130.

[250] Swinton, *Dementia*, 235.

[251] Ibid., 243.

were being present for the demented elder, which conferred a sense that they were valued, reducing the social isolation and mitigating the suffering.

In the third and perhaps the most touching example given in what is a very profound book on the subject, Swinton explains how an elderly woman with dementia was found in an agitated state, pacing the corridors repeating the word "God" over and over.[252] A particularly enlightened nurse walked alongside her for a while and then, in a flash of inspiration, asked her if she was afraid of forgetting God. When the older woman emphatically answered yes, the nurse told her, "You know, even if you should forget God, He will not forget you. He has promised that." The old woman, thus assured of God's continued love, became peaceful. This shows the importance of recognizing the agency of those with dementia as well as their capacity to attach meaning and purpose to their lives to ease suffering.

Unfortunately, this is often not the case. Athena McLean explains that the biomedical model, which is the dominant view of elderly senility, "prioritizes the body over the person's experience, attempts to control or suppress disturbed behaviors rather than to try to understand them and objectifies the person in order to carry out care tasks. Once labeled disease, behaviors that may express legitimate needs, discomforts and concerns are either disregarded or are marked as symptoms and targeted for treatment by chemical or physical restraints" (which are rare today).[253]

When people have dementia, like all terminal diseases, it gives them time to contemplate death and decide what is important to them. This is God calling them through suffering. Because

---

[252] Ibid., 196-197.
[253] McLean, *The Person in Dementia*, 34-35.

Alzheimer's progresses slowly, with increasing dependency and decreasing awareness, there is a "slow goodbye" that the patient might recognize as an easing into death while preparing the surviving family for its inevitability. It teaches patience and humility to both patients and caregivers and is clearly an opportunity for others to demonstrate love and for the sufferer to share in the sufferings of Christ in some way known only to God.

The Church offers valuable insight into the role of illness in God's plan in its prelude to the discussion on the sacrament of Anointing of the Sick in the *Catechism*:

> Illness and suffering have always been among the gravest problems confronted in human life. In illness, man experiences his powerlessness, his limitations, and his finitude. Every illness can make us glimpse death. Illness can lead to anguish, self-absorption, sometimes even despair and revolt against God. It can also make a person more mature, helping him discern in his life what is not essential so that he can turn toward that which is. Very often illness provokes a search for God and a return to him.[254]

These are important insights. Illness then exists as a vivid warning of human mortality and, as St. Thomas might add, of human sinfulness. Illness is universal for humans because death is universal. The *Catechism* is clear about the role of illness in the economy of salvation, noting that "illness becomes a way to conversion; God's forgiveness initiates the healing. It is the experience of Israel that illness is mysteriously linked to sin and evil, and that faithfulness to God according to his law restores life."[255] Understanding this

[254] CCC 1500-1501.
[255] CCC 1502.

can mitigate suffering. As its purpose becomes clear, joy can re-place suffering, but for those who do not believe, sickness and, in particular, dementia can be a terrifying experience when a person's existence is so severely threatened.

Jesus' ministry clarified the link between illness and evil. Healing the sick was a significant part of Jesus' ministry and, in fact, the Gospels record that it was the reason that He initially gained the attention of the crowds.[256] However, although Jesus is compassionate toward all who suffer and identifies with them, He did not heal all the sick: "his healings were signs of the com-ing of the kingdom of God."[257] In other words, Jesus healed for a greater purpose than temporal comfort; He healed in order to lead people to eternal life. The Catechism, under the title of "Christ the Physician," notes that "he has come to heal the whole man, body and soul."[258] This is the key to understanding the mystery of the linkage between illness and sin. Illness is a sign of human mortality, and suffering's role is to highlight goods that are needed for the person to exist and to flourish. Like all types of suffering, there are two ways to resolve it. The first is to attain the good that threatens the person's physical existence — to find a cure. The second is to find meaning in the suffering that allows the person to maintain their identity, even after death. This results in the person seeking God.

Suffering from illnesses leads people to salvation through the same four steps that are needed in the case of injuries. The first way that people react to illness is also the first way they react to injuries: they look for healing. The Church supports this,

---

[256] Matthew 4:23-25; Mark 1:23-34; Luke 4:31-41.
[257] CCC 1505.
[258] CCC 1503.

teaching that "part of the plan laid out by God's providence is that we should fight strenuously against all sickness and carefully seek the blessings of good health, so that we may fulfill our role in human society and in the Church."[259] This first response is consistent with human nature, focused on temporal goods. God uses suffering in this manner to direct man in the way to subdue the earth, highlighting the goods to be pursued and causing the strong sensation we know as pain to remain until the goods are attained. Yet even in this first step, suffering pushes men toward higher goals because as St. John Paul II notes, "It is suffering, more than anything else, which clears the way for the grace which transforms human souls."[260]

The more important work of suffering is not to motivate people to find temporal healing but to facilitate the healing of the soul. It does this through suffering by making people aware of their own mortality. As people come to understand that their particular injury or illness is life-threatening without a readily available cure, or if they face a long, painful convalescence, they often seek God for meaning and help, resulting in conversion.[261]

As discussed in section one, St. John Paul II attributes this to a special grace concealed within suffering that draws a person interiorly close to Christ. The pope notes that

> when this body is gravely ill, totally incapacitated, and the person is almost incapable of living and acting, all the more do interior maturity and spiritual greatness become evident, constituting a touching lesson to those

[259] Paul VI, Apostolic Constitution *Sacrament of the Anointing of the Sick*, 3.
[260] John Paul II, *Salvifici doloris*, 27.
[261] CCC 1501.

who are healthy and normal. This interior maturity and spiritual greatness in suffering are certainly the result of a particular conversion and cooperation with the grace of the Crucified Redeemer.... To the suffering brother or sister, Christ discloses and gradually reveals the horizons of the Kingdom of God: the horizons of a world converted to the Creator, of a world free from sin, a world being built on the saving power of love. And slowly but effectively, Christ leads into this world, into this Kingdom of the Father, suffering man, in a certain sense through the very heart of his suffering.[262]

This conversion is a reorienting of the will from selfish pursuits toward God's will for the sufferer. In some cases, the person is healed in body and soul and can take up the work of the "Good Samaritan," practicing charity and the other infused virtues in the aid of those still suffering. In other cases, where the illness or injury is so debilitating that the sufferer cannot practice charity in this way, the opportunity for redemption lies in understanding and rejoicing in the fact that his suffering is providing an opportunity for redemption for those that help the sufferer. This is the greatest act of redemptive suffering, because it is sharing in the suffering of Christ for the benefit of others. St. John Paul II says "it often takes time, even a long time, for this answer to be interiorly perceived.... It is then that man finds in his suffering interior peace and even spiritual joy."[263]

The Church recognizes this aspect of redemptive suffering most obviously in its explanation of the effects of the Sacrament

---

[262] John Paul II, *Salvifici doloris*, 26.
[263] Ibid.

of Anointing of the Sick. It makes it clear that it is the healing of the soul that takes priority, explaining that "this assistance from the Lord by the power of his Spirit is meant to lead the sick person to healing of the soul, but also of the body if such is God's will."[264] It further explains that this sacrament allows the sick person to participate in the saving work of Jesus by giving him the strength and the gift of uniting himself more closely to Christ's Passion. Thereby, "Suffering, a consequence of original sin, acquires a new meaning; it becomes a participation in the saving work of Jesus."[265] The *Catechism* concludes that the sick who receive this sacrament, by freely uniting themselves to the Passion and death of Christ, contribute to the good of the people of God.[266] This can be thought of as a way that a person recognizes that his suffering is for the benefit of others without knowing them or how they benefit. It is essentially a sign of faith in the goodness of the Lord to believe that God would not subject us to pointless suffering, but that whatever goodness we lack is borne for someone's benefit.

In the final analysis, what are perceived by humans as natural evils—disability, injury, illness, and death—are not only required, but are elements of particular providence providing an environment conducive to the acceptance of grace that leads to salvation. People who seem to be disabled from a human perspective were made perfectly for the role God has in mind for them. Illness is the way to conversion, and death is the gateway to eternal life. Suffering, the ability humans were given to sense when they are lacking some critical good, is a grace in that it is

[264] CCC 1520.
[265] CCC 1521.
[266] CCC 1522.

a free gift from God. It is a blessing because it relentlessly drives us toward the ultimate good, which is union with God Himself.

Natural evils, then, are a necessary part of the evolutionary design of the universe that relies on constant recycling of all living matter to bring it to its ultimate perfection in man. Suffering from natural evil can highlight ways for humanity to facilitate this evolutionary plan by taking its position as stewards of creation but, paradoxically, it also makes man aware of his mortal finitude and focuses him on the true purpose of his life, which is to share in the divine nature and unite with God in eternity. As counter-intuitive as it seems to those whose focus remains on temporal goods, these natural evils are actually part of God's particular providence, leading to beatitude those who are aligned with His will.

9

Suffering, Conscience, and the Evil of Sin

St. Thomas vigorously argues that God is rational and, thus, wills things toward an end, which is his own goodness. "In no way does he will the evil of sin, which is the privation of right order toward the divine good."[267] On the other hand, God does will the evil of punishment because it is attached to the greater good of justice. These two are interrelated in that they both are required accidentally for true free will and for freely given love to exist. God desires humans to have free will so that they can freely love. During man's earthly journey, freedom of choice is necessarily attached to the possibility of errant choices. Therefore, God permits sin. Perhaps just as importantly, if choices do not have ramifications, they are not meaningful choices, so punishment is a necessary requirement for both free will and love to exist.

The evil of sin differs from physical and natural evil in several important ways. The most obvious way is that unlike the other two, it is an act of man and not an act of God. In fact, at its most basic level, sin is man foolishly trying to usurp God's role despite lacking the knowledge, power, and goodness to do so. As the *Catechism* puts it: "Sin sets itself against God's love

---

[267] *ST* I, q. 19, art. 9.

for us and turns our hearts away from it. Like the first sin, it is disobedience, a revolt against God through the will to become 'like gods,' knowing and determining good and evil. Sin is thus love of oneself even to contempt of God."[268]

Unlike other evils, which are principally highlighted and resisted through suffering, the evil of sin is highlighted and resisted primarily through conscience. Conscience is a human competency to recognize right from wrong based on God's gift of reason, although the will can also use reason to rationalize sin.[269] Conscience is man's first line of defense against sin. This does not mean that suffering has no role in addressing the evil of sin concerning others. Far from it. In fact, suffering opposes the evil of sin through the evil of punishment, which is covered in the next chapter, and through the redemptive suffering of the victims of sin, which will be the subject of the rest of this chapter.

It is important at this point to explore suffering for sin from the vantage point of the victim. Whereas committing a sin separates one from God, being the victim of sin can provide a path to redemption in much the same way as being the victim of a physical or natural evil. Being the victim of a violent crime might seem unjust and random to many readers, but St. Thomas sees it as medicinal, since it is intended for the good of the victim's soul, if he bears it patiently.[270]

There are general and particular reasons for individuals to suffer for the sins of another, and an omnipotent, omniscient God can manage both simultaneously. The most obvious general reason people are allowed to suffer for the sins of others is that for free will

---

[268] CCC 1850.
[269] CCC 1778.
[270] *ST* I-II, q. 87, art. 8.

to exist, people have to be allowed to make free decisions, even if they result in crimes. On an individual level, however, there is a particular reason that is unique to each individual and contributes to God's providential plan: there are no accidents in God's plan. As St. Augustine explains, "When He subjects me to adversity, this is either to test my merits or chastise my sins; and He reserves an eternal reward for my pious endurance of temporal ills."[271]

Sometimes the victims are called to suffer for a cause they understand is greater than themselves. Such is the case for all Christian martyrs as well as battlefield heroes and those that suffer for a multitude of good causes. Others suffer because their lives need redirection unrelated to the sin that provides it. Still others suffer to give a third party the opportunity to aid them. As will be discussed later, this can be redemptive for the sufferer as well.

It is understandable that people find it hard to comprehend how anyone benefits by being murdered, maimed, or raped. In fact, it is hard to imagine any temporal scenario where this would be the case. But the point of suffering is to drive people to the ultimate good, which is union with God, while motivating virtuous behavior here on earth. Therefore, to understand how being the victim of a sin can be beneficial starts with the premise that eternal life is the goal for which temporal suffering can be accepted.

As discussed in the first section, suffering can be redemptive when someone willingly uses his suffering for the benefit of another. Being the victim of another person's sin can present this type of opportunity if the victim socializes his suffering in a way that activates the conscience of the sinner and causes the

---

[271] Augustine, *The City of God against the Pagans*, trans. and ed. R. W. Dyson (New York: Cambridge University Press, 1998), bk. 1, ch. 29.

sinner to repent and make amends. This powerful link between conscience and suffering was actually understood and leveraged by both the greatest of sinners and the most prominent social reformers of the last century.

In Hannah Arendt's classic study on the banality of evil, *Eichmann in Jerusalem*, she explains that to carry out "the final solution to the Jewish problem," Heinrich Himmler recognized he was giving the "most frightening order an organization could ever receive."[272] She reports:

> The problem was how to overcome not so much their conscience as the animal pity by which all normal men are affected in the presence of physical suffering. The trick used by Himmler—who apparently was rather strongly af-flicted with these instinctive reactions himself—was very simple and probably very effective; it consisted in turning these instincts around, as it were, in directing them toward the self. So instead of saying: "What horrible things I did to people!", the murderers would be able to say: "What horrible things I had to watch in the pursuance of my duties, how heavy the task weighed up my shoulders!"[273]

It was not only mass murderers like Heinrich Himmler who recognized the power of suffering to activate the conscience of another. This is the main principle behind the nonviolent re-sistance movement developed by Mahatma Gandhi[274] and used

---

[272] Hannah Arendt, *Eichmann in Jerusalem: A Report on the Banality of Evil* (New York: Penguin Books, 1994), 105.

[273] Ibid., 106.

[274] Mahatma Gandhi, *The Essential Gandhi: An Anthology of His Writings on His Life, Work and Ideas*, ed. Louis Fischer (New York: Vintage, 2002), 79.

successfully by Dr. Martin Luther King, Jr., in the American civil rights movement in the 1960s.[275]

Marilyn McCord Adams embraces these same fundamental concepts as forms of martyrdom. She describes a martyr as a witness who gives testimony about a person, some events, or an ideal and is made to pay a price for doing it. She notes that this price usually involves the loss of some temporal goods: for example, the experience of social disapproval or exclusion, the deprivation of educational and professional opportunities, economic losses, moral disapproval, imprisonment, exile, and death. Despite all of this, Adams makes a persuasive argument that "martyrdom is an expression of God's righteous love toward the onlooker, the persecutor and even the martyr himself."[276]

Adams explains that for onlookers, the event of martyrdom may function as a prophetic story and that martyrs who persevere to the end are inspiring. The onlooker, if sympathetic to the cause, may be inspired to a higher level of commitment. Alternatively, the onlooker may see himself in the persecutor and be moved to repentance. Either way, if the onlooker has ears to hear the martyr's testimony, he may receive God's redemption through it.[277] She explains that martyrdom is potentially redemptive for the persecutors by allowing them to see what they are really like: "the more innocent the victim, the clearer the

---

[275] Gary Commins, "Is Suffering Redemptive? Historical and Theological Reflections on Martin Luther King, Jr.," *Sewanee Theological Review* 51, no. 1 (Christmas 2007): 62.

[276] Marilyn McCord Adams, "Redemptive Suffering as a Christian Solution to the Problem of Evil," in *The Problem of Evil*, ed. Michael L. Peterson (Notre Dame, IN: University of Notre Dame Press, 2017), 219-220.

[277] Adams, "Redemptive Suffering," 220.

focus."[278] Given this view, some persecutors will reform their lives and avoid eternal punishment (and, in some cases, forge better relationships on earth by ceasing the persecution). Finally, Adams explains that martyrdom is beneficial to the martyr as a way to demonstrate the depth of his commitment to the cause and to build a relationship of trust with God, Who will redeem him.

This does not mean that everyone embraces the concept of redemptive suffering. In their essay, "For God so Loved the World?" feminists Joanne Carlson Brown and Rebecca Parker claim that "Christianity has been a primary—in many cases, *the* primary—force in shaping our acceptance of abuse."[279] They add that "any sense that we have a right to care for our own needs is in conflict with being a faithful follower of Jesus. Our suffering for others will save the world." Taking the position that "in order for us to become whole, we must reject the culture that shapes our abuse and disassociate ourselves from the institutions that glorify our suffering," they call for women to leave the Church.[280] They then attack King's use of the concept, saying "It asks people to suffer for the sake of helping evildoers see their evil ways. It puts concern for the evildoers ahead of concern for the victims of evil. It makes victims the servants of the evildoers' salvation."[281]

This is all true. That is what makes it so powerful. It begins with the victims showing love for their enemies in the face of suffering. This is a very profound type of love because by overcoming the

---

[278] Ibid., 220-222.

[279] Joanne Carlson Brown and Rebecca Parker, "For God So Loved the World?" in *Christianity, Patriarchy, and Abuse: A Feminist Critique*, ed. Joanne Carlson Brown and Carole R. Bohn (New York: Pilgrim Press, 1989), 2.

[280] Ibid., 3.

[281] Ibid., 20.

hatred and hurt of the oppressed, it appeals to the consciences of all men. In fact, it is the kind of love Jesus showed from the Cross as He forgave His executioners and those who aided them. When the oppressed suffer for the sake of their oppressors, they are very clearly sharing in the suffering of Christ, and that suffering is redemptive.

Delores Williams, a womanist theologian, also struggles with King's approach and the concept of redemptive suffering, albeit for different reasons, and, in fact, uses Carlson and Parker's quote verbatim in her book *Sisters in the Wilderness*.[282] Williams recognizes that King's strategy is consistent with the "moral suasion" argument used by Frederick Douglass a century earlier which assumed that black people could obtain their rights by appealing to the moral conscience of their white oppressors. In fact, she tacitly agrees that it worked when she says that this strategy is antiquated because "white America seems moved more by the loss of money than by any working of its moral conscience."[283]

Gandhi has a ready answer to this charge:

A Satyagrahi (supporter of passive resistance) bids good-bye to fear. He is therefore never afraid of trusting the opponent. Even if the opponent plays him false twenty times, the Satyagrahi is ready to trust him for the twenty-first time for an implicit trust in human nature is the very essence of his creed. Satyagraha is based on self-help, self-sacrifice and faith in God.[284]

---

[282] Delores Williams, *Sisters in the Wilderness: The Challenge of Womanist God-Talk* (Maryknoll, NY: Orbis Books, 1993), 200. Note, womanists call attention to the needs of black women, who are discriminated against for both race and gender.

[283] Ibid., 273-274.

[284] Gandhi, *The Essential Gandhi*, 81.

Gandhi's point is that Williams is selling her opponents short. He is adamant that with time and courage, his system of non-violent resistance will work. His view cannot be easily dismissed because his techniques have been successful in eliminating colonialism in India, apartheid in South Africa, and legal racial segregation in the United States, all highly entrenched forms of oppression in their individual societies. Additionally, redemptive suffering can be effective even in cases where the direct oppressor is unmoved if it moves the consciences of others who have the power to stop them.

Gary Commins addresses their combined concerns differently, when he observes:

> Much of the womanist-feminist critique of redemptive suffering is, of course, in reaction to its ubiquitous misuse: men in religious authority advise abused and oppressed women to endure their suffering like the cross. Nothing is done to confront the oppressor, end the abuse, heal the pain, or correct the injustice. Those with power nurture a cult of suffering in order to exploit others and justify oppression; redemptive suffering becomes an opiate for the oppressed — or, more precisely, a placebo.[285]

As Commins indicates, the feminist-womanist critique of redemptive suffering is typically a misstatement of the problem as the inappropriateness of redemptive suffering rather than an abuse of the use of the term by those in power to exploit others.[286] This

---

[285] Gary Commins, "Is Suffering Redemptive? Historical and Theological Reflections on Martin Luther King, Jr.," *Sewanee Theological Review* 51, no. 1 (Christmas 2007): 71.

[286] Ibid.

is unfortunate because these critics are actually undermining the very technique that will ultimately resolve the issue. Dorothee Söelle has it right when she says the first step in resolving societal suffering is to lament.[287] Calling attention to the moral good that is lacking through public suffering can activate the consciences of both bystanders and perpetrators and lead to lasting societal change. Gandhi called it transforming hatred to pity.[288] There is great power in the witness of the suffering to affect change, so it is important to highlight the problem that the womanists and feminists create for themselves when they attack redemptive suffering.

It must also be reiterated that Dorothee Söelle is absolutely justified in her assertions that the key to removing suffering is to socialize it, particularly in suffering caused by the sins of others.[289] She reminds us that "without the capacity to communicate with others, there can be no change."[290] Following Gandhi, we must be prepared to trust our oppressors because they too are children of God.[291] Following Jesus, we must be willing to love our oppressors and act for their salvation because in doing so, our own suffering can be redemptive, leading to eternal bliss.

As discussed in chapter 5, making the victims the servant of the evildoers' salvation is actually what is required for suffering to be redemptive. Is this not what Jesus did on the Cross? He died for the salvation of sinners, including those who crucified Him. Even more to the point, it ties together the concerns of both the oppressor and the oppressed. If the oppressed understands that his

---

[287] Söelle , *Suffering*, 92-98.
[288] Gandhi, *The Essential Gandhi*, 134.
[289] Söelle, *Suffering*, 71.
[290] Ibid., 76.
[291] Gandhi, *The Essential Gandhi*, 83.

suffering is being done for the good of the soul of the oppressor, the oppressed is sharing in the suffering of Jesus and will share in His glory. Furthermore, by seeking change in this way, one serves others who also suffer the same injustices. This must be active suffering, where the perpetrator is made to understand the impact of his actions, not passive suffering, where the victim silently absorbs abuse.

Because conscience is an apprehensive rather than a sensitive faculty, suffering must be articulated in a way that the oppressor's conscience can comprehend. Love and vulnerability will touch the conscience much more readily than hatred and anger. If the oppressor's conscience is touched and he removes the oppressive action, then everyone benefits, both spiritually and temporally. This is what Jesus called for when He said in the Sermon on the Mount, "love your enemies."[292] It challenges both the oppressed and the oppressor to be charitable toward the other and will fail if either side fails to love. If the oppressed cannot forgive, they cannot be saved. As the *Didache*, a first-century catechism succinctly puts it, "love those who hate you, and you shall not have an enemy."[293] In the case where the oppressed makes the effort to suffer bravely so that the oppressor can see the impact of his actions, and the oppressor is not moved by an inadequately trained conscience, it would seem that the victim's effort to love his enemy would still be spiritually rewarded while the oppressor's condemnation by both man and God would increase.

[292] Matthew 5:44.

[293] M. B. Riddle, trans., *The Didache*, from *Ante-Nicene Fathers*, vol. 7., ed. Alexander Roberts, James Donaldson, and A. Cleveland Coxe (Buffalo, NY: Christian Literature Publishing, 1886), revised and edited for New Advent by Kevin Knight, http://www.newadvent.org/fathers/0714.htm.

Some may ask why a good, omnipotent, and omniscient God would allow humans to sin, particularly now that man's technological capability is sufficiently "advanced" that a single sinner like Adolf Hitler can send millions of people to their deaths. The obvious answer is that God wants humans to be able to repond to His love freely, so He is willing to accept that people will abuse that freedom, some horrendously so. To mitigate that, as just discussed, God gave humans moral consciences to guide them, attached the debt of punishment to sin to deter it, and allowed the victims to suffer so that they too would be motivated to ignite the sinner's conscience through their witness. Furthermore, God's creative power is such that He can create something good where before there was only evil, the privation of good.

A perfect example of this is when the oppressed willingly activate the consciences of their oppressors by socializing their suffering with them, thus leading to the end of the oppression and the opportunity for redemption of both parties. As Martin Luther King, Jr., described in reference to his non-violence policy in the U.S. civil rights movement:

> We will match your capacity to inflict suffering with our capacity to endure suffering. We will meet your physical force with soul-force. ... We will soon wear you down by our capacity to suffer and in winning our freedom we will so appeal to your heart and conscience that we will win you in the process.[294]

Gandhi shows that leveraging redemptive suffering in this way is powerful. He calls it "soul-force," and asserts that "real suffering bravely borne melts even a heart of stone." He adds that

[294] Commins, "Is Suffering Redemptive?," 62.

"thousands, indeed tens of thousands, depend for their existence on a very active working of this force. Little quarrels of millions of families in their daily lives disappear before the exercise of this force. Two brothers quarrel, one of them repents and reawakens the love … lying dormant in him, the two again begin to live in peace."[295]

Contrasting the use of punishment with that of self-sacrifice and redemptive suffering to control evil, Gandhi comments that "the law of survival of the fittest is the law for the evolution of the beast but the law of self-sacrifice is the law of evolution of the man."[296] This is an apt description of how suffering from sin can be used creatively by God to bring humans to beatitude. Suffering bravely borne *can* melt the heart of stone. As discussed above, if Arendt is to be believed, even Heinrich Himmler, the notorious head of the Nazi Gestapo and one of those most responsible for the Holocaust, was susceptible to its powers.[297]

This "soul-force" can be wielded most effectively by the innocent. Whose conscience would not be moved to address the suffering of a young child beaten and raped, or that of an equally young and innocent child with Down syndrome, or one born without limbs, being ostracized by others simply for being different? The more one sees the humanity in another, the harder it is to oppress them.

While Gandhi and King espoused the need for individuals who suffer to stand up to their oppressors, they also recognized that lasting social change required movements in which the oppressed join together in solidarity to socialize their suffering.

---

[295] Gandhi, *The Essential Gandhi*, 79.
[296] Ibid.
[297] Arendt, *Eichmann in Jerusalem*, 106.

Söelle notes that "everyone's natural reflex is flight from suffering; but even when it succeeds it is at the same time the perpetuation of universal suffering."[298] She says that "to serve the pain of God by your own pain is to lead suffering out of its private little corner and to achieve solidarity."[299] This is not easy to do; it requires not only significant leadership skills but extreme courage and conviction. After all, both King and Gandhi were martyred for their causes, although as is often the case, their witness became even stronger and more effective in death. Oppressors understand this, and the more astute ones will make an effort not to make martyrs of their opponents.

It must also be pointed out that often the tactic used to circumvent or delegitimize the witness of the suffering victim is through their dehumanization: the Nazis depicted the Jews as an inferior race to justify their extermination; the same was said of black people when subjecting them to slavery. Unwanted pre-born children are labeled "fetuses" to justify abortion. The senile are described as no longer persons to justify "warehousing" and euthanasia. Such tactics must always be resisted to resolve suffering, both on the part of the victim and the oppressor.

As Gandhi asserts, socializing one's suffering and allowing the oppressor to witness the effects of his sins can activate the consciences of people at all levels and drive healing and repentance. This is true in individual families, where a person might not otherwise understand the hurt and damage their words and actions have on more vulnerable family members, as well as in the community, where structures of sin must be exposed by those that suffer from their effects in order for the responsible parties

---

[298] Ibid., 45.
[299] Ibid.

to recognize the lack of good in their actions and take the appropriate corrective action.

God has a specific plan for the universe that is sophisticated enough to account for disordered conduct (that is, sin) on the part of individuals and groups of all sizes. Sometimes this level of distortion to the good can be extreme, as in the case of wars, genocides, and nuclear fallout, causing widespread and deep levels of suffering. Other times it can be venial and isolated. In all cases, sin leads to suffering and suffering motivates people to seek change. Most of the time, this will result in temporal changes that, if successful, may be habituated to prevent future suffering, which results in virtues and a return to order. If no temporal changes can be made through human means, the person will often turn to God, even if it is a last resort. Sin can therefore result in good, through God's providential use of suffering.

10

The Evil of Punishment Rebuilds Goodness

Evil is defined in this work as the absence of good, and as such, it provides the opportunity for good to be attained. This is most easily understood in the case of the evil of punishment because punishment is about restoring the order lost through sin. Punishment is considered an evil because some good is withheld or taken from the person being punished, such as money, life, or liberty. As discussed previously, St. John Paul II's insight on punishment is that it "has meaning not only because it serves to repay the objective evil of the transgression with another evil, but first and foremost because it creates the possibility of rebuilding goodness in the subject who suffers."[300] This has two ramifications. First, in the repaying of one evil with another evil, punishment serves as a deterrent to future sin, not only in the one who is punished for the offense, but also in bystanders who might otherwise be tempted to do the same. Second, by creating the possibility of rebuilding goodness in the subject, punishment is shown as benefiting not only the punished but society as a whole. In this context, punishment is about rehabilitation, not vengeance.

---

[300] John Paul II, *Salvifici doloris*, 12.

Why All People Suffer

St. John Paul II notes that in the Old Testament, people began to recognize that suffering had meaning beyond that of simple punishment, and furthermore, that it had educational value.[301] He points out that "in the sufferings inflicted by God upon the Chosen People there is included an invitation of his mercy, which corrects in order to lead to conversion." He then demonstrates from the Second Book of Maccabees that the Israelites understood this, since the author wrote, "these punishments were designed not to destroy but to discipline our people."[302] The pope asserts that "the purpose of penance is to overcome evil, which under different forms lies dormant in man," and also "to strengthen goodness both in man himself and in his relationship with others and especially with God."[303]

Similarly, St. Thomas Aquinas assures his readers that God does not delight in punishments for their own sake but because they are required for the sake of justice.[304] He explains that punishment is essentially related to the disturbance of the order, and according to God's justice, it will last as long as the disturbance lasts.[305] The severity of the punishment will also be in proportion to that of the disturbance that caused it.[306] St. Thomas points out that people can create disorders that they cannot repair on their own, and that if they do not seek the help of God, Who can fix anything, they will incur a debt of eternal punishment. These would be true in the case of sins that turn a person away

---

[301] Ibid.
[302] 2 Maccabees 6:12.
[303] John Paul II, *Salvifici doloris*, 12.
[304] *ST* I-II, q. 87, art. 3, reply to obj. 3.
[305] *ST* I-II, q. 87, art. 3, reply to obj. 4.
[306] *ST* I-II, q. 87, art. 3, reply to obj. 1.

from God, his last end, so as to destroy charity.[307] The Angelic Doctor also notes that a similar dynamic occurs in terms of human suffering when a crime such as murder is committed that cannot be undone. In these cases, the criminal is often punished by imprisonment or banishment for life, or even death, thus removing the offender permanently from the fellowship of the living.[308]

The use of punishment to drive moral action is ubiquitous in all levels of human society. Parents have rules; organizations have bylaws; churches have commandments and doctrines; and governments have laws and regulations. These provide the order that is required for an organization to survive and prosper, and they also provide for the safety and preservation of the rights of its members. Because there are people who choose to disobey its rules and laws, an organization must take measures to enforce them and maintain order and consistency within its operations. Thus, some use of coercion is necessarily seen as beneficial for society and is in no way an intrinsic evil. The *Catechism* also makes clear, as did John Paul II, that punishment should be medicinal in that it improves the guilty party.[309]

This, of course, assumes that the punishment is just. This is clearly not always the case. At times, innocent people are punished to further the interests of those in power. Jesus Christ provides an example for consideration. The Jewish leaders felt threatened by His power and popularity and played on Pontius Pilate's insecurity in his position to have Jesus unjustly executed by the Romans for sedition.[310] This should be considered under

---

[307] *ST* I-II, q. 87, art. 3.
[308] *ST* I-II, q. 87, art. 3, reply to obj. 1.
[309] CCC 2266; John Paul II, *Salvifici doloris*, 12.
[310] CCC 596.

the evil of sin rather than the evil of punishment, as should all unjust punishments.

As discussed in the first section, punishment is required for there to be true freedom because decisions without ramifications are not meaningful. These ramifications are best understood as being direct outcomes from certain behaviors. An easy-to-understand example that has been discussed already is the case where, if someone drinks too much alcohol, the person will get sick and have a hangover in the morning. While not every sin has such an obvious cause-and-effect ramification, St. Thomas has noted that "Because sin is an inordinate act, it is evident that whoever sins, commits an offense against an order: wherefore he is put down, in consequence, by that same order, which repression is punishment."[311]

Thomas notes that there are three orders to which the human will is subject: his own reason; his human governors (and it matters whether they govern spiritually or temporally); and the universal order of divine government.[312] Because each of these orders is disturbed by sin, man can be punished by any or all of them, depending on the nature of his sin. In God's plan, punishment is for rehabilitation, not vengeance, so if a person's conscience is sufficiently active to drive the person to make restitution for his sins, then further punishment should not be necessary. It is when a person does not make restitution on his own that human or divine punishment becomes necessary.

St. Thomas next explains that sin can be self-propagating when it results in a fall from grace, allowing the person to be overcome by his disordered passions.[313] However, in this he recognizes

---

[311] *ST* I-II, q. 87, art. 1.
[312] *ST* I-II, q. 87, art. 1.
[313] *ST* I-II, q. 87, art. 2.

that even when God punishes people by permitting them to fall into sin, this is directed to the good of virtue. St. Thomas notes that sometimes it benefits those who are punished "when they arise from sin, more humble and more cautious," but its true purpose is for the amendment of others, "who seeing some men fall from sin to sin, are the more fearful of sinning."[314] St. Thomas defends this point by reminding the reader that even the punishment that is inflicted according to human laws is not always intended as a medicine for the one who is punished, but sometimes only for others. In his example, "when a thief is hanged, this is not for his own benefit, but for the sake of others, that at least they may be deterred from crime through fear of the punishment."[315]

He goes on to explain that suffering does not always cease when a person is absolved from their sins and returns to virtuous living.[316] He adds that sin is an act of the will to turn from God, and the resulting stain of sin cannot be removed from people unless they voluntarily take upon themselves the punishment for their past sins or bear patiently the punishment inflicted upon them by God. In either case, the punishment is called "satisfactory," since it satisfies the debt of punishment as regards the will. St. Thomas cautions that even after the stain of sin has been removed from the will, punishment still may be suffered in order to heal other powers of the soul that may have been disordered by the sin committed, to restore the equality of justice and to remove the scandal given to others, so that those scandalized might be edified by the punishment.[317]

---

[314] *ST* I-II, q. 87, art. 2, reply to obj. 1.
[315] *ST* I-II, q. 87, art. 3, reply to obj. 2.
[316] *ST* I-II, q. 87, art. 6.
[317] *ST* I-II, q. 87, art. 6, reply to obj. 3.

St. Thomas denies that anyone can suffer spiritual punishment for the sins of another, quoting Augustine's interpretation of Scripture.[318] As for physical suffering, St. Thomas also denies that anyone can suffer penal punishment for the sins of another, except in the case of children or servants who are themselves complicit in the sin in some way. However, he says that if one is united in some way with the sinner, one may voluntarily bear their satisfactory punishment. St. Thomas notes that Christ bore a satisfactory punishment for *our* sins, not for His.[319] He also notes that out of a union of love, even in human affairs, people willingly take on the debts of another, bearing their punishment.[320] A good example of this is Maximilian Kolbe, who, as discussed in section one, willingly took the place of a man he did not know who was randomly picked to starve to death in the Nazi death camp at Auschwitz in 1941.

Thus, combining the teaching of St. Thomas and the *Catechism*, one can see that punishment is the use of coercive force by an organization to keep order within it. The responsibility to punish in the civil context rests with the lowest effective level of authority acknowledged by government officials and the convicted criminal for this purpose.

St. Thomas warns, however, that things are not always as they appear, and that sometimes people mistake God's purpose when they suffer. Indeed, he notes that what people assume is a punishment can actually be God redirecting them to greater goods. As examples, he suggests that one can lose money for the sake of bodily health, or lose of both of these, for the sake of his

---

[318] *ST* I-II, q. 87, art. 8.
[319] *ST* I-II, q. 87, art.7, reply to obj. 3.
[320] *ST* I-II, q. 87, art. 7.

soul's health and the glory of God.[321] As noted above, St. Thomas also observes that suffering from punishment is not always for the direct benefit of the sufferer, although it can be.[322]

Finally, it can often be the case that sins go unpunished by human authorities. This is because most sins disrupt human enterprises and thus depend on human authorities to administer temporal punishment. There can be many impediments to this being done correctly. The first is that only an acknowledged authority can rightly punish, and there are many sins by people who are not under the control of an authority. For instance, when it is the governing authority that is exploiting its own citizens, there is no one who has the wherewithal to punish the offenders. Secondly, the authorities often do not know of sins within their jurisdiction unless someone brings them to their attention. Third, the authority may simply not see fit to punish the sinner for a variety of reasons, from mercy to corruption. In all these cases, it remains important that the sufferers are vocal about their needs, just as it was in the case of sin discussed in the last chapter. In each of these cases, resolving the suffering will need to occur through touching the conscience of the sinner and not through punishment, since in the first case there is no applicable authority to protect the sufferers, and in the second and third, the applicable authority is not in a position or is not motivated to act on their behalf.

This lack of efficiency in human punishment does not, however, suggest that sin does not have ramifications. There remains God and our consciences to provide deterrence and ramifications when we sin. As discussed in the previous chapter, the suffering

---

[321] *ST* I-II, q. 87, art. 7.
[322] *ST* I-II, q. 87, art. 3, reply to obj. 2.

of others that results from sin, whether we are the sinner or just a bystander, can activate our consciences and cause changes in behavior. Granted, some people, including Heinrich Himmler, can devise arguments that can cause our consciences to err, as was also discussed in the last chapter, but even he was not oblivious to what he was doing.[323]

Even if our consciences can be fooled and our human authorities are unreliable in instilling punishment, God can be trusted to be just in His judgments and punishment. Granted, that threat does not mean much to an atheist and may not deter one from committing crimes. Yet it is important for the righteous to know that justice will be served and that sin has ramifications so that they take heed, even though the wicked do not. As St. Paul wrote to the Romans:

> By your stubbornness and impenitent heart, you are storing up wrath for yourself for the day of wrath and revelation of the just judgment of God, who will repay everyone according to his works: eternal life to those who seek glory, honor, and immortality through perseverance in good works, but wrath and fury to those who selfishly disobey the truth and obey wickedness.[324]

As has been described throughout this book, suffering involves uncertainty and isolation in addition to physical discomfort. While death itself presents all humans with a certain sense of uncertainty and isolation, the potential for judgment with eternal consequences can add to the concerns, even among the devout, who are trained not to be presumptuous. Such a judgment is part

---

[323] Arendt, *Eichmann in Jerusalem*, 106.
[324] Romans 2:5-8.

of divine revelation and thus is an article of Christian faith. As previously discussed, Jesus Himself described its reality and the judgment criteria in the passage in Matthew's Gospel typically titled "the Judgment of the Nations."[325] In it, He describes separating all the nations into two groups. The ones to His right are offered entrance into the Kingdom of God for caring for those who are suffering, while those to the left are condemned into the eternal fire for failure to do the same. The *Catechism* teaches that "Each man receives his eternal retribution in his immortal soul at the very moment of his death, in a particular judgment that refers his life to Christ: either entrance into the blessedness of heaven through a purification or immediately — or immediate and everlasting damnation."[326]

In addition to the particular judgment at the hour of a person's death, the Church teaches that at the end of time, there will be a Last Judgment. The *Catechism* explains that "on the last day, God through his son Jesus Christ will pronounce the final word on all history. We shall know the ultimate meaning of the whole work of creation and of the entire economy of salvation and understand the marvelous ways by which his Providence led everything toward its final end. The Last Judgment will reveal that God's justice triumphs over all the injustices committed by his creatures and that God's love is stronger than death."[327]

The *Catechism* then explains that the message of the Last Judgment calls men to conversion while God is still giving them the time and opportunity for salvation. This is the point of temporal punishment. It inspires a holy fear of God and commits men

---

[325] Matthew 25:31-46.
[326] CCC 1022.
[327] CCC 1040.

to the justice of the Kingdom of God. It proclaims the "blessed hope" of the Lord's return, when He will come "to be glorified in his saints, and to be marveled at in all who have believed."[328]

The punishment of Hell is the permanent separation of the damned from God, the source of all that is good. This is actually a voluntary punishment on the part of the damned, since they have rebuffed God's call to them and have failed to heed their suffering. In some cases, God gave them their wish and allowed some people to live their lives with a minimal amount of suffering. Without God's direction, these people never learned to love and had no desire to unite with God, and so remain separated according to their desire. In other cases, people were given ample direction through suffering but chose not to follow it, choosing their own path rather than the one that leads to God. In these cases, too, God honors the choice of the damned to be separated. God also honors the choice of those who want to be with Him as demonstrated by their efforts to share in His nature.

---

[328] CCC 1041.

11

Divine Action

In addition to the problem of evil, the other issue identified by David Fergusson as key to the theological debates concerning providence is whether God takes an active role in carrying out His plan in specific circumstances related to individuals, called "particular providence." The alternative is that His role limited to "general providence," operating only through the fixed rules established at the time of creation with any appearance of concern for, or attention to, any specific individuals being strictly accidental. Fergusson maintains that most people now deny that particular providence exists, aligning themselves with the Deists, who hold that God, having created the universe, acts as a disinterested observer. His view is driven by three considerations.[329] The first is the perception of modern man that science can explain what was formerly attributed to divine agency in natural terms. The second assumes that God's original design was sufficiently robust that no particular divine action is necessary to "fine-tune" the workings of the plan. The third consideration is that there is no decisive criterion for determining which events are acts of God and which are not, so many default into a denial of particular providence in favor of the Deist view.

---

[329] Fergusson, *The Providence of God,* 218-219.

Further, some apologists, including Harold Kushner, whom we discussed in chapter 6, deny the existence of particular providence in an effort to protect God from the charge of being the author of evil.[330] They argue that God is not responsible for the evil experienced from events related to the way the universe functions if God does not take specific steps to cause the evil. As was previously discussed, this concern results from a misunderstanding of the nature of evil and in God's intentions toward man. There are no accidents for an omnipotent and omniscient God; everything is part of His plan. To deny this is to deny the nature and capabilities of God, Who lives outside of time and can create anything out of nothing. Evil exists only as a privation of good, and God withholds or takes away goodness either to redirect or to improve mankind in some way.

St. Thomas Aquinas has a different view of providence than what is described by Fergusson. First, he separates the development of the plan (providence), which is solely God's purview, from its execution (governance), which God assigns to secondary sources, whether it be to physical laws such as gravity or to creatures, who each have their roles.[331] Unlike the Deists, however, St. Thomas recognizes that governance still remains under God's control, since He retains and utilizes the ability to reward and to punish those He has assigned as intermediaries.[332] St. Thomas's view is that God extends His providence in a more excellent way with the righteous, preventing anything from happening

---

[330] Kushner, *Why Bad Things Happen*, 56-61. As discussed in chapter 6, it is theists such as Kushner, and the proponents of open and process theodicies, that deny the power of God to affect the outcome of daily events.

[331] *ST* I, q. 22 art., 1.

[332] *ST* I, q. 22, art. 2, reply to obj. 5.

that would impede their final salvation, whereas He does not restrain the wicked from the evils of sin.[333]

St. Thomas also holds that God plans not only for each individual but also at a universal level and that universal plans supersede individual ones. In this transaction, St. Thomas notes that at times, the good of the individual is compromised for the greater good of the universal plan. In his example, the lion needs to eat, so other animals will be prey. However, an omnipotent and omniscient God does not need to sacrifice the individual for the greater good, and, because there is an afterlife, not all the benefits have to be corporeal. He can accomplish this by putting in place scenarios where both parties benefit, even in the face of death. In fact, Jesus demonstrated this when He suffered on the Cross to reconcile mankind with God, opening up Heaven for us while completing His own mission. In a similar way, when a person is martyred as a sign for others, the martyr will benefit eternally, even though the people on earth may not realize it.

When we offer up our own suffering to Jesus for the sake of others, we share in the nature of Christ, and if we accept His grace, we will share in His glory. This links particular and universal providence by making it clear that while each individual has his own path to salvation, these paths are interlinked and communal in nature. In fact, in Christ's parable of the Last Judgment, He explicitly says that those who will be saved will be those who served the least of their neighbors in their hour of need.[334] The parable also acknowledges that each person is responsible for his own decisions and will be held accountable for them. At the same time, the goal of union with God begins with union

---

[333] *ST* I, q. 22, art. 2, reply to obj. 4.
[334] Matthew 25:31-46.

with Christ through Baptism into His Church, and therefore there is no salvation outside of the Church.[335]

Although God is the master of His plan, He makes use of His creatures' cooperation to carry it out, not because He is weak, but because He is good, and allows them the dignity of acting on their own.[336] The Church understands this as being most fundamentally a statement of the dignity of man, as explained in the *Catechism*:

> To human beings, God even gives the power of freely sharing in his providence by entrusting them with the responsibility of "subduing" the earth and having dominion over it. God thus enables men to be intelligent and free causes in order to complete the work of creation, to perfect its harmony for their own good and that of their neighbors.[337]

This statement has important ramifications in a theology of suffering because it makes it clear that God deliberately left creation in an unfinished state (that is, with physical evil) to allow humanity the opportunity to perfect it. This allows mankind to grow and evolve in virtue and beatitude. While this might appear to be a statement of general providence, it actually shows how

---

[335] CCC 894, 1257. Note: The Church recognizes the Baptism of Blood for those who die as martyrs of the Faith prior to Baptism (CCC 1258), and the Baptism of Desire for those who were not able to be baptized but had they known about it, would have desired it (CCC 1260). It also recognizes that God is not bound by His sacraments, so others may be saved by God's mercy (CCC 1257, 1261).

[336] CCC 306.

[337] CCC 307.

God uses suffering to bring about particular providences, which, in aggregate, lead to universal providence. The explanation in the *Catechism* continues, noting that "though often unconscious collaborators with God's will, people can also enter deliberately into the divine plan by their actions, their prayers, and their sufferings. They then fully become 'God's fellow workers' and co-workers for his kingdom."[338]

Within this simple statement from the *Catechism*, one can find the seeds of the four tasks through which suffering acts on men for their salvation, as discussed in section one. To reiterate, the first task is for people to develop the cardinal virtues even as they collaborate with God in an unconscious way to subdue the earth in response to their sufferings. The second task is for suffering to cause them to experience a change of heart and to reorient their wills toward God, which causes them to enter deliberately into the divine plan by their actions and prayers in response to the needs of others. This response to the needs of others relates to the third task of suffering, which is to release love by providing opportunities to utilize the infused virtues in the service of others. Finally, the fourth task is fulfilled when people willingly suffer for the sake of others, becoming " 'God's fellow workers' and co-workers for his kingdom."[339]

In this section, it was shown how these four tasks of suffering are carried out to lead humans to salvation in the face of each of the four types of evil. These are clearly acts of particular providence, with God taking specific action in the lives of individual people to bring about their salvation. This salvation inevitably involves serving and often suffering for the benefit of others,

[338] Ibid.
[339] Ibid.

sharing in the nature of Christ. It is possible through the grace of Christ, made available through His Church.

Another important element to consider in understanding divine providence is how God carries out His plan in light of man's freedom, of which the *Catechism* has this to say:

> God created man a rational being, conferring on him the dignity of a person who can initiate and control his own actions. "God willed that man should be 'left in the hand of his own counsel,' so that he might of his own accord seek his Creator and freely attain his full and blessed perfection by cleaving to him."[340]

It also adds this insight from St. Irenaeus's *Against Heresies:* "Man is rational and therefore like God; he is created with free will and is master over his acts."[341]

The Catechism explains that God is the primary cause of all actions, Who operates in and through secondary causes, including humans.[342] St. Paul added slightly more clarity in his Letter to the Philippians when he told them that "God is the one who, for his good purpose, works in you to desire and to work."[343] This can be understood to mean that God carries out His plan, not by forcing men to do His bidding by controlling their thoughts, but by providing them with the motivation to make that choice on their own. This is not to deny that an omnipotent God could control a person's thoughts, but instead recognizes, as the Catechism states, that God in His goodness, "grants his creatures not

---

[340] CCC 1730.
[341] CCC 1730, quoting Irenaeus, *Against Heresies* 4, 4, 3.
[342] CCC 308.
[343] Philippians 2:13.

only their existence but the dignity of acting on their own."[344] An omniscient God, living outside of time, sees all of eternity at once and therefore knows with complete accuracy what each person will do given a specific set of stimuli, particularly given the fact that He made them and knows them better than they know themselves. Further, an all-powerful God has no limitations on how to provide these inducements to act. Therefore, God's plan will be executed according to His wishes, without having to infringe upon human free will.

God can carry out His plans without infringing on human free will in the following manner: God creates an environment that will motivate each person to act in accordance with His plans. Environmental changes often are perceived as evil by humans, particularly those who have established habits based on the old environment. The change could be an illness that threatens the person or a loved one; or it could be an earthquake that devastates a community. It can be an act of God or a human act, such as a war or the rise of an oppressive government that God anticipates. God's desire is for man to share in His divine nature and His life, just as in the parable of the Prodigal Son, so His actions toward man reflect that desire. What men sometimes perceive as evil intent on the part of God are actually acts of love designed to bring us to our greatest happiness.

As stated repeatedly in this book, evil is not an entity in opposition to God but is the absence or privation of good. This is not to deny the existence of Satan and the other fallen angels. The *Catechism* is very clear that they were created as good but freely chose to sin, rejecting God and His reign.[345] It is equally

---

[344] CCC 306.
[345] CCC 391-392.

clear that despite their malevolence, their action is permitted by divine providence and cannot prevent the building-up of God's reign.[346] Further, it states unequivocally: "The truth that God is at work in all the actions of his creatures is inseparable from faith in God the Creator. God is the first cause who operates in and through secondary causes."[347] This is no less true for sinful angels than it is for sinful man.

God in His omniscience can foresee their every action, just as He can predict every sin that man will commit. His plan anticipates this and can use it for good, regardless of the intentions of the fallen angel. The greatest example of this is how He turned Satan's greatest apparent accomplishment, the Crucifixion of Christ, into the Greatest Good, with the Resurrection. In a similar way, in the Book of Job, God allows Satan to bring down tremendous calamities upon Job, despite Job's righteousness, and then uses the story as a teaching lesson for mankind. He then rewards Job with double what he lost and an enhanced reputation as a righteous man.[348]

When God withholds a good from us, which we perceive as an evil of some sort through our suffering, whether directly or through some secondary source like Satan or one of our neighbors, it is to motivate us to attain that good or to redirect us to something else. In fact, God continues to present us with these opportunities throughout life as appropriate to lead us to salvation. As St. Thomas notes, God presents more of these opportunities to

---

[346] CCC 395.

[347] CCC 308.

[348] Job 1:13-22 describes the first set of trials, Job 2:1-10 describes the second set of trials, and Job 42 describes the outcome of it all.

those who will be saved than to those who will be condemned.[349]
This dynamic is also noted in the book of Wisdom:

> The souls of the righteous are in the hand of God,
>   and no torment shall touch them.
> They seemed, in the view of the foolish, to be dead;
>   and their passing away was thought an affliction
>   and their going forth from us, utter destruction.
> But they are in peace.
> For if to others, indeed, they seem punished,
>   yet is their hope full of immortality;
> Chastised a little, they shall be greatly blessed,
>   because God tried them
>   and found them worthy of himself.
> As gold in the furnace, he proved them,
>   and as sacrificial offerings he took them to himself.[350]

Perhaps the best example of how God motivates action by providing the necessary environment and inducements is that of the reluctant prophet, Jonah. Called by God to preach repentance to the Ninevites, Jonah objects to helping his enemy and chooses to flee instead, taking passage on a ship to Tarshish, which is to go in the opposite direction.[351] God first raises up a storm to make the environment hostile to Jonah's plan and uses suffering in the form of fear for their lives to motivate the sailors to toss Jonah overboard.[352] God then saves Jonah by having a whale swallow him up and vomit him out on the shore, and again asks him to

---

[349] *ST* I, q. 22, art. 2, reply to obj. 4.
[350] Wisdom 3:1-6.
[351] Jonah 1:1-3.
[352] Jonah 1:4-16.

preach in Nineveh.[353] At this point, Jonah decides that doing so is the path of least resistance for him, and he proceeds to preach repentance in Nineveh, which to his shock and dismay, the Ninevites heed, taking on sackcloth and ashes.[354]

In the narrative, God employs physical evil, in the form of a storm, to create an environment of fear that motivates the sailors to do what He needs them to do for His plan to succeed.[355] God also makes it clear to the sailors that Jonah is the reason for their danger, when He implicates him as the guilty party through the casting of lots.[356] When Jonah confesses to them that he is fleeing the Lord God of Heaven, the sailors are afraid of God's wrath and ask Jonah for a solution that will placate God.[357] As St. Jerome notes in his commentary, Jonah knows that he is responsible for putting the sailors in danger, so he tells them to throw him into the sea.[358] After praying for forgiveness, they do just that.

God then acts again, showing that throwing Jonah into the water was His desire by calming the sea immediately after they threw him in. This stops their suffering and has the added benefit of serving as a catalyst for conversion for the sailors because "seized with great fear of the Lord, the men offered sacrifice to the Lord and made vows."[359] Finally, suffering from the evils of

---

[353] Jonah 2:1-3:2.
[354] Jonah 3:3-10.
[355] Jonah 1:5.
[356] Jonah 1:7-9.
[357] Jonah 1:10-12.
[358] Jerome, "Commentary on Jonah," *Aquinas Study Bible* chapter 1.11, https://sites.google.com/site/aquinasstudybible/home/jonah/st-jerome-on-jonah/chapter-1.
[359] Jonah 1:1-14.

the storm, being thrown into the raging sea, and then being swallowed by the whale was clearly enough to get Jonah to reconsider his decision and to align himself with God's will.

In the story of Jonah, it is made clear that God was taking specific action to ensure that His plan remained intact by employing the storm and the whale to do His bidding. The appearance of the storm and the whale at precisely the time they were needed is not accidental. This is a prime Scriptural example of particular providence, utilizing evil to provide the environment desired and suffering to motivate the desired behavior in the affected individuals (in this case, both the sailors and Jonah). As St. Jerome says in his commentary, God's plan not only led Jonah to align himself with God's will, but also led the sailors on the boat and the people of Nineveh to do the same.[360] In each of these cases, there was a particular plan for each individual, with an omnipotent and omniscient God capable of integrating them for efficiency. Jerome goes further:

> The flight of the prophet can be related to man in general, who, forsaking the commands of God, flees from his face and goes out into the world. But in consequence a storm of wickedness and the shipwreck of the entire world are sent against him, and he is made to pay attention to God and to return to that which he had fled. From this we can understand that what appears to be advantageous to mankind, turns into their downfall by God's will.[361]

As should be obvious, there is no need or reason for a person's salvation to be a matter of chance or accident when in the hands

---

[360] Jerome, "Commentary on Jonah," chapters 1, 2.
[361] Ibid., chapter 1.

of an omnipotent, omniscient God, Who cares deeply about His creation.

It must be emphasized at this point that God is actually using evil, which is the privation of good, to provide the environment He knows is needed for humans to grow spiritually. People need challenges to grow. Eleanor Stump notes that human experience in child-rearing supports this claim: spoiled children often grow up into unpleasant adults, whereas those who grew up facing challenges are more prepared to prosper as adults.[362]

Because they are accustomed to thinking about evil as being in opposition to God, some will be uncomfortable with a position that God actively makes use of evil actions and circumstances to bring about good, not merely that He allows it as a prerequisite of free will. However, such a position is well-attested to in the Church, embraced by Doctors of the Church, the Magisterium, and Scripture itself. As already discussed, the defining act in Sacred Scripture, the Resurrection of Christ, was making use of the greatest evil: His Crucifixion. In the story of the blind man in the book of John, chapter 9, Jesus is explicit in saying that the man was born blind specifically to be used as an instrument of God's glory.

St. Thomas Aquinas explains that evil would never be sought after, not even accidentally, unless the good that accompanies the evil was more desired than the good of which the evil is a privation.[363] He further explains that God in no way wills the evil of sin because that represents a loss of right order toward His own goodness, which God wills most highly. On the other hand, God does will natural evil because He wills the preservation of

---

[362] Eleonore Stump, "The Problem of Evil," *Faith and Philosophy* 2, no. 4 (October 1985): 410.

[363] ST I, q. 19, art. 9.

the natural order, which requires that some things must be corrupted. For example, one generation must die to leave resources for the next one. St. Thomas also notes that God wills the evil of punishment because it is attached to justice, which God desires more than the comfort of the sinner. This includes illness and birth defects, which are the effects and punishments for Original Sin.[364] However, God punishes to heal, not to hurt. Indeed, St. Thomas says that birth defects are given to people for the good of their souls or those around them.[365]

Note that although God makes use of evil, it is never out of malice, but always to serve a greater purpose. St. John Paul II in *Salvifici doloris* is clear that although God is responsible for punishment, it is not for the purposes of destroying a person, but to rebuild goodness.[366] When God called up the storm to reroute Jonah, He did it not out of malice to Jonah, but to redirect him to the path of righteousness that He had planned for him. The storm was perceived by Jonah to be an evil because it was an impediment to his desired actions. He suffered as a warning that he was pursuing a path contrary to God's will. Actually, though, as we come to see as the story unfolds, the storm is an instrument of salvation for Jonah, the sailors, and the Ninevites—a much greater good than the temporary loss of comfort and the loss of material goods experienced by Jonah and his shipmates.

Scripture obviously supports the concept that God is active in our lives and that He desires for us, His prodigal sons and daughters, to become like Him so that we can join Him in eternal life in the glow of His Beatific Vision. Tradition, as seen in the

---

[364] *ST* I-II q. 85, art. 5.
[365] *ST* I-II, q. 87, art. 7, reply to obj. 1.
[366] John Paul II, *Salvifici doloris*, 12.

works of the Magisterium, the Church Fathers and the saints, builds on this, to show how God uses suffering to call us back to Him. While this can be hard to understand because of our pre-conditioning to avoid what is uncomfortable for us, and the fact that the theology of suffering requires extracting from the vast deposit of faith maintained by the Church, it is true nonetheless and has been made more accessible by St. John Paul II in *Salvifici doloris*. The next chapter will define the theology of suffering succinctly, and the third section will provide some ideas about how it calls us to eternal life and how to respond appropriately to the suffering we experience both personally and through others.

12

The Theology of Suffering

The purpose of this theology is to make Catholic moral teaching more accessible to those both inside and outside of the tradition by linking St. John Paul II's teaching on suffering to the *Catechism*, thus filling a gap in current Catholic resources concerning suffering. More importantly, it is meant to provide hope and solace to those who suffer and to assure them that God loves them and is calling them to participate in His nature and His life, in both this world and the next.

This theology of suffering is consistent with Catholic doctrine, having been based on ten key teachings of the Catholic Church as related in the *Catechism*, augmented by three specific insights from St. John Paul II's apostolic letter *Salvifici doloris*. They are as follows:

1. God must be omnipotent and omniscient to be able to build the universe out of nothing and to keep it orderly (CCC 288-300).
2. God is rational; everything is done for a reason; therefore, God cares about His creation (301-303).
3. Because God is omniscient, omnipotent, and rational, everything He made is perfect for its purpose (299).
4. God made man in His image so that man could become like Him and then be with Him in heaven (356).

5. God gave man free will so that he could freely choose to unite with God (357-358).

6. God became man so that "man could become God," giving us a model and the grace for which to do so (359).

7. Suffering is an experience of evil, warning us when we are threatened and motivating us to attain the missing good (John Paul II, *Salvifici doloris*, 7).

8. There are four tasks of suffering to bring man to be like God (derived from CCC 307 and *Salvifici doloris*).

9. God left the universe incomplete and left man as its steward to help bring it to completeness, giving purpose to man's life (CCC 307).

10. Evil is the privation of good, either through corruption, misuse, disorder, or incompleteness, of something that ought to be there (John Paul II, *Salvifici doloris*, 7).

11. God completes His universal design at the optimal time, thus making good from the consequences of evil, even moral evil (CCC 312).

12. God loves us and is actively working to perfect us so that we can be fulfilled and happy (CCC 313).

In the *Catechism*, it explains that the origins of evil must be approached by "fixing the eyes of our faith on him, who alone is its conqueror." It quotes St. Augustine as saying that "the mystery of lawlessness is clarified only in the light of our religion."[367] Another way to understand this is that to understand the nature of evil and suffering properly requires it to be understood in the context of all the other existential questions about the nature of

---

[367] CCC 385.

God, the nature of man, man's purpose in life, and the question of life after death. If the solution to one of these questions is not self-consistent with the answers to all the rest, then at least one of the answers is wrong. To have a theological system like that of the Church, which can answer all these existential questions in a way that they all make sense simultaneously, is a very strong proof of their truth.

Jesus shows us in the parable of the Prodigal Son that God's greatest desire is to be united with His wayward children and to provide us the happiness that He had always intended for us.[368] Like the father in the parable, He is always reaching out to us, ready to celebrate when we come to our senses and to welcome us home. Like the Prodigal Son in the parable, many pursue a life of dissipation and will not notice that they have lost everything until they suffer. And just as in the parable, suffering will make them aware that the Father has every good thing they need and motivate them to return to Him, where they will find happiness and fulfillment in the Beatific Vision.

An omniscient, omnipotent Father Who desires nothing more than to be united with His wayward children certainly reaches out to each and every one of us to encourage our return to the life He has planned for us. Ironically, evil has a prominent place in God's plan for salvation, even when we sin. God created everything and it was all perfect for its purpose. Evil does not exist as an entity: it is the lack, loss, or privation of good that ought to be present.

To provide humans with a sense of purpose, God left the universe in an unperfected state, with physical evils reflecting opportunities for human growth and initiative.[369] He also made

[368] Luke 15:11-32.
[369] CCC 310.

humans interdependent so they would learn to love.[370] He gave man free will as a sign of his dignity, knowing that man would abuse the freedom in sin. But God also endowed humanity with reason so we could learn and grow.[371] In His providential plan, God provides physical and natural evils at appropriate times for humans to develop the virtues consistent with the divine nature that leads to beatitude.[372] In fact, God in His omniscience also uses the evil of sin to perfect the victims and the evil of punishment to perfect the sinner in much the same way.[373] Finally, God gave us suffering, which is the ability to detect these evils, and it motivates us to avoid evil by attaining the good that suffering shows us is lacking.

Despite the fact that God can make use of our sins for the sake of others, He does not wish it or condone it because, for the sinner, the evil of sin is an intentional deviation from the path of righteousness and joy. Sin is to choose our own path versus the one God laid out for us. It is to choose the way of the Prodigal Son, abandoning the father and a life of growth and fulfillment for a life of dissipation.[374] In doing so, we foolishly believe that we know better than the Creator of the Universe what will bring us joy. Or perhaps, we just do not believe God has our best interest at heart, failing to recognize it is God Who sustains our existence. Indeed, as the parable shows, God mourns for sinners as the father mourned for his Prodigal Son, and He is anxious for our redemption.[375] Because of His great love and respect for His children, He

---

[370] CCC 340.
[371] CCC 356-357.
[372] CCC 306-307.
[373] CCC 312.
[374] Luke 15:3.
[375] Luke 15:32.

allows us the freedom to choose, but He also provides suffering as a beacon to light our way home should we choose to return.

In a very real way, suffering is the divine beacon God has set up for us, showing us the existential dangers that surround us, providing a warning we cannot ignore when we deviate from the path of righteousness and joy. It illuminates the path home to Him, where we can bask in the eternal joy of the Beatific Vision. People incorrectly associate suffering with evil, when it is in fact in opposition to it, warning us whenever evil is present in our lives. Unfortunately, those who cannot believe what is beyond their senses recognize only the discomfort it causes and never even consider that the meaning of this discomfort is to warn us of the lack of goodness that evil represents, as well as to motivate us to attain the good we are missing.

This theology of suffering also allows us to perceive the sufferer differently, not as a whiner or a sinner, but as a messenger of God, with a profound responsibility to reveal to others the lessons of his suffering. This witness serves to bring those who suffer back into the community, to give them a sense of purpose, and provide solidarity with those around them. Their witness can provide onlookers with an opportunity for spiritual merit if the onlookers provide them aid. It can also warn others of both spiritual and material dangers that lead to suffering and show others the path to faith and virtue.

For those engaged in the debates around divine providence, this theology makes it clear that God is active in everyone's life, using what humans understand as evils to provide challenges and opportunities at precisely the time that they are needed to help us grow in virtue. God also uses suffering to direct us back on the path to eternal life when we stray from it. This is not done in a malicious or sadistic manner, but out of love. While it is true that those focused on temporal goals alone may come to doubt in God's providence, it is equally true that God will persist in His attempts to steer us back on the road to beatitude until we either see the light and return to virtue, or we die in our sins. After all, this is the God Who so loved the world that He gave His Only Begotten Son to save it. It is also the God portrayed by the father who ran to the Prodigal Son, ecstatic that the son who had been lost had returned. As much as He loves us and wants us to return to Him for our own good, God does not force us to do so. However, because suffering is uncomfortable and persistent, it motivates men to choose the right path by giving them an example of what life is like without God.

Evil and suffering, then, with the exception of when we turn away from God in sin, are instruments of God's providence, leading to men's happiness. Evil, understood properly as the absence of good, presents opportunities for man to develop and practice faith and virtue in imitation of God, and suffering makes the choices clear and motivates men to act properly toward God, themselves, and others. To the extent that men take action spurred on or prompted by suffering and to the extent that they align themselves with God, they share in His providence and His perfection of the universe, bringing forth His Kingdom. On the other hand, if they fail to act, the suffering will have been endured in vain, and when men sin, they create their own evil, separating themselves from God and adding to the suffering borne by their neighbors.

In the book of Genesis, we are told that our first parents were willing to risk death to be like God, partaking of the fruit of the tree of the knowledge of good and evil.[376] God, in His omniscience,

[376] Genesis 3.

surely understood that His human children would want to be like Him and in fact, like human fathers, wanted this as well. But God also knew that humans would need help and training to share in the divine life and that the kind of love required must be freely given. He put the tree easily within their reach so that they could demonstrate their willingness to put God's desires above their own. Knowing that they were not ready to accept that true love requires putting others' desires before their own, He warned them that choosing their way over God's way came with suffering and death, which the serpent denied. The serpent tricked our first parents into reaching out for deification before they were ready for it by emphasizing the gain while denying the costs—a classic half-truth. In essence, our first parents had chosen to steal what God was already preparing for them, and in doing so, they separated themselves from the Father.

Once the choice was made, they experienced evil because they separated themselves from the good provided by God, much as the Prodigal Son did when he left his father to pursue a life of dissipation. As warned, the choice was coupled with suffering and death, not merely as a punitive measure but as the kind of punishment that causes a growth in goodness and results in rehabilitation.

Ironically, suffering *is* the fruit of the tree of the knowledge of good and evil, and at the same time it is the divine beacon of joy, highlighting evil and motivating us to seek the missing good that it implies. Through its four tasks, suffering takes men on the journey to conform them to God's will so they can become like God. To make it easier to understand, God also became incarnate in the person of Jesus Christ, demonstrating the divine nature for us, including the need for selfless love that He displayed on the Cross. He demonstrated through His Crucifixion and Resurrection that death is the pathway to eternal life in the presence of the Father, and He explained how this could be achieved with the Beatitudes and parables, perhaps none more profound than that of the Prodigal Son. In the words of St. Irenaeus, "God became man so that man might become God."[377] If we follow Him, we can become like Him, and if we fall off the path, suffering will highlight it and show us the way back, like a divine beacon of joy.

[377] Irenaeus, *Against Heresies*, bk. 3, ch. 19.

Section III

Answering the Call to Share
in the Nature of God

13

All People Suffer in Life

Everyone suffers in life because the universe in which we live is not yet perfected. This is a deliberate part of God's plan. He saw value in creating humans in His own image, capable of love and reason and endowed with free will, and so He created the universe in a way that would provide the challenges that would allow us to exercise and grow physically, intellectually, spiritually, and morally. In fact, without challenges, people quickly become bored and develop their own challenges. In God's plan, humans can aspire to be like God, not in infinite power or knowledge, but in their ability to love,[378] which, as St. John wrote in his first epistle, is the very nature of God (God is love).[379]

Humans cannot reach such a lofty ideal of being like God on their own, but only with God's help and guidance. In fact, people can even become immortal and partake of the Beatific Vision (which is man's last end and results in eternal joy) if they are willing to follow God's lead, as demonstrated by Jesus Christ, God Incarnate, and partake of the grace of the sacraments. As an additional aid, God provides humans with suffering to point them on the path to eternal salvation whenever we stray.

[378] 2 Peter 1:3-11.
[379] 1 John 4:8.

Why All People Suffer

This is analogous to divine revelation, since God uses suffering to communicate not only evils to be avoided but also the goods that must be attained. In a very real way, suffering can be seen as the fruit of the tree of the knowledge of good and evil that Eve craved enough to risk death for herself and all who followed her. It can just as easily be thought of as a divine beacon, which God has set up to lead us to Him by making any deviation from the desired path extremely uncomfortable to us.

When people suffer, they have two fundamental responsibilities. First, they must heed the message they receive, avoiding evil and attaining the good of which evil deprives them. This puts them on the path to eternal life and is, in essence, a personal repudiation of Original Sin, which drove humanity off that path at the beginning. Second, they must share what they experience, becoming messengers of God. This will allow others to gain the same knowledge without having to suffer themselves in the same way. In fact, in certain circumstances, such as when they are victims of another person's sin, passing on the message to the sinner is their full responsibility. It is in doing so that suffering takes on meaning because unheeded suffering is suffering in vain.

Interpreting the Message of Our Own Suffering

When people suffer, they are uncomfortable, and this can make it hard to discern what is happening to them or to ascribe to it a reason. The thing to remember is that God is like the father that Jesus describes in the parable of the Prodigal Son, who not only forgives his son for wasting half his property on prostitutes and a life of dissipation, he literally runs to him to welcome him back.[380]

---

[380] Luke 15:11-32.

We therefore need to trust that despite our sins, God also wants to welcome us with open arms.

The key to understanding God's providential plan and the role of suffering in it is to orient one's will to that of God, to see it as much as possible from His perspective. Because an omniscient, omniscient God has infinitely more power and insight than humans, this would be impossible unless He reveals it to us. Fortunately, He has done exactly that through his Son, Jesus Christ, Who as fully God and fully man can enlighten us about God's will through His own words and actions.[381] Thus, when considering why we suffer, we must consider how it would lead us all to conform our wills to God's and ultimately lead us to beatitude in the Eternal Kingdom through the building up of virtue and cleansing of past sins.

The first consideration that we should examine when we suffer is whether we have separated ourselves from God, the greatest good and the source of all that is good. If so, we should work to reconcile with Him with complete contrition, sacramentally if possible, and be thankful that He cares enough about us to warn us of our danger so stridently and continuously. If we understand the meaning behind this suffering and rectify it, we will see that our lives have purpose and that we have dignity as children of God. By grasping this, we turn aside the social isolation of feeling unwanted and the psychological trauma associated with the unknown, leaving only physical pain to deal with, which is a much easier task.

It is important to understand that our suffering is not always a warning or a punishment for our sins, nor is every sufferer a sinner. Indeed, Jesus was the sinless Son of God, and yet He suffered grievously for other's sins. Mary, His Mother, also sinless from the

---

[381] CCC 480.

day of her conception,[382] suffered through Jesus' Passion; one of her titles is therefore "Our Lady of Sorrows." The saints often suffered. St. Bernadette Soubirous, the visionary of Lourdes, said of her discussion with the Blessed Virgin on February 18, 1854, that "She could not promise to make me happy in this world, only in the next."[383] Her suffering was in the form of physical illness, rather than the result of injuries, as in the case of Jesus, or mental anguish, as in the case of Mary. In all these cases, the suffering was not on account of personal sin, but was for the benefit of others and is therefore redemptive.

It is often not possible to discern who is benefiting from the suffering of another, because people are interconnected in a multitude of ways and human perspective and insight can be quite limited. What is possible to do is to recognize that suffering is always for the spiritual benefit of someone, whether it be the sufferer or someone else who is moved toward true happiness, which is union with God. Even if the details cannot be established, the message that his suffering has meaning for someone can be uplifting for the sufferer and lead to spiritual joy. This joy increases along with spiritual merit if the sufferer is willing to bear it for the love of others.

Giving God the "benefit of the doubt" in this way is actually practicing the theological virtue of hope. As St. Thomas notes, the object of hope is eternal happiness, and by trusting that God is using suffering to lead us to that goal is to experience hope.[384] It is a theological virtue, which cannot be earned or acquired, but must be infused by God. But like all infused virtues, it must

---

[382] CCC 411.

[383] Tejvan Pettinger, "Biography of Bernadette Soubirous," Oxford, UK, www.biographyonline.net, updated March 21, 2017.

[384] *ST* II-II, q. 17, art. 2.

also be acknowledged and accepted by us. Confronted with the insight that our suffering is part of God's plan to reorient mankind to Himself and to allow it to experience the Beatific Vision, every person must decide whether he is willing to accept his role in it. For those who do, there is recognition that their suffering has meaning and purpose, which will turn their suffering to joy in knowing they are sharing in the suffering of Christ, just as St. Paul articulated in his Letter to the Colossians.[385]

Those who interpret the messages of suffering through a temporal lens will not appreciate this because the point of suffering is to show us the deficiencies inherent in the material world and to point us to the greatest good, which is union with God. If a person's goal is comfort, it is easy to see why the person would reject a God that makes temporal life uncomfortable. On the other hand, if the person understands that true happiness is having access to all that is good, true, and beautiful through the Beatific Vision, then God's efforts to extract the person from an exorbitant and unhealthy desire for material goods and focus the person on Himself can be appreciated. As such, the meaning of suffering is intimately tied up with the meaning of human life and the providential plan of God. If one uses the right interpretive lens, one that understands that God's will is to share the divine nature with man, then the message that joy is achieved through suffering will be interpreted in a way that can become actionable.

Heeding the Message of Our Own Suffering

Ultimately, suffering demands more of us than to recognize its message. Its intensity and persistence demand that we heed its

---

[385] Colossians 1:24.

message and take action to love ourselves, God, and our neighbors in everything we do. Because it highlights the goods we lack, suffering directs us on the path to joy, to the attainment of spiritual goods that lead us to our greatest good, union with God. What we sense as suffering is God's warning that something more is needed from us, and the sensation is harsh and persistent to ensure we act upon it.

Sometimes we suffer because we are being punished for our sins, but sometimes we are being called to be instruments of another person's salvation. In either case, we are being called to love more fully, which is to act in accordance with the divine nature. Indeed, Jesus Himself suffered as an instrument for the salvation of others. It is the willingness to suffer for the benefit of others that makes it redemptive in that it is most in keeping with the nature of Christ.

Perhaps paradoxically, it is by willingly accepting suffering for the benefit of others that the suffering will ultimately be relieved — first, temporally, since, as has been the witness of many commentators, finding meaning in suffering will mitigate it by providing a sense of purpose; then, eternally, as a share in the sufferings of Christ. At the same time, those who resent being called against their will to suffer for their neighbor lack the good of charity which is required to attain the Beatific Vision. If they are lucky, the terrestrial suffering will continue until they are converted, thus sparing them eternal suffering.

This does not mean that we should not seek a cure for our suffering. Indeed, suffering itself compels us to do so. What needs to be remembered as we heed our own suffering is that the soul is eternal and hence it is more important than the body, so we need to attend to our spiritual needs as well as seek physical healing. Perhaps the right way to think about it is that pursuing physical healing enhances our ability and extends our time to work on those spiritual needs and thus has spiritual benefit. On the other hand, if we are physically cured without heeding our own spiritual needs, then the suffering we endured was pointless.

The sufferer should not automatically assume that he or she is being punished for sin, nor should anyone assume that someone else's suffering means he or she is a sinner. In fact, in the story of Job, he suffered precisely because he was indeed righteous, and God wanted to use him as an example of how to behave under duress.[386] It is not necessary for the sufferer to judge himself or those around him, heeding the Lord's admonition to "judge not, lest you be judged."[387] Instead, the sufferer should heed the message of suffering to increase charity and love those around him; to look for opportunities for spiritual attainment, which brings joy.

In some cases, sufferers can readily discern that they are the direct or indirect cause of their own suffering because they failed to heed the warnings of fellow sufferers not to eat certain foods or to avoid certain places or activities that posed dangers. This category includes those who suffer punishment for their crimes. In these cases, the way to show love is to warn others to the best of one's ability about what could happen to them, in order to save them from similar suffering. St. Thomas believed that such suffering, if willingly accepted for the good it could do for others who were deterred from future sin, could remove the stain of sin.[388]

In other cases, the sufferers can readily discern that another person or organization is causing them to suffer. This can range in intimacy from an abusive spouse or parent to an uncaring

---

[386] Job 1:8; Job 2:3.
[387] Matthew 7:1.
[388] ST I-II q. 87, art. 6.

public utility that pollutes one's drinking water, causing the person to be ill. Whatever the case, the person who suffers must act out of love for those causing the person harm, alerting them to the harm they are causing and appealing to their consciences to modify their actions. In most cases, the most charitable way to communicate one's suffering to an oppressor is to simply let them see the evil they are causing, trusting in the good of human nature. If they fail to respond, it is still a work of mercy to seek out advocates who might help to convince the offender of the injustice of their actions, since the good to their soul will be worth more than the embarrassment they might feel to be confronted by a third party. The last option to be pursued is to bring one's grievances to an authority whose role is to protect its citizens. This will result in temporal punishment for the offender, which will likely be resented, but if it stops him from sinning, there is spiritual benefit or at least a lessening of the spiritual demerits for the offender, and it would be therefore considered an act of mercy. As discussed earlier, there is spiritual benefit and the potential for joy as long as the sufferer persists in charitably witnessing to the truth, even if the oppressor does not take action. In fact, Tertullian famously said, "the blood of the martyrs is the seed of Christianity,"[389] because even if the oppressors did not desist in their persecution, others may have a spiritual awakening from the sufferer's charitable actions on behalf of their oppressors.

Finally, there are cases where the suffering appears to be the result of an act of God, whether it be as rare and obvious as being hit by lightning or as ordinary and subtle as contracting an

---

[389] Tertullian "Tertullian quotes," Brainyquote.com, https://www. brainyquote.com/authors/tertullian-quotes.

illness. As discussed in the first three sections, many people have a hard time reconciling how a benevolent God allows, let alone dispenses, suffering to bring about good. In the fifth century, St. Augustine explained: "When He subjects me to adversity, this is either to test my merits or chastise my sins; and He reserves an eternal reward for my pious endurance of temporal ills."[390]

John Paul II, writing at the end of the twentieth century, saw other reasons that God subjects us to suffering that would require a different response to suffering than pious endurance:

> Suffering must serve for conversion, that is, for the rebuilding of goodness in the subject, who can recognize the divine mercy in this call to repentance. The purpose of penance is to overcome evil, which under different forms lies dormant in man. Its purpose is also to strengthen goodness both in man himself and in his relationships with others and especially with God.[391]

In John Paul II's theology, suffering is about love. Above all, it is about the fact that God's love for us that is so great that "He gave his only Son, that whoever believes in him should not perish but have eternal life."[392] It is also about leading us to love God, through the "special grace" contained within suffering that leads to profound conversion.[393] Finally, suffering unleashes love in the human person on behalf of other people.[394]

---

[390] Augustine. *The City of God against the Pagans*, edited and translated by R. W. Dyson. New York: Cambridge University Press, 1998. Book 1, Chapter 29.

[391] John Paul II, *Salvifici doloris*, 12.

[392] Ibid., 14 quoting John 3:16.

[393] Ibid., 26.

[394] Ibid., 29.

Suffering is not something to endure, it must be embraced. When we suffer, we must respond with love toward ourselves, toward our neighbors, and toward God. How we do so may in fact be dictated by how we are made to suffer. For instance, if we suffer from material losses, it is already a sign that we are too attached to material things. This type of suffering can be resolved with a change in perspective in which we are willing to get by with less and to embrace the charity of others, who can benefit spiritually by helping us materially. In fact, if we willingly accept our losses for the spiritual opportunity it provides for those who help us, our suffering becomes tied to that of Christ and is redemptive. If we can reach this state, we may also realize that God took away our material wealth to focus us on spiritual wealth, and we will understand it as an unexpected blessing and an act of love by the Father.

Job gives us a pertinent example to follow when he lost all his livestock and all his children in a single day. His response was to tear his cloak, cut off his hair, and lay prostrate on the ground and then say: "Naked I came forth from my mother's womb and naked shall I go back. The Lord gave and the Lord has taken away, blessed be the name of the Lord."[395] For this, Job was lauded by God, Who said to Satan, "Have you noticed my servant Job? There is no one on earth like him, blameless and upright, fearing God and avoiding evil. He still holds fast to his innocence although you incited me against him to ruin him for nothing."[396]

If we are struck with physical suffering from illness or injury that is not the result of a human mistake or sin, the *Catechism* reminds us that:

[395] Job 1:13-21.
[396] Job 2:3.

In illness, man experiences his powerlessness, his limitations, and his finitude. Every illness can make us glimpse death. Illness can lead to anguish, self-absorption, sometimes even despair and revolt against God. It can also make a person more mature, helping him discern in his life what is not essential so that he can turn to that which is. Very often illness provokes a search for God and a return to him.[397]

To suffer illness, then, is a call for conversion, which must be heeded to attain joy in the unconverted. When the already devout become ill, it can be for other reasons. In the case of Job, it was simultaneously a test of his devotion and an opportunity to give him and his companions a more accurate view of the nature of God.[398] When the devout bear their illnesses well, it adds to their credibility as witnesses for the goodness of God and can help in the conversion of others. If their suffering is willingly accepted because they recognize it is for the benefit of others, it will be redemptive.

No matter how we are called to suffer, regardless of whether we can perceive its purpose or beneficiary, we should recognize it as a call to love those around us. The first way we can show love is to bear witness charitably to what we feel. This should not be done as a complaint against God or man, but as a lament of the situation that serves to warn people about the danger, highlight opportunities for "Good Samaritans" to help, and engage the consciences of the responsible parties to repent. We should also

---

[397] CCC 1500-1501.

[398] Job 2:1-10, which describes Job's test at the hands of Satan, and Job 42, wherein he admits that he misunderstood God's works, and where God explains to Eliphaz that he and his companions had not spoken rightly concerning God.

recognize it as an opportunity and a message to take stock of our lives and recommit ourselves to the development of virtue.

Finally, when we are called to suffer, we should recognize it not as a condemnation by God, but as a religious calling. First, it is calling us home to God, Who is waiting on the other side of death with open arms, anxious for us to return to Him. This is not just a physical calling but a call to align our thoughts and desires with His as well. Being united to Him means more than being in God's presence; it means partaking in His nature, becoming loving as He is loving. Becoming like God is the ultimate joy to which humanity has always aspired, despite not really understanding what this joy means. It is not about having the power to create from nothing or to see the entire history of the world at a glance. These abilities present a responsibility and a burden that is incredibly heavy; one which none of us would enjoy if we actually had to do it. Instead, it is about sharing in that responsibility where we are in time and place and helping those whose needs are presented to us by their suffering. This is love, and it is the nature of God.

What God does on a universal scale, we are called to do on a personal scale, building up virtue in ourselves and others. We do this by following His example, shown to us in human form by Jesus; and by heeding suffering, avoiding those acts and situations that lead to suffering, and alleviating any suffering we encounter to the best of our abilities. God reveals His plan to us in these ways: showing us the path to righteousness directly through the words and actions of Jesus and those that follow Him, and by showing us the ramifications of separating ourselves from Him through sin with suffering, which is a more painful way of learning what was available to us through divine revelation, the deposit of faith.

14

The Role of the Church

Sometimes the lessons of suffering are very obvious and straight-forward, while at other times they are more difficult to discern. The closer we are aligned with Christ and His Church, the more obvious the lesson will be, because having the right perspective is critical in interpreting the lessons of suffering. For instance, without life after death, terminal suffering can never be justified. Without Jesus' example, we would have great difficulty surmising the nature of God or the value of redemptive suffering. Without the Christian interpretation of evil as a privation of good, we would be misled into thinking that evil was opposed to good, which would make the co-existence of God and evil problematic. Without the understanding that the purpose of life is union with God, we would not be able to understand that human suffering leads to a greater good.

The greatest advantage to understanding this theology is that it focuses our attention on the message of the suffering rather than on the sensation of suffering itself. It also gives us a set of parameters to consider that makes the discernment process more manageable. For instance, we know that God loves us and is using suffering to guide us into His company, teaching us how to share in His nature. That eliminates the possibilities that are punitive in nature and it also eliminates other possibilities, namely that suffering is random and meaningless because God either does not exist, is indifferent to the lives of His children, or is powerless to change anything.

Although God makes His presence known to us through suffering, it is not the only way to understand the divine nature. As discussed earlier, the Church also reveals that Christ, because He is truly God, can make us sharers in His divinity. Because He is truly man, He can also be our model of holiness.[399] Said simply, to know Jesus is to know God, because as Jesus stated, "The Father and I are one."[400] The Church provides both Scriptural and Traditional sources to reveal the human and divine natures of Christ to us and therefore the nature of God to us as well.

People come to believe in God and His Church in different ways. Many are born into it based on decisions made perhaps even centuries earlier by others. Being "born into it" is a misnomer, however, because for a person to be a meaningful member of the Church, he will need to make a personal decision to participate in a way that will lead to the Beatific Vision. Some will enter based on the witness of others. Some will come to faith after a catastrophic life event leaves them nowhere else to turn. For others, it requires suffering from a series of problems that motivate a person to pursue goods, and then ultimately the greatest good. Suffering's purpose is to lead us back to God, and He gave us the Church to facilitate that. Therefore, the first and best way to answer the call of suffering is to engage with the Church, taking part in its liturgy, following its doctrines and moral direction, partaking of its sacraments, and engaging in its social ministries.

[399] CCC 459-460.
[400] John 10:30.

As stated in the Great Commission at the end of St. Matthew's Gospel, the Church was tasked with teaching what Jesus taught the apostles.[401] What it teaches is that mankind was designed in the image and likeness of God, and that God became man so that mankind could share in His nature and His life. The Church, as the Body of Christ, provides not only the knowledge and understanding of what it takes to become like God, but also the graces required, which it is authorized to bestow through the sacraments. Thus, the Church is essential in developing the virtues that lead to true happiness.

This begins with building faith in God. God accomplishes this in different ways with different people. Some, like St. Augustine, are converted through appeals to the intellect, without much recourse to suffering. Others, like St. Paul, who was thrown from his horse and blinded on the road to Damascus, are converted through overwhelming force because nothing else would suffice. Many, however, require something in between: an incremental process that raises a person first from vice to natural virtue, which in turn prepares him to accept the grace that leads to theological conversion. Some, of course, do not convert at all, never having been exposed to the type of suffering that would have driven their conversions. Ironically, those who think they have been blessed with a happy life with minimal suffering have been in fact cursed with a lack of divine correction. Like spoiled children, they think themselves privileged, only to find they are ill-prepared for the life that awaits them.

The infusion of faith itself has two prerequisites in the Thomistic tradition.[402] The first is that the things to be believed must be

---

[401] Matthew 28:18-20.
[402] *ST* II-II, q. 6, art. 1.

proposed to a person, and the second is the assent of the believer to the things that are proposed. Because the things which are of faith surpass human reason, they must be revealed by God. This is either done directly, as in the case of the prophets and apostles, or indirectly, through their witness to others, which has been passed down through the centuries by the Church through Sacred Scripture and Tradition.

This is where the Church is valuable to mankind. Jesus established the visible Church to carry out His work on earth. The Church holds and teaches from the deposit of faith left by the apostles, who were witnesses to Christ's teaching and actions and were guided by the interpretations of the Holy Spirit. It also has the power to dispense the Lord's grace through the sacraments, which is required to elevate fallen men to sons of God, partakers of the divine nature. Finally, in keeping with the theme of unity, the Church provides charitable, spriritual, social, youth, and other ministries in which each individual has something to offer and also has some need to be filled.[403] Together, we can make each other better, just as is the case with a husband and a wife. To love charitably, as God loves, is to unite in goals with another, both seeking the best for the other.[404] This is the goal of the Christian life, made possible by the gifts of the Holy Spirit and reinforced by the love of fellow parishioners.

This final point is important. Theologian Therese Lysaught reminds us that "at all times, sacraments must be understood as actions whose fundamental purposes are Christological — the building up of the body of Christ, the Church, and the ongoing

---

[403] 1 Corinthians 12:12-31.
[404] *ST* II, q. 23, art.1.

formation of those who worship as embodied images of Christ."[405] Indeed, this is also true of suffering, which, as will be shown, pushes us toward each other as an ecclesial community as it pushes us toward God. Our ultimate happiness depends on our decisions in life. When we are baptized, we become members of the Body of Christ, united with God through the sacraments and the grace of Christ. The *Catechism* states: "The Lord himself affirms that Baptism is necessary for salvation."[406] This is a precursor to the ultimate union with God, which becomes perfect after death. So too, if we do not unite ourselves with God in this life but are separated from Him, we will remain separated after death.

If one does try to engage with the Church and comes away dissatisfied, this is a message to approach it differently. Many feel that the Church is too restrictive in its rules, too impersonal in its relationships, too mechanical in its practices; that it does not meet their needs in one way or another. This, too, misses the point. The Church describes itself as the Bride of Christ and also the Body of Christ, the two being interchangeable because in marriage, the two become one body. The same relationship exists between the Church and its members: they become one, each seeking out the best for each other. The object is not to get something out of the relationship, but to give something to the relationship, which is to show love. Our responsibility is to

---

[405] M. Therese Lysaught, "Suffering in Communion with Christ" in *Living Well and Dying Faithfully: Christian Practices for End-of-Life Care,* ed. John Swinton and Richard Payne (Grand Rapids, MI: Eerdmans, 2009), 84.

[406] CCC 1257. The *Catechism* quotes John 3:5: "Jesus answered, 'Amen, Amen, I say to you, no one can enter the kingdom of God without being born of water and spirit,'" but notes that God is not bound by His sacraments.

make the Church better, and in doing so, we make ourselves better. Not everyone in the Church understands this, but those who do understand it experience joy in their encounters as they share in the divine nature.

God loves and respects His creation enough to let us choose our own paths, but there are ramifications. When we turn our back on the Church, we turn our back on God's plan for us. Jesus Himself warned in the parable of the Sower that in many cases, faith is not deep enough to withstand the trials that inevitably come.[407] In other cases, worldly desires and the lure of riches choke out the Word, and people turn away from the Church. Suffering will inevitably follow, not to harm us but as God's warning to His prodigal sons and daughters of the hollowness of life without Him. If we are lucky, it will be intense enough or we will be alert enough to take notice and amend our lives accordingly.

However, in the absence of the Church's guidance, it will be difficult for most people to discern the message of their sufferings. Some will contemplate this and return to God through the Church in search of answers. Others, however, will refuse to do so, many becoming increasingly bitter toward God, in effect, reenacting the Original Sin of choosing their own way rather than following God's plan for them, which ironically would provide them with the happiness they desire had they decided to follow it.

Outside the Church, there is no salvation, because salvation comes from Christ through His Body.[408] To the extent that one is in communion with the Church, one is in communion with Christ. For instance, with the Orthodox Churches, "the communion is so profound that it lacks little to attain the fullness that

---

[407] Matthew 13:18-23.
[408] CCC 846.

would permit a common celebration of the Lord's Eucharist."[409] People from other Christian churches that share a valid Baptism but deviate from Church sacramental practice and doctrine in other ways will have those deficiencies to overcome in order to understand and heed properly the suffering they encounter; non-Christians even more so. Because Jesus asserted the necessity of Baptism, which is entry into the Church, those who understand this and still refuse to enter or remain in the Church are denying Christ's command and cannot be saved.[410] This is the reason the Church is so serious about its missionary mandate.[411]

But what of those who, through no fault of their own, do not know of Christ and His Church? The Church itself teaches that they too can be saved:

> "Since Christ died for all, and since all men are in fact called to one and the same destiny, which is divine, we must hold that the Holy Spirit offers to all the possibility of being made partakers, in a way known to God, of the Paschal mystery." Every man who is ignorant of the Gospel of Christ and of his Church, but seeks the truth and does the will of God in accordance with his understanding of it, can be saved. It may be supposed that such persons would have *desired Baptism explicitly* if they had known its necessity.[412]

Since the Enlightenment, men have been increasingly skeptical about the role of organized religion in human salvation,

[409] CCC 838.
[410] CCC 846.
[411] CCC 849.
[412] CCC 1260.

trusting more and more in their own ability to discern a path forward that leads to happiness. Many people today believe that the Church is not necessary for salvation, preferring to reach out to God in their own way.[413] This is simply an extension of Original Sin, to value our will above that of Jesus Christ, God Incarnate, Who established the Church for the salvation of men, under the leadership of St. Peter.[414] As will be shown, this individualistic path deviates from God's plan and therefore causes its own brand of suffering.

Pope Benedict XVI identifies the modern tendency toward individualism, and with it the idea that Jesus' message is aimed at only one person singly instead of as a community serving each other, as an outgrowth of science. Benedict explains that the Enlightenment ideas that drive it are rendered with particular clarity by Francis Bacon, "who claimed that the new correlation between science and praxis would mean that the dominion over creation—given to man by God and lost through original sin—would be re-established."[415] Benedict explains further that up to this time, the recovery of what man had lost through sin was expected from faith in Jesus Christ. Now, redemption, the restoration of the lost

---

[413] Pew Forum, "In U.S., Decline of Christianity Continues at Rapid Pace: An Update on America's Changing Religious Landscape," October 17, 2019, https://www.pewforum.org/2019/10/17/in-u-s -decline-of-christianitycontinues-at-rapid-pace/. Pew reports that the religiously unaffiliated has grown from 12 percent of those polled in 2009 to 17 percent in 2019, while atheists and agnostics have increased from 5 percent to 9 percent over the same time period.

[414] Matthew 16:16-19.

[415] Benedict XVI, *Spe salvi (Saved in Hope)* (San Francisco: Ignatius Press, 2008), 16.

Paradise, would be made through the application of science. Faith in God has been replaced by faith in progress.[416]

Benedict then points out the modern view of progress is primarily associated with the growing dominion of reason, and that the goal of progress is to overcome all forms of dependency, to become perfectly free.[417] He explains that in 1792, Immanuel Kant applied these concepts to religion, claiming that "the gradual transition of ecclesial faith to the exclusive sovereignty of pure religious faith is the coming of the Kingdom of God."[418] But if the Kingdom of God were to be the perfection of the earth by man, progress could no longer come only from science, but must also come from politics, which required a revolution. Karl Marx set this revolution in motion with his *Communist Manifesto*, and real revolution followed in Russia.[419] With it followed real suffering, which is a reliable indicator that we have deviated from the path of righteousness. As Ilya Somin wrote in an article commemorating the centennial of Communism, "Communist regimes killed as many as 100 million people in the last century, more than all other repressive regimes combined in the same time frame." He continues, saying that "Even those fortunate enough to survive were subjected to severe repression, including violations of freedom, of speech, freedom of religion, loss of property rights and the criminalization of ordinary economic activity."[420]

---

[416] Ibid., 17.

[417] Ibid., 18.

[418] Ibid., 19.

[419] Ibid., 20.

[420] Ilya Somin, "Lessons from a Century of Communism," *Washington Post*, November 7, 2017, *https://www.washingtonpost.com/ news/volokh-conspiracy/wp/2017/11/07/lessons-from-a-century -ofcommunism/*.

It should be noted that the folly of the Enlightenment was, in essence, a misreading of the state of man and the purpose of our life's journey. Sir Francis Bacon's project was focused on the need for man to improve the world to make it more hospitable to our needs and desires.[421] What it failed to recognize is that fallen man is too self-centered to manage the world effectively in his current state, which is a fact that has been demonstrated all too effectively by the wars, corruptions, environmental decay, and mass genocides of the last few centuries. Granted, humanity has made huge technical strides over that timeframe, improving human comfort on many fronts, but it has also increased man's danger to himself and his neighbors because the increased technical capability did not come with a corresponding increase in moral judgment.

In contrast to the goal of the secular humanists to create a new Paradise on earth, the Church, benefitting from the truth revealed by God to the apostles, understands that the goal is not to perfect the world, but to perfect mankind, morally and spiritually.[422] Suffering is not something to be overcome, but it is to be heeded as it points out how mankind needs continual conversion to become like God so that we can truly share in His life. God uses temporal suffering to bring about moral growth, which is more lasting than our corporeal bodies. As is clearly evident from the history of the last century, the improvement required of man is not the power of technology, which can be used for good or evil, but in the wisdom and charity needed to control it.

Benedict XVI notes that in Enlightenment thinking, a kingdom based on reason and freedom would seem to guarantee, by

---

[421] Benedict XVI, *Spe salvi*, 16.
[422] CCC 358.

virtue of their inherent goodness, a new and perfect human community. It was also viewed that the shackles of faith and of the Church inhibited reason and freedom.[423] However, when people complain that the guidance of the Church is inhibiting their freedom, they fail to recognize the difference between freedom of indifference and freedom for excellence.

As explained by theologian Servais Pinckaers, O.P., "we can compare freedom for excellence with an acquired skill in an art or profession; it is the capacity to produce our acts when and how we wish, like high-quality works that are perfect in their domain."[424] Freedom to excel, then, involves having the capability to excel. Said another way, without the capability to excel, we are bound to something less. St. Paul describes the situation to the Romans as being dominated by sin.[425] Indeed, the true limitation on man is not the ability to choose, which is the definition of freedom of indifference, but in the ability to bring to fruition what we choose, which is freedom for excellence.

Answering the call to reorient ourselves to God and His Church, the second task of suffering is critical for our journey to salvation. This is, in effect, the personal repudiation of Original Sin, choosing to unite our wills to the will of God, thus reducing the separation that previously existed. In this way, we emulate Christ Who prayed to God in Gethsemane, "not as I will, but as you will."[426] Like Christ, we need to put our love of God into action through our love of neighbor and, as in the life of Christ, suffering will provide the opportunity and context for this to

---

[423] Benedict XVI, *Spe salvi*, 18.
[424] Pinckaers, *Morality*, 69.
[425] Romans 3:9.
[426] Matthew 26:39.

occur. It begins with the unleashing of our love toward our suffering neighbors, as we provide aid and comfort. It culminates in our own redemption when we realize our own suffering provides an opportunity for the redemption of others and we embrace it out of love for them, thus uniting ourselves with Jesus, Who suffered on the Cross for the love and benefit of humanity.

15

Finding Joy with Chronic Illness

While all forms of suffering are difficult to deal with, suffering from an injury or an illness is different because it directly threatens our existence. When it reaches this level, we experience our powerlessness, our limitations, and our finitude.[427] It is natural when facing the possibility of death to consider the key existential questions: Why do we die? What happens next? Is there a God? What is He like? Why do we need to suffer like this? What did I do to deserve this?

People react to injury and illness in different ways. Some will react with anguish, self-absorption, despair, and even revolt against God, but others will be chastened by the realization that death is near and this will provoke a search for God and a return to Him.[428] This is the main emphasis of God's use of natural evil to provide a catalyst for conversion, which is the goal of the second task of suffering.

Suffering can and does lead to joy when people understand its purpose. This realization can be hard to grasp, particularly in cases of chronic illness because there is no expectation of cures,

[427] CCC 1500.
[428] CCC 1501.

presenting challenges both to the chronically ill and to those who care for them. Constant discomfort is very difficult to manage in these cases, but people can learn to manage it through the four tasks of suffering. It is worthwhile at this point to revisit three of the stories discussed previously in this book from the perspective of the person with the illness to provide insight into their call to conversion and the role of bystanders and loved ones in that conversion.

The biblical story of Job is quite applicable to understanding this case, since Job was stricken with a chronic illness that resulted in very uncomfortable boils.[429] Beyond the agonizing pain of the illness, Job also had to endure the speculation, from even his wife and his closest friends, that his illness was punishment for sins he committed. This threatened his self-identity as a righteous man and made him question the righteousness of God while exposing him to social isolation.

Job speaks effectively for those who suffer from chronic illness through no fault of their own. In his first reply to Eliphaz, who had just tried to comfort him with the words, "Happy is the man whom God reproves,"[430] Job laments his weakened state but holds firm in declaring his innocence. But interestingly, he sees that despite his pain, he could still have joy, stating:

> Oh, that I might have my request, and that God would grant what I long for: Even that God would decide to crush me, that he would put forth his hand and cut me off! Then I should still have consolation and could exult

---

[429] Job 2:4-10.
[430] Job 5:17.

through unremitting pain, because I have not transgressed the commands of the Holy One.[431]

Job's primary concern is to remain faithful to God's commands, and he senses that if he dies in that state, he will be joyful. He is afraid, however, that his illness is a signal that God has counted him among the wicked, and it is against this that he protests:

I will give myself up to complaint; I will speak from the bitterness of my soul. I will say to God: Do not put me in the wrong! Let me know why you oppose me. Is it a pleasure for you to oppress, to spurn the work of your hands, and shine on the plan of the wicked? Have you eyes of flesh? Do you see as mortals see? Are your days like the days of a mortal, and are your years like a human lifetime, that you seek for guilt in me and search after my sins, even though you know that I am not wicked, and that none can deliver me out of your hand? Your hands have formed me and fashioned me; will you then turn and destroy me?[432]

It is interesting that in the epilogue of the Scriptural account which discusses Job's restoration, it does not say that he is healed of his disease. Instead, his position as a righteous man is restored by God, Who informs Eliphaz:

I am angry with you and with your two friends; for you have not spoken rightly concerning me, as has my servant Job. Now, therefore, take seven bullocks and seven rams, and go to my servant Job, and offer up a holocaust for yourselves; and let my servant Job pray for you; for

---

[431] Job 6:8-10.
[432] Job 10:1-9.

his prayer I will accept, not to punish you severely. For you have not spoken rightly concerning me, as has my servant Job.[433]

It is only after Job prays for them, restoring his sense of self, that we are told that his family and friends come to dine with him, comforting him in his suffering and giving him money. We are then told he was given twice as many possessions as he lost; beautiful daughters; and that he lived to be one hundred and forty years old, twice the normal lifespan; but never is it said he was cured of the boils.[434] Some might assume that the cure is implied, but this is not necessarily so. Many people learn to live joyfully even in the face of chronic disease, once they learn that they can live productively with it. In Job's case, his self-identity was that of a righteous man. Once it became clear that he had further established that identity with his reaction to suffering, he may have been able to see his disease as confirming that position, and thus it could be seen as a source of joy for him.

Granted, not everyone is addressed directly by God as Job was, but it is possible to see one's limitations as focusing the person on what is important. It is also possible to recognize chronic illness as a change that brings out opportunities even as it restricts others. Borne bravely, suffering can be inspiring to others and can also provide an opportunity for others to demonstrate true charity toward the sufferer. It can also be redemptive if it is willingly accepted as God's plan for us, even if we cannot see clearly who benefits from it. To be able to do so is in itself a sign of our faith in the goodness of God, which has spiritual merit and can lead to joy.

[433] Job 42:7-8.
[434] Job 42:10-17.

It is important to remember that suffering involves physical, psychological, and social elements. Like Job, people with chronic illnesses are more concerned with the loss of their personal identity and social status than with their physical discomfort. Probably in most cases, the illness will force a resetting of expectations, but it is not necessarily so. After all, polio kept Franklin Roosevelt off the golf course but not out of the White House. What is important for those with chronic diseases to recognize is that their lives have purpose and that they deserve to be loved like everyone else. If they can attain this, there can be joy in their lives. In fact, when a person has dignity and purpose, he is not suffering. For sure, the pain and limitations of a chronic illness remain a constant irritant to the person, but it need not threaten the person's existence or challenge the person's dignity. It is incumbent on those around them to help the chronically ill to feel loved and to find a sense of purpose. Those that fail to do so cruelly add to the suffering of the chronically ill.

The message of joy to the chronically ill is that they can overcome their impediments, and when they do, they provide a vivid example for others to follow. Overcoming hardship is inspiring and can lead others to follow the path to righteousness. Seen in this light, chronic illnesses can provide an enhanced sense of purpose, like it did for Job, which will make the suffering bearable in life and redemptive in death.

Another important lesson from the book of Job is that chronic illness is not a sign of guilt, as many (including Job's friends and even Job himself) suppose. In fact, Job is made ill specifically because he is righteous and God wants to use him as an example for others.[435]

---

[435] Job 2:1-7.

At the same time, God uses Job's suffering to bring both Job and his friends to a better understanding of God.[436] This is surely true in cases other than Job's, perhaps in the majority of cases. Bystanders and especially caregivers should take this to heart and assume that those with chronic illnesses are not only not guilty, but in fact are messengers of God, showing how we can live productive lives even with constant discomfort. Further, when devout sufferers like Job keep the faith, it draws others to it as well. Recall what the *Catechism* maintains: illness is a catalyst for conversion.[437]

The fact that chronic disease, even dementia, is a catalyst for conversion is displayed effectively in John Swinton's poignant story of the elderly Alzheimer patient who roamed the hallways of her institution muttering "God" repeatedly so as not to forget Him. Like many with chronic illnesses, she was searching for God, and as with her, sometimes it is only with the help of others that we come to understand that God truly loves us. It was an attentive nurse who understood this elderly patient's concern and comforted her by saying, "You know, even if you should forget God, He will not forget you. He has promised that."[438] And the woman, thus assured of God's love, became peaceful.

It is likely that the nurse also felt joy in that moment, having provided spiritual aid to the woman. In this way, the chronically ill and those who aid them are drawn together in love and joy, with the ill person being the instrument by which others are saved by practicing charity, while at the same time benefitting from the aid and becoming closer to God.

---

[436] Job 42:7-9.
[437] CCC 1501.
[438] Swinton, *Dementia*, 196-197.

The final case to revisit is that of Nancy Mairs, the writer with MS we met in chapter 8. There is much to be learned from her story, for both chronic sufferers and those around them. As we learned, her first response to her diagnosis was self-destructive: leaving her family, having a series of affairs, and even attempting suicide. This did not decrease her suffering; it made it worse. The *Catechism* in its wisdom explains that "illness can lead to anguish, self-absorption, sometimes even despair and revolt against God."[439] Mairs definitely exhibited that in her initial response.

Suffering, however, is unrelenting in carrying out its tasks, and as the *Catechism* notes, "It can also make a person more mature, helping him discern in his life what is not essential so that he can turn toward that which is. Very often illness provokes a search for God and a return to him."[440] Kathleen Norris, in a *New York Times* review of Mairs's book *Ordinary Time*, recognizes that Mairs experienced this, writing:

> Like many a contemplative before her, Nancy Mairs finds that it is an inescapable decrease in physical capacity that most clearly sharpens her sense of the all-encompassing love of God. In a passage that perhaps only a saint could have written, she states that "the extraordinary benefit of death, one unrecognized in the secular world, lies in its redemptive quality. Horribly constrained in a body that can no longer roll over in bed reliably, much less be trusted to arise and get to the toilet before the flood, I have never felt freer to cherish and celebrate my husband

---

[439] CCC 1501.
[440] Ibid.

and children and the smelly old man who comes on his trash-picking rounds to take away my aluminum cans, and even (please God, one day soon) Jesse Helms."[441]

Mairs's illness was indeed a catalyst for conversion. As Norris notes, *Ordinary Time* "is primarily a book of essays about conversion in the broadest sense: not only to Roman Catholicism, to feminism and the importance of marriage, but also to life itself."[442] For Mairs, her disease was both a curse and a blessing, in that while it limited her mobility, it expanded her horizons and her audience. In fact, this was recognized in a laudatory obituary in *The New York Times* upon her death in 2016 at the age of seventy-three, which said in part:

> Ms. Mairs was a budding poet in her late 20s, suffering from agoraphobia and depression—she had once attempted suicide—when she was told that she had MS. The inexorable progress of the disease provided her with her richest subject, as she wrote of her fears and hopes, her resolve to push against her limitations and her aversion to such euphemisms as "differently abled."[443]

Mairs was particularly adept at witnessing to her suffering, serving as we all should as a messenger of God. In Mairs's *Times*

---

[441] Kathleen Norris, "The Gift of a Difficult Life," *New York Times*, June 13, 1993, sec. 7, https://www.nytimes.com/1993/06/13/books/the-gift-of-a-difficult-life.html.

[442] Ibid.

[443] William Grimes, "Nancy Mairs, Who Wrote About Infirmities, Dies at 73," *New York Times*, December 8, 2016, sec. A, https://www.nytimes.com/2016/12/07/books/nancy-mairs-dead-author.html.

obituary, the poet Kathi Wolfe is quoted as saying of Mairs, "She's not telling these stories to inspire people or induce our pity. The author (Mairs) is coming out from behind the curtain to make visible the experience of being disabled in America."[444] In her own words, Mairs describes that her interest lay in "the role of affliction in perfecting human experience." Viewed from a spiritual perspective, she adds, it is "simply an element in the human condition, to be neither courted nor combatted. To refuse to suffer is to refuse to live."[445]

When we first become aware of a chronic disease, the first reaction is inevitably to ask "Why me?" as Job did, and to wonder what the future holds. Some will react with anger, assuming the worst as Nancy Mairs did, and some will successfully kill themselves, which she did not. However, as both of them learned, God was redirecting them to more fruitful endeavors with their illnesses, not despite their illnesses. Granted, not everyone will experience these benefits in life with a chronic illness, but they have shown that it is a possibility, so we should not give up on life. More importantly, however, as the elderly woman with Alzheimer's learned, God has not and will not abandon us. Sometimes, we are given illnesses to reorient us to what is important.

It can be particularly hard on the loved ones of those who are stricken with a chronic illness. Not only is it tough to see a loved one suffer, but it also inevitably restricts their own activities since their partners have new limitations and they will be called upon to provide aid. The thing to recognize in these situations is that a loved one's illness is a joint opportunity for salvation.

---

[444] Ibid.
[445] Nancy Mairs, "A Necessary End," quoted by Grimes in "Nancy Mairs, Who Wrote About Infirmities, Dies at 73."

The loved one has the opportunity to demonstrate love through their care and support of the one who suffers, while the one who suffers demonstrates redemptive love by accepting his role as the instrument of God's outreach to unleash the love of his loved ones. This is particularly true of the devout person who gets a chronic illness who does not need a catalyst for conversion. Like Job, these devout sufferers are being used by God as instruments of salvation for others, including their loved ones. The truly devout will understand this to be an unparalleled opportunity to share in the redemptive suffering of Christ and to subsequently share in His glory. If they bear their suffering well, they will inspire others and be the catalyst for their conversions. This knowledge also provides a sense of purpose for the chronic sufferer, and reflection on it can bring joy, even amidst the pain.

The point is that chronic illnesses are catalysts for conversion. They are not punishments for sins against God or man meant to destroy us. While it is true that they are uncomfortable and limiting, it is also true that this is what is often required to re-orient us to God's plan for us. Recognize it for what it is: God calling out to us in the only way we are sure to take notice. God loves us, like all creation, and He wants nothing more than for us to join Him in the Beatific Vision where we will experience the joy that He always wanted for us.

16

Living with a Terminal Illness
and Dying Well

As discussed in chapter 8, natural evils exist in part to remind us of our mortality and to serve as catalysts for conversion, which is the second task of suffering. While this is clearly a consideration with chronic diseases, along with the potential need to refocus our lives, it takes on an entirely different sense of urgency when we are diagnosed with a terminal illness. Amy Plantinga Pauw writes that "death is a frightening prospect because it destroys any illusion that we are in full control of our lives and we are our own makers and keepers."[446] Yet, although there are a variety of opinions on the nature of death, there are times when death is considered by most people to be a blessing.

Some will judge a death by the status of the person at the time of death. Many judge death to be a good, if the person is old and it relieves the person's suffering. The same people will see death as a tragedy if the person is young and full of potential. Others will judge a death based on how it comes about.

---

[446] Amy Plantinga Pauw, "Dying Well" in *Living Well and Dying Faithfully: Christian Practices for End-of-Life Care*, ed. John Swinton and Richard Payne (Grand Rapids, MI: Eerdmans, 2009), 17, 259.

Most people will judge a peaceful death in one's sleep as far better than a violent, painful death, whether inflicted by God or man. Others, however, desire to go out in a blaze of glory on the battlefield. Some will judge the nature of a death by the witnesses: dying surrounded by loved ones is generally considered a good death, while dying alone is generally regarded as a sad way to die. A good death would be one where the person gets closure on all outstanding business and is able to reconcile and say goodbye to all who are dependent on the dying person. Leaving unfinished business and broken relationships is an undesirable way to die.

While all these things feel important, they are as nothing compared with a soul's final disposition after death. Even if all the circumstances above were good, a person would still have a very bad death if the person found himself separated from God in Hell. At the same time, even if a person dies a violent, painful death all alone and never gets to say goodbye to loved ones, that person will have a joyful death if he finds himself in the presence of God in Heaven.

While we can and should always work on conforming ourselves to God's will so that we can share in God's life, there are two dying situations that lend themselves to this purpose. The first is martyrdom, which is the supreme witness a person can give to the truth of the Faith because it requires the most to be given up.[447] However, most people are not called to die in this way, and it is not martyrdom if one actively seeks it.[448] The second is to be diagnosed with a terminal disease, which gives humans a

---

[447] CCC 2473-2474.

[448] Substitution cases like Maximilian Kolbe are not sought but present themselves as opportunities to practice charity.

sense of urgency to take action toward reconciling with God by warning us of our impending deaths.

Many will find it difficult to understand that there can be joy in having a terminal illness, but it is clearly a matter of perspective. As John Swinton and Richard Payne put it, "Suffering, death, and dying have meaning, and the shape of these meanings has a profound impact on how a person approaches these experiences."[449] As discussed previously, death for a Christian is not an evil, but in fact is understood as a transition to a better life, one with the Beatific Vision. It might be most properly seen as a graduation from the world of suffering to the world of joy. Like graduations on earth, there can be excitement in the undertaking of a new adventure coupled with anxiety of the unknown and some sadness for the world left behind. But there is also the exhilaration at having successfully completed an arduous task, that of living a good life in a world full of temptations. This is joy.

The priority of the healing of the soul and the benefits of sacramental strengthening when suffering from a serious illness has long been a position of the Church. In fact, as discussed in the last chapter, the Fourth Lateran Council stipulated in 1215 that physicians called to the bedside of the sick were to call for a priest before starting treatment because "the soul is more precious than the body."[450] This was still the practice being taught by the Church in the *Ars Moriendi*, or "art of dying," literature in

---

[449] John Swinton and Richard Payne, "Christian Practices and the Art of Dying Faithfully" in *Living Well and Dying Faithfully: Christian Practices for End-of-Life Care*, ed. John Swinton and Richard Payne (Grand Rapids, MI: Eerdmans, 2009), xviii.

[450] Schroeder, "The Canons of the Fourth Lateran Council, 1215," Canon 22.

the late fifteenth century that was designed to advise the faithful on how to die a good or blessed death.[451] "Self-help literature, or conduct literature as it was called then, was popular in the late medieval period and not surprisingly in an age where death was rampant, the *Ars Moriendi* was a best-seller."[452] Based on a pastoral handbook, *Opusculum Tripertitum*, published early in the fifteenth century by Jean Gerson, the chancellor of the University of Paris, variations on the *Ars Moriendi* theme were soon published in every major European language.[453] The most popular variant, the *Tractatus Artis Bene Moriendi*, contained six parts: a commendation of death; a warning of the temptations of the dying and advice on how to resist them; a short catechism concerning repentance; instructions and prayers focused on imitating the dying Christ; a call to both the dying and the caregivers to prioritize these matters; and finally, the prayers for the Anointing of the Sick.[454] The genre remained popular for three hundred years, lasting well into the eighteenth century.[455]

The emphasis of the *Ars Moriendi* is clearly on reconciling the dying with God. For Christians, this should be the highest priority of those dying as well as for their loved ones. However, this is clearly only available to those who know in advance that they are dying: those that are terminally ill. The warning that a

---

[451] Verhey, *The Art of Dying*, 164-167. The *Ars Moriendi* literature were pamphlets published by the Church throughout Europe in the late Middle Ages to advise people on how to die well.

[452] Ibid., 79.

[453] Ibid., 85-87.

[454] CCC 1514: In current sacramental practice, the faithful are encouraged to seek the anointing of the sick as soon as any one of the faithful begins to be in danger from sickness or old age.

[455] Ibid., 87.

terminal illness provides for both the dying and their friends and family to prepare emotionally for their separation can be invaluable. Most importantly, the terminally ill have an opportunity to partake of the sacraments and reconcile with God, which is not available to those who die suddenly.

Granted, to be told that one is going to die soon is shocking and distressing for most people, and few would initially see it as the blessing it is. Many would prefer not to face the prospect of dying at all, preferring to pass away peacefully in their sleep. That might work for people who are exceptionally well-prepared, but most people would benefit from the warning to get their affairs, both spiritual and material, in order. Even for the most proactive people, having some warning is beneficial to allow them to reconcile their affairs and say their goodbyes. As hard as the message is to deliver, and to receive, it is an act of love toward the patient when a doctor lets the patient know that death is imminent. Further, with the exception of suicide and terminal illness, one does not get the opportunity to choose the circumstances of one's death. Many people die tragic deaths. Given that death is inevitable, being given a warning to get affairs in order should be considered a blessing once the shock wears off.

At this point, it should be reemphasized that God is the Master of life and death and will call us home at exactly the right time according to His plan. When people interject themselves into this dynamic, whether it be an overzealous doctor taking matters into his own hands to relieve a patient's suffering or the patient himself trying to maintain control over his destiny by ending his own life, they are effectively ending the person's journey prematurely without realizing the potential impact. Suppose in the remaining time that the person had left, he would have contemplated his situation and reconciled with God? Or what if a long-estranged relative was on the way to reconcile with the person, only to arrive a half-hour too late? We do not know God's plan for us, but we can trust that it is benevolent, so it is best for us to leave our deaths in His hands. This trust in the Lord is paramount to dying well because without it, how can one truly be in union with Him?

Nevertheless, to be given a medical death sentence is unwelcome news to virtually anyone who receives it. Such a diagnosis is naturally earth-shattering to most people, and it will take time to accept and embrace it. This is particularly true in a medical culture that views death as a medical failure, not to be accepted until it actually occurs.[456] In fact, in many if not most cases, the doctor will deliver that terminal illness diagnosis with hope for a cure and assurances that they will fight this disease together and the odds are in the patient's favor that he will be cured. This is not unwarranted in many cases. Indeed, the American Cancer Society claims that "more than 15.5 million Americans with a history of cancer were alive on January 1, 2016, most of whom were diagnosed many years ago and have no current evidence of cancer."[457]

The reality is that there is wide variability in the nature of terminal diseases. Some ailments, like Parkinson's disease, are slow to act but ultimately not curable, leaving those with this diagnosis to degrade physically and mentally over years and even decades before their ultimate but assured death. Others diseases, like some forms of liver and pancreatic cancers, are virulent, killing patients within a matter of months or even weeks after diagnosis. Some are totally debilitating, while others are less so,

---

[456] Swinton, "Why Me, Lord?," 122-123.

[457] American Cancer Society, *Cancer Facts & Figures 2019* (Atlanta: American Cancer Society, 2019), 1.

allowing patients to live fairly normal lives until close to the end. In fact, some will actually not prove to be terminal at all, with modern medicine delaying the effect of the disease long enough for the person to die of something else.

Regardless of the nature of the terminal diseases, all patients with such a diagnosis are immediately faced with two undeniable facts: they are going to die, but they are not dead yet. Granted, this is true for every human, but the person with the diagnosis of a terminal illness has been confronted with it in a very tangible way that cannot be ignored, including a prediction of when and how the person will die. This is only a prediction, of course, because medical science is not exact enough to predict time of death with any real certainty, nor can it account for unexpected situations like the patient getting hit by a bus on the way to the doctor's office. Nevertheless, it is natural for someone given an estimate of, for example, six months to live to consider what he will do in his remaining time on earth, as well as what awaits the person when he dies.

When confronted with the diagnosis of a terminal disease, a person has three basic tasks to prioritize: to fight the disease to extend and improve the quality of his life; to continue to live his life; and to prepare for his death. It is important to keep these three in balance as the journey progresses and to keep in mind that God is using this illness to call the person to Himself. Many will initially resent this call, thinking it unfair, and become angry with God. This will not stop the suffering, and eventually some of them will come to understand this and will instead turn to Him for answers. Others will die in misery, eternally separated from God.

Some will actively try to defy God, putting all their energy into the effort to prolong life on earth only to die in the end in despair, perhaps realizing that they had wasted a great gift by failing to get their spiritual and material plans in order, but more often they are disappointed that they couldn't have things their way. Ironically, even those people who are able to extend their lives often do so at a very high cost in additional temporal suffering, tied to a ventilator or other life-prolonging machine in an intensive care unit, while also potentially undergoing painful, nausea-inducing therapies. And, of course, this is nothing compared to an eternity separated from God, with no hope of happiness.

In contrast, the person who uses his terminal diagnosis as an impetus for resetting his life and does so by reconciling with God through His Church, and by taking the time left to him to help those left behind to adjust to his loss, will experience joy in the process. This is not to say that a person diagnosed with a terminal disease should merely accept it and never seek a cure or to improve his quality or length of life through medical means. Suffering has four tasks, and they all apply to cases of terminal illness. The first, developing proper self-love, includes looking for aid to mitigate one's symptoms so that one can carry out one's duties toward God and neighbor. This desire comes naturally to all people, but it needs to be balanced with the other priorities. If the person finds that seeking a cure is not likely to work or that it is getting in the way of his two other responsibilities, living his normal life and preparing himself and his survivors for his ultimate death, then he should give up seeking a cure and focus his attention on those matters. On the other hand, if the person is cured or at least had his life improved or extended through medical action, then the person should consider it a second chance at life, and, having been warned in a very vigorous way by his suffering, proceed in a way that will lead to the Beatific Vision for himself and others.

The second task also comes naturally to people with terminal illnesses because, faced with certain death, most will seek answers as to what is next and search for God.[458] This should not take the form of a bargain with God because, truly, we have nothing to offer Him. Instead, we should recognize that He is waiting for us with open arms and is beckoning us home. Being with Him means that we must unite with Him, and that means reconciling within the Church that is His Body, through the sacraments if possible. That the terminally ill patient has the chance to do this before death is a true benefit to him, and this benefit is unavailable to those who die without warning.

When a person fully reconciles with God, he will experience tremendous peace. Those who have not been to a good sacramental Confession will have a hard time understanding the depths of this experience. Granted, even a heartfelt confession to someone one has hurt can be cleansing to the soul, but it is not nearly the same. Now it is true that not everyone feels the same release in Baptism, sacramental Confession, or Anointing of the Sick, the three sacraments that most apply to reconciling with God, but that is God's way of drawing each person into a more complete relationship with Him. When a person has given himself completely, he will experience joy in a way that will be unambiguous, and he will no longer fear death. While there may still be physical pain, the suffering will end once the person is fully aligned with God.

The third task, to unleash love, is a very important part of the journey of the terminally ill as they seek to reconcile with the people they have hurt or became estranged from, as they put their affairs in order for their family, friends, and all who depend on

[458] CCC 1501.

them to carry on after they are gone. Every person must recognize that he is a part of many communities—including his family and the social, business, spiritual, and political communities in which he participates—and that when he dies, he leaves a void in the hearts and the activities of those around him. It is an act of love to prepare these communities for one's own death, and a blessing to be given the chance to do so.

One of the first challenges that a person who has been diagnosed with a terminal illness must confront is how, what, and to whom to communicate his experiences. There is a balance to be struck between the desire to communicate the needs of the sufferer and the concern about overburdening those around them with his suffering. Indeed, when a person shares his suffering with another, it is much more than words; he is literally making himself feel better by making the other person feel worse, if that person has any empathy at all. This does not mean that the sufferer should not share what he is going through; in fact, he should. As will be described in more detail in the next chapter, it is imperative that he does so for a variety of reasons. What is being recommended here is discretion on how that is done, so as to optimize the experience of both the terminally ill patient and that of those around him.

In reality, people in this situation fail to recognize that they are in fact communicating a lot of what they are feeling unintentionally through body language that even the most unempathetic among us will pick up on. One simply can't hide the signs of physical distress that come with terminal diseases: pallid skin tone, tremors, grimaces from pain, gauntness, and a whole host of other "tells" communicate to everyone that someone is not well. Given this, the suffering person should be open about his situation, particularly with those who are dependent on him, those on whom he depends, or those on whom he might depend in the future. Included in this group would be parents, children, spouses, and siblings, along with close business, church, and social associates. This group has a vested interest in the suffering person and will see the non-verbal clues indicating how he is feeling, but they may want more information. If they ask, he should tell them. He should also tell them when he has a particular need or when some proposed activity appears to be too much for him, for this is information that they need to help him. However, it is also important for the sufferer to remember that there still is life to be lived, both by him and by those around him, and that should be the focus of most of the discussions; not the illness. If the illness dominates every discussion, then the sufferer makes that his very essence, and this makes it hard for those not suffering to relate; this will inevitably lead to isolation. Instead, by focusing on living rather than dying, the terminally ill patient can stay part of the social fabric of the community, which is important to everyone. This can take some discipline on the part of those whose suffering is omnipresent, but those around him can help by redirecting conversations and being sympathetic to the sufferer.

The second challenge facing the terminally ill is to decide how and when to discharge their affairs in a way that benefits their loved ones. The person diagnosed with a terminal disease must use discretion on when to take these steps. Some diseases are slow to take their toll, and as we have seen, some with cancer may actually go into remission and live for years after the initial diagnosis. There is no doubt that the person should immediately reconcile with God and those estranged from them because one never knows the hour or day when one will be taken. To take these steps would be good to do in any case. However, the timing of material transfer of goods and information can be parsed out over time as seems appropriate to those involved. The person still has to live his life, which clearly does not end on the day he receives his terminal diagnosis. This can be giving loved ones mementos of a person's life to hold on to when they are missing them after they die. It can be giving them advice that they gained in their life's journey and telling them what they meant to them. It can be seeking forgiveness from others they have hurt, knowing that by forgiving the dying, the survivors can be at peace. Once the person dies, that peace cannot be gained. It can even be sharing the more mundane things of life, like where the financial records are kept or sharing secret favorite recipes. Doing these things personally before the person dies will be more appreciated by all the parties, rather than simply leaving them in a will.

The fourth and final task is to accept one's death for the good of others that may benefit from it. This includes people who, by caring for the dying, are sharing in Christ's mission by demonstrating mercy and charity. It might also include people who, in seeing someone die a good death, are motivated to seek reconciliation with God and His Church. This is the final and most spiritually rewarding statement of love that a person can achieve, because it shares fundamentally with the sacrifice of Christ and is thus redemptive. Unlike what has been described previously in this chapter, which applies to the terminally ill while they are still able to live relatively independently, this last step generally comes at a time in most people's lives when this will no longer be possible and they will need some form of institutional care.

Institutional care, while necessary for many people in the end stages of life to manage their physical needs, must be chosen with care to ensure that the patient's spiritual needs are respected. Dying well must be consistent with life's goals of knowing, loving, and serving God in this life and being with Him in the next, and that means that religion must play the primary role in the ministry to the dying. [459] To be sure, this does happen at times. Lisa Sowle Cahill applauds the Catholic Health Association for their work with the dying. She also notes the work of the Sisters of Charity, who have established homes around the world for those dying in abject poverty, as well as that of religiously led hospice centers who help people die well.[460] But this is often not the case without putting forth the effort to find a suitable environment from which the dying can reconcile with God.

Just finding a place that will make the sacraments available, while it can be mildly challenging, is of course insufficient to allow a person to die well. If the dying person has not done so already, he needs to settle his earthly accounts, both financial and social, as well as make his peace with God. Family, friends, and caregivers all have a role in this, making themselves available to help with the details and to support the person in their last weeks and hours. As in the *Ars Moriendi* tradition, emphasis should be placed on a commendation of death; a warning of the temptations of the dying and advice on how to resist them; a short catechism concerning repentance; instructions and prayers focused on imitating the dying Christ; and a call to both the dying and the caregivers to prioritize these matters. Unlike what was proposed in the *Ars Moriendi* tradition, the prayers for the Anointing of the Sick should be done at the beginning of the process of dying rather than saving them until the point of death. This is to give the person the sacramental grace to go through the entire process well. The Anointing of the Sick can also be given periodically as the dying person's condition worsens.

---

[459] *Compendium to the Catechism of the Catholic Church*, 79.
[460] Cahill, *Theological Bioethics*, 125-127.

The first grace of this sacrament is one of strengthening, peace, and courage to overcome the difficulties that go with having a terminal illness or the frailty of old age. This is a gift of the Holy Spirit to renew faith and trust in God and to strengthen us against the temptation of discouragement and anguish in the face of death. By partaking of this sacrament, the dying person receives the strength and the gift of uniting himself more closely to Christ's Passion, which gives new meaning to his suffering because it becomes a participation in the saving work of Jesus. This is not only a grace for the recipient but for the Church as a whole, which is strengthened and sanctified when it comes together in support of the dying. Finally, it completes the sacramental sequence that began at Baptism, fortifying us for the final struggles before entering the Father's house.[461]

As we focus on ourselves and our loved ones as death approaches, we should imitate Christ, living according to the Beatitudes as best we can because, by conforming our lives to His, we can share in God's life. This is true of both the dying and those accompanying them on the journey. We need to remind ourselves that suffering is a message from God, a shining beacon on a hill, directing us home to Him. It is reminding us of the frailty of this life and pushing us away from the mundane things we thought were important to the promise of the Beatific Vision, which will bring us joy while experiencing all that is good and true. Death is not to be feared, but seen instead as the gateway to glory. It should be embraced as a friend. When it arrives for our loved ones, properly prepared, we should be encouraged by the thought that they are with God and hopeful of joining them when we ourselves are called.

[461] CCC 1520–1523.

17

The Role of the Sufferer
as a Messenger of God

If suffering provides a "type" of revelation from God, then the sufferer can be thought of as a messenger of that revelation. This calling to serve God in communicating what He reveals to us through suffering is not unlike the angelic mission or that of the prophets. This role of the sufferer is important for the safety and the salvation of others and, therefore, must be taken with the utmost diligence and sincerity. As a divine messenger, the one who suffers in union with Christ is actively building the Kingdom of God, his fate tied up with the fate of all those who hear His message. If the sufferer does not transmit the message of his suffering, whether out of spite, laziness, fear, or some other reason, or fails to take some specific action associated with it, then the suffering he endured will have been pointless.

There are two distinct types of witness that the sufferer can give. First of all, the person who is actively suffering gives others the opportunity to love them. This can be by actively soliciting help through lamentation, or by suffering more passively in public, for either will engage the consciences and compassion of those who are charitable. This does not mean that the sufferer needs to understand why he suffers, nor does it mean that the sufferer fails in his role as a messenger of God if the person cannot articulate what has happened. In fact, sufferers act as witnesses in most cases, and they merely are required to show the effects that suffering has had on them.

This message in not always delivered verbally. Indeed, the most powerful witness of evil and injustice is often through visual evidence: the scarred back of an antebellum slave, the protruding belly and skeletal features of a starving child, the dismembered remains of an aborted child, the bald head of a child cancer victim, the tears of a mother whose child was just gunned down by a street gang, the cries of an uncomfortable infant ... Often without words, the simple presence of the sufferer can ignite the consciences of others to aid those who suffer and to right social injustices. For instance, the man who was left beaten and naked on the side of the road in the parable of the Good Samaritan did not ask for help, but "the Samaritan traveler who came upon him was moved with compassion at the sight."[462] If done in charity, this can lead to spiritual growth and result in joy for both the sufferer and those who are moved by their suffering to take action, including the people causing the suffering.

The human capacity for pity and compassion is great, and, unfortunately, people sometimes seek to exploit the charitable by feigning suffering themselves to get handouts or by using images of the truly suffering to get donations, which are subsequently misused or stolen, or even used to support various political agendas. Those who prey on the generous unrepentant will eventually be punished in this life or the next, but the charitable will get their reward as well, even if they are the victims of fraud. For this reason, those who suffer must continue to be true messengers of

[462] Luke 10:29-37.

God, and the charitable, while being vigilant against fraud and corruption, should not be dissuaded from helping those they judge to be in need.

Many people feel uncomfortable asking for help, and, indeed, a perceived lack of autonomy is the reason that most people give for requesting physician-assisted suicide.[463] This is most unfortunate because in asking for help they would be announcing an opportunity for spiritual merit to those who would help them, and if the sufferers embrace their role in the redemption of others, it can be redemptive for them as well.

All suffering has meaning unless the sufferer fails to act on it. This is why the sufferer must be a messenger, sharing his experience with those who can either cease activities that cause suffering or who can take action to relieve or resolve the suffering. It is for this reason that Dorothee Söelle finds lament, the articulation of suffering, to be critical to its resolution.[464] It is also the reason that Martin Luther King, Jr., describes the mute non-resistance of the oppressed as "consummating the sin of the oppressor" in his funeral sermon in Birmingham.[465]

Witnessing after one's suffering has already been addressed is also important, particularly when it takes on the aspect of sharing faith in God and in His holy Church. The *Catechism* asserts that "Faith is a gift of God, a supernatural virtue infused by him."[466] Quoting the *Summa*, it adds that "in faith, the human intellect and will cooperate with divine grace: 'Believing is an act of the

---

[463] Lisa Sowle Cahill, *Theological Bioethics: Participation, Justice, Change* (Washington, DC: Georgetown University Press, 2005), 94-95.

[464] Söelle, *Suffering*, 74.

[465] Commins, "Is Suffering Redemptive?" 73.

[466] CCC 153.

intellect consenting to the divine truth by command of the will moved by God through grace."[467] As discussed in section 1, it is St. John Paul II's great insight that in suffering is concealed a special grace to which many great saints owe their profound conversions.[468] Taken together with the *Catechism's* own assertion that "very often illness provokes a search for God and a return to Him,"[469] it becomes clear that suffering is a vehicle used by God to infuse faith into the sufferer, a faith that will provide the perspective to understand suffering. Suffering, particularly in the form of injury and illness, "can make a person more mature, helping him discern in his life what is not essential so that he can turn to that which is."[470] In other words, suffering can provide the focus and an environment conducive to faith. It makes sense, also, to acknowledge that suffering would be best understood by one who suffers.

But as St. Thomas taught in the *Summa* as quoted earlier, faith requires more than just the openness to God that results from suffering. It requires access to the divine truth to which the will and intellect must consent. This comes from divine revelation, either directly or indirectly, in the form of the accounts of credible witnesses of that revelation. Because God speaks directly only to a limited number of people, the rest must rely on the accounts of those people who can credibly prove that what they teach is true. Often, the willingness to suffer plays a large role in demonstrating that credibility, starting with Jesus Himself, Who had to rise from a horrific death to demonstrate

---

[467] CCC 155, quoting *ST* II-II, q. 2, art. 9.
[468] John Paul II, *Salvifici doloris*, 26.
[469] CCC 1501.
[470] CCC 1501.

His own credibility as the Son of God, a God "who so loved the world that he gave his only Son, so that everyone who believes in him may have eternal life."[471]

The credibility of the willing sufferer extends far beyond Jesus, of course. It includes His apostles like St. Paul, who was given thirty-nine lashes five times, beaten with rods three times, and stoned for the Faith, yet persevered in the Faith to provide the credibility that encourages others to believe.[472] Likewise, if the believer in the next hospital bed bears his suffering gracefully, it can lead the non-believer to faith and to the Church.

The act of relieving suffering can also increase the credibility of the message of faith. Indeed, many people came to believe in Jesus because of His ability to heal, and His apostles also were deemed credible for the same reason.[473] In addition, there are multiple examples of conversions in Scripture attributed to the testimony of the healed people themselves, including the man born blind whom Jesus healed, as well as the lame beggar who was healed by St. John and St. Peter, both of whom gave effective public testimony in service of the Gospel message.[474] In a similar way, the testimony of those who find joy in their suffering today has the power to bring others to faith.

We are all called to be honest witnesses to our suffering, passing on what is revealed through our own suffering to others for their benefit. This can range from warnings of physical dangers, which serve to protect other people and their possessions, to

---

[471] John 3:16.

[472] 2 Corinthians 11:24-25.

[473] The healing accounts of the apostles in Acts include conversions of the witnesses as described in Acts 9:34-35 and 9:41-42.

[474] John 9 (the man born blind) and Acts 3 (the lame man healed by St. John and St. Peter).

warnings against sinful action, which can save their souls. The most important witness sufferers can give, however, is a description of how suffering was a catalyst for their own conversion, for suffering's ultimate purpose is to lead us back to God, through Christ and His Body, the Church.

18

The Call to Help

We are all called to aid the suffering people whom we encounter. St. John Paul II refers to two parables taught by Jesus to show the importance of providing aid to the suffering. The first is the parable of the Good Samaritan, who stops and cares for a man left for dead by bandits while the respected priests and Levites of the community simply passed him by. As Jesus says, showing such compassion to the sufferer is to love one's neighbor.[475] In the second parable, that of the Final Judgment, Jesus says that showing or not showing mercy to the least of one's brothers is to do the same to Him. Those who showed mercy to their neighbors would be given entrance into God's Kingdom, while those who failed to do so would be condemned to Hell.[476] St. John Paul II's commentary on these two parables is as follows:

> One could certainly extend the list of the forms of suffering that encountered human sensitivity, compassion and help, or that have failed to do so. The first and second parts of Christ's words about the Final Judgment unambiguously show how essential it is, for the eternal life of

[475] John Paul II, *Salvifici doloris*, 28-29, quoting Luke 10:29-37.
[476] Matthew 35:31-46.

every individual to "stop" as the Good Samaritan did, at
the suffering of one's neighbor, to have some compassion
for that suffering and to give some help. In the messianic
program of Christ, which is at the same time the program
of the Kingdom of God, suffering is present in the world
in order to release love, in order to give birth to works of
love towards neighbor, in order to transform the whole
of human civilization into a "civilization of love." In this
love the salvific meaning of suffering is completely accomplished and reaches its definitive dimension. Christ's
words about the Final Judgment enable us to understand
this in all the simplicity and clarity of the Gospel.[477]

St. John Paul II makes it clear, as does Jesus, that we are to
aid the suffering in our midst when we encounter them, just as
the Good Samaritan did. However, as our own experience with
people who beg on the streets of most cities in the modern world
show, not all the people who present themselves as suffering actually are in need. This is not a new concern. Indeed, the *Didache*
deals with the issue specifically in describing the "Way of Life"
to the first generation of Christians:

Give to everyone that asks you, and ask it not back; for
the Father wills that to all should be given of our own
blessings (free gifts). Happy is he that gives according
to the commandment; for he is guiltless. Woe to him
that receives; for if one having need receives, he is guiltless; but he that receives not having need, shall pay the
penalty, why he received and for what, and, coming into
straits (confinement), he shall be examined concerning

[477] John Paul II, *Salvifici doloris*, 30.

the things which he has done, and he shall not escape thence until he pay back the last farthing. But also now concerning this, it has been said, Let your alms sweat in your hands, until you know to whom you should give.[478]

Said another way, we should take care in the giving of unsolicited alms to make sure we give to those who are truly suffering. However, we should give to those who ask us without question, knowing that God will hold them responsible for fraudulently receiving if they are not truly needy. Therefore, it is critical that we heed the laments of the suffering and tend to their needs as Jesus taught in the parable of the Good Samaritan and practiced through the many and varied healings that are recounted in the Gospel accounts.[479] This too is conforming ourselves to God's will in a real and obvious way, as we copy the actions and follow the commandments of Christ to feed the hungry, give drink to the thirsty, clothe the naked, shelter the homeless, care for the sick, and visit the lonely and imprisoned.

One thing to remember is that when others suffer, it may well be for our benefit. Granted, this role of suffering for another's benefit is rarely recognized by those who are doing it according to God's plan, but it does not keep us from recognizing it. In doing so, it is important not to rob the person of his dignity by turning him into an object of our salvation, rather than a person who is sacrificing something for our benefit and is thus deserving of our gratitude. This is particularly true of those who suffer under

---

[478] Riddle, *Didache*.

[479] There are at least sixteen accounts of healing in Matthew's Gospel alone, including 4:23-24, 8:3, 8:13, 8:15, 8:16, 8:28-34, 9:1-7, 9:18-26, 9:27-31, 9:32-34, 9:35, 12:10-13, 15:21-28, 15:29-31, 17:14-20, and 20:29-34.

our oppression and are brave enough to show us the results of our sins. In other cases, where we are not directly responsible for their suffering, it may be solely for the purpose of giving us an opportunity to help them. When we fail to do so, not only do we miss a chance for our own spiritual merit, we cause them to suffer pointlessly.

No matter what the initial cause of the suffering is, the sufferer and the person who comes to his aid are both drawn into a relationship where each stand to have spiritual benefit when the sufferer willingly provides the opportunity for us to aid him and we willingly provide the aid. It must be remembered also that it is the sufferer who initiates the relationship by making the other aware of his needs and the opportunity to help, even if it is done passively. This is the sufferer acting as a messenger of God.

Unfortunately, just because sufferers are called to be messengers does not mean that others are motivated to listen to them. Indeed, there is often great resistance to it for a variety of reasons, including discomfort with the topic of suffering and also with the responsibilities that it implies, like the need to care for those afflicted or to cease from activities that cause suffering in others. This can often lead to ostracism and social isolation for the sufferer, adding to his need to lament.

There are several reasons that bystanders should make the effort to hear what the sufferers have to say. The first is that the act of listening to the sufferers is an act of mercy in itself because, as Dorothee Söelle notes, this is what the sufferer needs to relieve his suffering. Söelle, borrowing liberally from Simone Weil's definition of *malheur* (affliction or suffering), asserts that suffering typically begins with physical pain and then, because people worry about the unknown impact of their new pain, psychological trauma follows, leading ultimately to social trauma when people who are suffering are ostracized by others.[480] Söelle believes that suffering is relieved by unwinding this process through the use of language.

"The first step towards overcoming suffering," according to Söelle, "is to find a language that leads one out of the uncomprehended suffering that makes one mute, a language of lament, of crying, of pain, a language that at least says what the situation is."[481] This brings the sufferer out of social isolation and allows the person to begin to work on active solutions to the psychological trauma and, ultimately, the physical ailments that were responsible for the suffering to begin with. To the extent that we do not hear the sufferer, we are adding more social trauma to their situation. We can thus be a help or a hindrance to those who are suffering.

The story of Job offers some valuable insight that applies to this situation. At the beginning of their engagement with Job, his three friends (Eliphaz, Bildad, and Zophar) "sat down with him for seven days and seven nights, but none of them spoke a word to him because they saw how much he was suffering."[482] Their solidarity with him allowed Job to lament his condition.[483] However, when Job wished that he had never been born, his friends turned on him, each assuming that Job was suffering as punishment for some sin. Job denied this and was disturbed that they would not listen to his pleas of innocence, saying, "At least listen to my words and let that be the consolation you offer. Bear with me while I speak and after I have spoken, you can mock."[484]

---

[480] Söelle, *Suffering*, 62-69.
[481] Ibid., 70.
[482] Job 2:13.
[483] Job 3:1.
[484] Job 21:2-3.

This Scriptural exchange shows that when the witnesses to suffering listen in solidarity with the sufferer, it provides consolation, but if the witness of the sufferer is ignored, no one benefits. The sufferer continues to suffer without redemption and the witnesses lose their opportunity to act in that charity that is their calling.

Hearing the sufferer at times must extend beyond the verbal to interpreting body language, because often that is the way by which suffering is most effectively expressed. Tears and anguished facial expressions are almost always more moving than words. Sometimes, as is the case with both infants and dementia patients, there is no adequate way for them to express their suffering other than simply to cry out in pain and then frustration when their needs are not met. In the case of infants, good parents will run through a checklist of items (is the baby tired or hungry, or does he need to be held or changed?) to stop the crying, but in the case of those with dementia, the approach may often be to sedate rather than using an approach of "hearing" the sufferer through nonverbal clues and evaluating whether they lack the universal human needs for love, food, rest, warmth, and cleanliness.[485] It is no wonder that some people with dementia react violently out of frustration when their caregivers make no attempt to *hear* them, ignoring the nonverbal clues that are their only means of communicating and, thus, do not help them find the things they lack.[486]

Suffering can bring people together in unique ways. As discussed previously, when the oppressed deliver the message of their suffering to their oppressors for the good of their souls, it has the important effect of linking the salvific interests of both

[485] McLean, *The Person in Dementia*, 34-35.
[486] Swinton, *Dementia*, 108-109.

the sinner and the victim together. Similarly, when the sufferers come to understand that others (including those who care for them) benefit from their suffering, and that this has salvific benefits to both parties, it drives them together in love. Witnessing the suffering of others activates the conscience, as well as compassion for them, within the soul. Suffering can bring those who suffer in similar ways to commiserate, creating a sense of community and support. Finally, because suffering can lead people back to God, people of all backgrounds become part of the Body of Christ, His Church.

The message of suffering is that our salvation is intertwined with that of others, and this is radically opposed to the human tendency toward selfishness that survives from the Original Sin. As St. John Paul II teaches about the parable of the Good Samaritan:

> Following the parable (of the Good Samaritan), we could say that suffering, which is present under so many different forms in our human world, is also present in order to unleash love in the human person, that unselfish gift of one's "I" on behalf of other people, especially those who suffer. The world of human suffering unceasingly calls for, so to speak, another world: the world of human love; and in a certain sense man owes to suffering that unselfish love which stirs in his heart and action. The person who is a "neighbor" cannot indifferently pass by the suffering of another: this in the name of fundamental human solidarity, still more in the name of love of neighbor. He must "stop," "sympathize," just like the Samaritan of the Gospel parable.[487]

---

[487] John Paul II, *Salvifici doloris*, 29.

Why All People Suffer

Every person has a role to fill in God's plan, and how we fill our roles will affect others. All legitimate occupations serve to support the greater good and, when carried out authentically, will avoid or alleviate suffering since they are attaining some real good. Unfortunately, if we fail to carry them out efficiently and justly, we can increase the suffering of others. This is particularly true in professions that are devoted specifically to the care of the sick and injured. Understanding the theology of suffering is highly beneficial for these vocations, highlighting the specific needs of the suffering while also warning of things that are harmful.

Suffering and the Primary Caregiver

Being the primary caregiver for one who suffers can be many things, often all at once. While it is well beyond the scope of this book to discuss the infinite varieties of caregiving scenarios that are possible, there are five points that are of particular relevance to the theology of suffering and of such universal applicability that they need to be mentioned. People who are truly suffering will have physical pain, anxiety about their condition and their future capabilities, concern about their continued purpose in life, concern about their social acceptance, and fear about what will happen to them when they die. Each of these needs should be addressed by the primary caregiver. The sufferer will probably feel them in the order given above, but the priority should be in the inverse order, starting with spiritual needs.

As in all human endeavors, the caregiver's guiding principles will condition the way that the person will approach the role and carry out the responsibilities. To be a successful caregiver, the person must be doing it for the love of the patient as a child of God. A person who is caring for someone who suffers out of sheer obligation or for pay will not have the same relationship with the sufferer as someone authentically practicing charity.

People who have chronic and, particularly, terminal injuries or illnesses will almost by definition experience their powerlessness, limitations, and finitude, as the *Catechism* states.[488] While it can lead to anguish, self-absorption, and even revolt against God, it can also be a catalyst for conversion as they contemplate what is important in life and come to grips with the reality that there must be a better place than earth. This can be a very difficult time for the sufferer in a spiritual sense, and it is incumbent on the primary caregiver to try to procure the necessary catechetical and sacramental support to help the sufferer make their peace with God. Harold Koenig and Andrew Weaver caution that caregivers must bring God into the solution when sufferers are going through crises because psychological principles and theories, while helpful, cannot replace the power of spiritual healing.[489]

This should be the highest priority for the caregiver, who should suggest the support but not push it on the sufferer. It will be ineffective and counterproductive to offer spiritual support before the sufferer is ready for it. Koenig and Weaver suggest that this begins with clergy addressing the meaning and purpose of suffering in sermons and meetings that the sufferers attend and allowing them to "progress at their own pace to lead them closer to God, closer to their fellow human beings, and closer to God's purpose for their lives."[490]

---

[488] CCC 1500.

[489] Harold Koenig and Andrew J. Weaver, *Pastoral Care of Older Adults* (Minneapolis: Fortress Press, 1998), 23.

[490] Ibid.

The next greatest need for all sufferers is that of social acceptance. Suffering can be very isolating, particularly for the elderly, so it is exceptionally important for primary caregivers to "be there" for the sufferer. This means more than being physically present; it means being emotionally attached in a way that the sufferer understands that he is important and is loved. It is heartbreaking and counterproductive when friends and family convey a sense of obligation but not a desire to be with the sufferer. It is also good to help the sufferer keep a sense of normalcy about his social life, helping him maintain ties to existing groups and engage with new groups conducive to his new situation.

The third thing that every person needs is a sense of purpose. Helping the sufferer find that purpose is a true work of mercy on the part of the caregiver. One thing that the sufferer can normally claim as a purpose is that their suffering is providing the potential to make the caregiver a better person, more compassionate and loving than before. Sufferers can also make their purpose be to set a good example for others on how to bear their suffering. Koenig and Weaver point out that an extreme example might be when an elderly woman who is completely disabled and dependent on the caregiver because of a stroke can give the caregiver a smile of appreciation as her service to others. They rightly conclude that "such a pleasant and considerate attitude in this woman's situation is likely to have a real impact on her caretakers in many ways."[491] Although it may not be as apparent as a smile to her caregivers, the woman could also pray for them. Of course, based on the sufferer's malady and background, there could be a great many more ways that she can add value to the community.

[491] Ibid., 61.

The fourth thing that suffering people are concerned about is the sense of uncertainty that clouds a suffering person's existence. The first big question is whether the person will survive whatever ails them and for how long. Almost as disconcerting is the question of what type of capability the person will be left with if he survives. The caregiver should be aware that this is a major concern for almost all who suffer and should try to help the sufferer get whatever answers are available. Pain is much more tolerable if the person understands what drives it and what to expect.[492]

The fifth concern is that of physical comfort. Suffering is, by definition, uncomfortable, and finding a way to reduce or eliminate the discomfort, while often not the most important need of the individual, usually is the first that presents itself. The caregiver should help the sufferer get treatment without neglecting the other tasks mentioned earlier. This means that the patient is not sedated to the point where he is not able to interact with others or to contemplate the meaning behind his suffering.

It is worthwhile to reiterate the overwhelming importance of spiritual care at this point, for good spiritual care can actually provide for all the other needs. Effective spiritual care will involve the community, providing social acceptance. It will also provide a sense of purpose for the person and will assure him that even in death, his existence as a child of God will continue. This will, in turn, mitigate suffering and create an expectation of joy, if not joy itself, as they progress spiritually.

A caregiver who completes these five tasks will make the person's suffering significantly easier to bear. To do this willingly and without expectations of return is highly charitable and is

[492] Cassell, *The Nature of Suffering*, 34.

conforming oneself to God's will, ultimately leading to beatitude and eternal life. To do this well is a source of great joy, both for the sufferer and the caregiver.

Conversely, the caregiver can also create additional suffering for their charge if the caregiver is unresponsive to the person's discomfort. The caregiver can cause actual despair if she makes the sufferer feel like a burden or if she devalues or does not acknowledge the person's ability to contribute. A person's sense of autonomy is critical, so a caregiver must allow the patient to make all decisions that are appropriate but should protect the patient by stepping in when the decision at hand endangers the patient who does not understand the consequences. As discussed in the second section, John Swinton argues that when dementia is treated as a malignant social pathology, then a person's positive view of their roles in the community cannot be maintained because the only persona now recognized by society is "dementia patient."[493] The caregiver also has it in her power to crush the sufferer's personal dignity by causing social isolation and inhibiting spiritual and religious activity.

Ironically, professional caregivers are among the lowest-paid workers in society, yet they may have the most fundamental impact on the well-being of the people in their care. The fact that people carry out this most important role for little or no pay is substantial proof of the vocational nature of this calling.

Suffering and the Physician

Because true suffering always has a physical component, many people incorrectly associate suffering solely with medical issues,

[493] Swinton, *Dementia*, 98.

ignoring the spiritual reasons that are often its true basis. There-fore, the expectations to end suffering have typically rested within the medical community. This view, however, is tantamount to equating suffering with physical and perhaps psychological pain, which it is not, as demonstrated in the first section. People suf-fer because they sense that evil, the privation of some good, is threatening their existence. The purpose of suffering is to drive people to the good and ultimately to the greatest good, which is God. The good that has been lost or taken away could be spiritual, emotional, psychological, social, or physical, but they all have some physical manifestation to alert the sufferer to the fact that some good is missing. Obviously, the medical profession cannot provide all of these goods to their patients. As Farr Curlin sug-gests, what they can do is provide enhanced function that will allow their patients a better opportunity to attain the spiritual goods they lack, and perhaps procure for them a longer life in which to do so.[494] To those healed, their work can seem miracu-lous, relieving pain and sometimes impediments that handicap them from being the best versions of themselves.

Because the underlying reason for suffering is to drive spiritual growth, the expectation that the physician can eliminate all suf-fering is misplaced. As discussed earlier, the physician does not even have the most important healing role. According to the Fourth Lateran Council, that role belongs to the priest, whom the physician is to call to the bedside of the sick before starting treatment because "the soul is more precious than the body."[495]

[494] Curlin, "Hospice and Palliative Care," 60.
[495] H. J. Schroeder, "The Canons of the Fourth Lateran Council, 1215," in *Disciplinary Decrees of the General Councils: Text, Trans-lation and Commentary* (St. Louis: B. Herder, 1937), Canon 22.

This, however, is not how English Enlightenment philosopher Sir Francis Bacon envisioned it. Bacon suggested in the early seventeenth century that medicine had a goal beyond healing and avoiding harm: the preservation of life.[496] Bacon was emphatic in his belief that a cure could be found for all human diseases and that the scientific method should be used for the advancement of learning. The resulting Baconian project was to eliminate human mortality and vulnerability to suffering by means of technology.[497]

This seems like a reasonable and worthwhile goal to many people, given that God had given man the responsibility of subduing nature in the first chapter of Genesis and the Lord Himself had stated that the caring for the ill was one of the works of mercy that distinguished the saved from the damned.[498] In much the same way, the human reaction to avoid death is consistent both with self-love and the description of death as the last enemy to be destroyed.[499] Because of this, it is not surprising that Bacon saw medicine as a Christian vocation and a way to serve God in the world.

The problem is that Bacon's viewpoint fails to acknowledge that God is Lord over life and death, so it places too much faith in humanity's ability to conquer death through technology.[500] This is, of course, impossible, since man is made of nothing but the dust of the earth and his whole being is sustained by the

---

[496] Allen Verhey, *The Christian Art of Dying: Learning from Jesus* (Grand Rapids, MI: Eerdmans, 2011), 28-31.

[497] Ibid., 31.

[498] Matthew 25:31-46.

[499] 1 Corinthians 15:26.

[500] CCC 2258.

breath of God.[501] This single-minded drive toward an unattainable goal resulted in distorted views of the role of humanity in God's providential plan and a loss of recognition of the eternal values and goals to which a good life is rightly ordered. Ironically, it is by rightly ordering one's life to God that death is actually conquered and eternal life is achieved, according to God's providential plan.[502]

In fact, what Bacon was offering was an alternative vision for immortality than the one presented by Christ through His Cross and Resurrection. The Christian version offers an eternity of bliss in Heaven, partaking of all that is good and true in the Beatific Vision for those who choose to follow Christ, sharing in the divine nature. Bacon's project requires nothing more for immortality than submission to medical science, but then it offers nothing more than extending the life of the body indefinitely, with no soul to drive it or goal to give it purpose. This type of life is its own version of Hell: soulless, devoid of all goodness, and separated from God. It has been dubbed "medicalized death."[503]

Allen Verhey asserts that the medicalization of death became triumphant after World War II, and into the third quarter of the twentieth century, as advanced technologies, laboratories, and pharmacies consolidated into hospitals.[504] When people became seriously ill, they would go to the hospital in hope of a cure. Sometimes that happened, while other times the patient died, sometimes with a lingering death in pain or in a coma. Verhey says that the first characterization of a medicalized death is that it

---

[501] Genesis 2:7.
[502] CCC 1010.
[503] Verhey, *The Christian Art of Dying*, 13.
[504] Ibid.

occurs in a hospital. In 1945, 40 percent of the population died in a hospital. By 1995, 90 percent of all deaths occurred in hospitals.

Verhey notes that when dying moved to the hospital, there was a profound change in attitudes.[505] In an earlier time, the dying prepared for death, whereas now the patient was merely sick and getting treatment. Often heroic measures would be taken and the battle against death would be fought right up until the patient died. Instead of priests and family accompanying the dying on their final journey with prayers and sacraments, the patient would instead spend his last moments with doctors and nurses scrambling to save his life. The salvation of the soul and any higher meaning of suffering was pushed aside in an all-encompassing effort to keep the physical body in motion.

Because the business of the hospital was to avoid death, an effort was made to stop mentioning it.[506] In fact, many physicians refused to tell their patients that they were dying so that they would not give up hope. In doing so, they did their patients a huge disservice by not letting them prepare spiritually and emotionally for death. This was also true of their survivors, who not only were deprived of the chance to pray for the dying and to procure the sacraments, but whose mourning was suppressed by the climate of silence around death.

Jeffrey Bishop asserts that medicalized death is manifested most acutely in the intensive care unit (ICU), which is designed with the imperative to intervene in a failing physiology.[507] In his telling, it is a place for those who are dying where specially trained personnel make care decisions and family involvement is

---

[505] Ibid., 14.
[506] Ibid., 15.
[507] Bishop, *The Anticipatory Corpse*, 112-113.

limited. In a highly impersonal way, patients move either toward health, or, depending on the patient's level of functioning, to intermediate-level facilities where families are persuaded to allow their loved ones to die. Despite any efforts from the caregivers to provide comfort, patient life is reduced to physiological function, for the sake of which both disease and patient effectively disappear. Furthermore, dead and dying organs are replaced by machinery, masking death, and, because the machines are so hard for loved ones to turn off, patients are left in a state where life is defined as non-living matter in motion with no hope of returning to human thriving.

The problem was not in Bacon's desire to make use of scientific knowledge to cure diseases. This in itself is commendable, and, as Verhey himself notes, humanity is in Bacon's debt for the advancements in medicine over the last three hundred years that resulted from his insight and leadership.[508] The problem was that Bacon's framing of his initiative focused exclusively on physical healing, disregarding the spiritual needs that are the basis for all suffering. As this framing became more incrementally ingrained in the medical community's thinking, concern for the soul became increasingly limited. Instead of being in the service of God, the medical establishment presented itself as a kind of alternative to God, capable of providing immortality to its patients through advanced tools and techniques. Over time, this created an environment in which dying in a way that reconciled one with God was first ignored and then forgotten.

As discussed in length in the second section, God uses illness and injury to make humans aware of their mortality and to provide a catalyst for conversion. However, this second task

508 Verhey, *The Christian Art of Dying*, 31.

of suffering is mitigated by what John Swinton calls "glorious medicine." Swinton explains that "glorious medicine strives to use human power and reason to gain victory over death and to end suffering, tasks which can only ever be achieved theologically by God alone."[509] Nevertheless, he points out that both practitioners and patients have come to expect that "if human beings use their powers well enough, all will be well." They have, as Pope Benedict XVI put it, "faith in progress."[510]

Unfortunately, such expectations can lead to tragic results. Swinton describes a situation in which a young mother with advanced cancer was planning to write stories for her young children to remember her by after she died. However, because both the patient and the doctor were too optimistic about the power of technological intervention to save her life, she put off doing it. Tragically, two weeks later she was dead, having never created her legacy stories.[511]

Swinton describes this as a clash between what the patient saw as a fundamentally important dying task, to leave her children a legacy, and what both the doctor and the patient saw as the goals of medicine, to resist death at all costs. Swinton asserts that the right course of action was to enable a good and meaningful death, focusing her remaining time and energy on creating the stories for her children, rather than what turned out to be a futile attempt to delay the inevitable.[512]

---

[509] John Swinton, "Why Me, Lord?" in *Living Well and Dying Faithfully: Christian Practices for End-of-Life Care*, ed. John Swinton and Richard Payne (Grand Rapids, MI: Eerdmans, 2009), 121-122.

[510] Benedict XVI, *Spe salvi*, 17.

[511] Swinton, "Why Me, Lord?," 112-113.

[512] Ibid., 113.

Swinton further describes this as a clash between a theology of glory, which denies death, and a theology of the Cross, which understands that God's power is perfected in weakness and that death has meaning.[513] To maintain the theology of glory in a medical setting, the "glorious" doctor can never let on that a cure is not available and that death is inevitable. Indeed, death is seen by the "glorious doctor" as a failure of medicine to be resisted at all costs. Conversely, the theology of the Cross is a theology of reconciliation and redemption. Swinton concludes that "the comfort and consolation of the theology of the Cross comes not from naïve optimism or malignant stoicism, but from the knowledge that where there is suffering, there is God and where God is, there is the hope of redemption."[514]

Swinton's view is compatible with the theology of suffering offered here in that each recognizes that suffering is linked both to God and redemption and that death is inevitable in God's plan. In the theology of suffering, suffering motivates a return to God in part because it reminds humans of their mortality. The theology of glory that Swinton describes militates against this because people are led to believe that medical technology can cure any problem, robbing suffering of its motivational power to drive people to God. Therefore, both physicians and patients must recognize that God is the Master of life and death, Who will ultimately decide when to call a person home. This forces medical practitioners to think of their role in a different way.

Largely in reaction to and as an antidote for what Swinton calls "glorious medicine," notes Farr Curlin, hospice and palliative medicine (HPM) has risen up as an alternative form of treating

[513] Ibid., 116-126.
[514] Ibid., 127.

the dying.[515] He observes, however, that when HPM seeks to end rather than mitigate suffering, it frustrates and even circumvents the possibility of dying well by removing the capacities that make suffering possible.[516] In other words, rendering a person terminally unconscious through sedation, while it relieves the suffering, also precludes the patient from carrying out any of the activities associated with a good death. He advocates focusing HPM care on creating the conditions needed for patients to engage in the tasks of dying well.

To be sure, not all physicians view themselves beholden to the Baconian project. In contrast, Edmund Pellegrino and David Thomasma describe the role of the Christian physician as a special relationship with their patients that carries with it significant moral obligations.

> A Christian physician has the same vocation as all Christian persons: to fulfill oneself in giving oneself to others: to family, friends, neighbors, strangers. In addition, as a physician, the Christian person is called to a special way of love, of giving oneself in one's daily works of healing, helping, curing, and caring. Physicians and patients are persons interacting in a specific existential situation in which one is vulnerable and suffering and seeks healing for another who offers to help and heal. By its nature, the healing relationship is unequal. The patient's personhood is exposed to and by the physician—bodily, spiritually,

---

[515] Farr A. Curlin, "Hospice and Palliative Medicine's Attempt at an Art of Dying" in *Dying in the Twenty-First Century: Toward a New Ethical Framework for the Art of Dying Well*, ed. Lydia S. Dugdale (Boston: MIT Press, 2015), 47.

[516] Ibid., 60.

and emotionally. The patient's need for affirmation as a person in the face of this exposure is intense and a source of moral obligation for the physician.[517]

If these obligations are not met, physicians can inhibit spiritual growth when they promise more than they can medically deliver and take on spiritual roles they were unqualified to fill. They can also cause suffering when they use their knowledge to harm (for example, via abortion, euthanasia, mutilation, or terminal sedation) or to exploit their patients for their own purposes. Medical professionals can cause great distress in their patients when they are insensitive to their insecurity about what is happening to them, especially when they deliberately keep the patient in the dark about his condition. Medical professionals can also damage a person's sense of dignity when they fail to treat him in a dignified manner or inhibit social support mechanisms. This, of course, puts considerable pressure on physicians to meet each patient's physical, emotional, and spiritual needs within a medical structure that is unsuited to support them.

All of this contributes to the suffering of the medical professionals themselves. There is a crisis in the medical community today that is commonly referred to as "physician burnout," but some experts believe a more accurate understanding is that they suffer from "moral injury."

Wendy Dean, MD, formerly a psychiatrist and now senior medical officer at the Henry M. Jackson Foundation for the Advancement of Military Medicine, says moral injury

---

[517] Edmund D. Pellegrino and David C. Thomasma, *The Christian Virtues in Medical Practice* (Washington, DC: Georgetown University Press, 1996), 144.

occurs when doctors feel they are impeded from doing what is best for their patients. Impediments can take a variety of forms, such as an insurer's unwillingness to pay for a medication or procedure, limits on appointment times set by the doctor's employer, or the need to score highly on patient satisfaction surveys.[518]

It is clear from the pervasiveness of the physician burnout and moral injury crises that substantive changes must be made in the way that both the public and the medical community see the role of the physician. This is suffering carrying out its task of determining when good is lacking and motivating the community to attain it. There are, of course, many people with theories to solve it. Part of the underlying problem that is not generally part of the discussion is that the failure of the medical community to recognize that the reason for suffering is a lack of spiritual good and that the physical aspects are symptoms. The reason many physicians cannot find joy in their work is that joy is the result of spiritual attainment which they are not currently pursuing.

Indeed, it would help if the medical practitioners saw themselves as instruments of God's mercy who can mitigate symptoms and delay death to allow people the opportunity to meet their familial, ecclesial, and societal obligations. If they behaved according to this principle, they would never use terminal sedation or euthanasia, for each inhibits patients from fulfilling their obligations, nor would they simply keep their bodies alive in "medicalized death." Further, by offering nothing more than a mitigation of symptoms

---

[518] Jeffrey Bendix, "The Real Reason Docs Burn Out," *Medical Economics* 96, no. 2 (January 16, 2019), https://www.medicaleconomics.com/business/real-reason-docs-burn-out.

and a delay in death, the medical practitioner does not decouple illness and injury from the sense of finitude that they should impart to the patient, which is the source of its power to bring people to search for God. Instead of treating death as a failure of medicine, they ought to take the opportunity of impending death to facilitate a good death for their patient. This would generate joy for them, for their patients, and for their patients' loved ones.

Ultimately, the change that is required is for physicians to recognize that the person is a unity of body and soul and that healing must encompass both. This can be done most readily in the Catholic Health Care System, which by directive is pre-disposed to this view, even if many of the people utilizing it are not. In fact, in the general introduction to the current (sixth) edition of *The Ethical and Religious Directives for Catholic Health Care Services*, the USCCB notes that "the Church has always sought to embody our Savior's concern for the sick."[519] It goes on to remind us that:

> Jesus' healing mission went further than caring only for physical affliction. He touched people at the deepest level of their existence; he sought their physical, mental, and spiritual healing (Jn 6:35, 11:25-27). He "came so that they might have life and have it more abundantly" (Jn 10:10).[520]

It further says:

> The healthcare professional has the knowledge and ex-perience to pursue the goals of healing, the maintenance

---

[519] USCCB, *The Ethical and Religious Directives for Catholic Health Care Services*, 6th ed. (June 2018), 6, http://www.usccb.org/about/doctrine/ethical-and-religious-directives/.
[520] Ibid.

of health, and the compassionate care of the dying, taking into account the patient's convictions and spiritual needs, and the moral responsibilities of all concerned. The person in need of healthcare depends on the skill of the healthcare provider to assist in preserving life and promoting health of body, mind, and spirit. The patient, in turn, has a responsibility to use these physical and mental resources in the service of moral and spiritual goals to the best of his or her ability.[521]

This final point is important because it highlights the responsibility that physicians have in healing the soul of the patient in a way that can be translated to other Christian vocations. As Pellegrino and Thomasma pointed out, all Christian vocations are fulfilled in the giving of one's self to the other.[522] This service to the other is consistent with Jesus' teaching the apostles to serve one another through the washing of their feet at the Last Supper.[523] Thus, it is part of the Christian calling to serve those in need and it can be done in any job or vocation that is aligned to God's Kingdom. This is true whether someone is a doctor, or a plumber, or a farmer, or a member of any other profession which has the potential to alleviate suffering in others. As St. Paul said in his First Letter to the Corinthians, "There are many parts but only one body."[524]

Suffering and Spiritual Care

As discussed throughout this book, the reason suffering exists is to drive us from material to spiritual goods, with the ultimate goal

[521] Ibid.
[522] Pellegrino and Thomasma, *Christian Virtues*, 144.
[523] John 13:1-20.
[524] 1 Corinthians 13:12.

being the attainment of the joy associated with sharing in the life and nature of God. For this reason, it is the clergy, chaplains, and catechists who provide spiritual care that potentially have the greatest impact on reducing human suffering. Because we cannot aspire to complete self-giving on our own, particularly in our fallen state, we need sacramental aid to attain the graces that are required to progress fully in the pathway of the Lord. But to educate and prepare people for the sacraments, we also need good catechesis.

In the last half-century, many secular medical institutions, including hospices and hospitals, have begun to employ chaplains as part of their total care for the patient. Because these institutions serve a religiously diverse clientele, these chaplains are restricted from espousing any particular religious beliefs so as not to offend any patients. Their role as part of the full medical team is generally to assess the spiritual needs of the patient and to provide comfort and counseling using generic humanist techniques. The major supporter of "generic" chaplaincy is the medical community itself, which has an interest in managing all aspects of patient care including their spiritual needs. Jeffrey Bishop describes this as "totalizing" care.[525] Chaplains in the system have goals, measurements, and improvement plans like all other members of the medical team and must produce tangible benefits in terms of patient outcomes, compliance, and satisfaction in order to stay employed.[526]

---

[525] Bishop, *Anticipatory Corpse*, 255.

[526] H. Tristram, Engelhardt, Jr., "The Dechristianization of Christian Hospital Chaplaincy: Some Bioethics Reflections on Professionalization, Ecumenization, and Secularization," *Christian Bioethics* 9, no. 1 (2003): 139-160.

Beyond the medical community, generic chaplaincy has some support from religious communities, particularly those with limited resources and personnel. Christopher Swift says that in England, secular institutions provide an outlet for the Church of England to place pastors who are not suitable for parish work at no cost to the Church.[527] Others believe that the opportunity to be with the sick and the dying, even under the constraints of "generic" chaplaincy, is beneficial.

Generic chaplaincy can be appealing to those patients who are hostile to religion but who will be comforted by generic counseling without the threat of proselytization. As Dorothee Söelle describes in *Suffering*, the first step necessary to resolve suffering is to talk about it.[528] Some people are content with having someone there to listen, which is the main role of a generic chaplain. As described previously, being there to listen is important because it recognizes the dignity and worth of the sufferer. However, it does not help the person get to Heaven.

The critics of generic chaplaincy, and there are many, start with the problem that secular institutions will allow no real religious content, limiting chaplains to psychology instead of theology. Allen Verhey describes a dying friend's experience with the Catholic chaplain in a secular hospital as an example.[529] The friend was looking for the priest to help him reconcile with God, but all the priest would do, per his charter with his employer, was discuss how the man was feeling. This is a devastating indictment of the generic chaplains and the institutions they serve because

---

[527] Christopher Swift, *Hospital Chaplaincy in the Twenty-first Century* (New York: Taylor and Francis, 2014), 171-172.

[528] Söelle, *Suffering*, 70-71.

[529] Verhey, *The Christian Art of Dying*, 71-72.

they fail to comprehend the reason that they are needed. Many people suffer because they lack the greatest good in their lives: the presence of God. When they finally seek Him in the waning moments of their lives, the generic chaplain may lack the charter and sacramental authority to help them. With their eternal souls in the balance, this failure is a tragedy and a travesty of the highest magnitude.

Beyond the fact that generic chaplains cannot meet the religious needs of their patients, commentators like Corrina Delkeskamp-Hayes and H. Tristram Engelhardt are concerned that they are also doing damage to their own souls.[530] This occurs in two ways. The first is that the generic chaplain can only give advice that is approved by the employing institution. In most cases, this means that the chaplain is propagating a religious view consistent with secular humanism as opposed to what he truly believes. This is not only a lie but an abdication of his missionary mandate. Secondly, the chaplain may be party to actions that are opposed to his own religious beliefs. For instance, a Catholic chaplain employed by a secular hospital might be forced to advocate for terminal sedation if he wants to keep his job. This would put him in the position of cooperating with evil to maintain his employment.

Anthony Fisher points out that the Catholic Church's interest in hospitals is to heal both body and soul. To do that, the Church

---

[530] H. Tristram Engelhardt, "Generic Chaplaincy: Providing Spiritual Care in a Post-Christian Age," *Christian Bioethics* 4, no. 3 (2010): 231-238; Corinna Delkeskamp-Hayes, "The Price of Being Conciliatory: Remarks about Mellon's Model for Hospital Chaplaincy Work in Multi-Faith Settings," *Christian Bioethics* 9, no. 1 (2003): 69-78.

must resist secular influences in its hospitals.[531] In much the same way, the Church must resist the temptation to permit Catholic chaplains to work for secular institutions. Instead, it must negotiate guest privileges in these institutions that allow them to minister to Catholics as Catholics and to any others who are interested in their services. It should not accept any limitations in this mission because to do so would prevent chaplains from carrying out their missionary mandate and, more importantly, it would not allow them to provide adequately the spiritual resources that the terminal sufferers so desperately need. This means that the devout can get sacraments from their pastor and the agnostics who are searching for God can talk to a Catholic priest rather than a "generic" chaplain provided by secular institutions, who can provide neither specific religious content nor any sacraments in their last chance to reconcile with God.

Ultimately, good spiritual care requires effective catechesis, the sacraments, and an understanding of the theology of suffering. These will set people on the path to righteousness and will help them understand when suffering arises that it exists to put them back on the path when they start to deviate from it. The Church must ensure that these tools are available to all, but it is the responsibility of the people to make use of these tools since they have free will.

As the three examples (physical, medical, and spiritual caregivers) showed, an increase of suffering, whether experienced by us or by the people we serve, is an indication that we are not fulfilling our purpose, and it should motivate us to refine how we are doing the job or to find one that has meaning for us. When

---

[531] Anthony Fisher, *Catholic Bioethics for a New Millennium* (Cambridge: Cambridge University Press, 2011), 275-301.

we find our role, whether it be what we do to make a living or some separate activity such as coaching, teaching, or working in a soup kitchen, it leaves us energized and happy. Look for that sense of joy, because that is the sign that God gives us when we are fulfilling His plan for us, just as we will suffer with an empty feeling and fatigue when we fail to carry out God's plan for us.

19

The Joy in Finding Meaning in Suffering

Joy is our ability to sense spiritual attainment, the carrot to the stick of suffering, which guides us home along the path of righteousness as surely as a beacon in a stormy harbor. At the beginning of our spiritual journey, it can be hard to see the joy; particularly when we are experiencing suffering as God guides us toward His plan for us. However, as we proceed through the four tasks of suffering, learning to love, while at the same time learning of God's love for us, our suffering begins to take on meaning. In the very first paragraph of *Salvifici doloris*, St. John Paul II asserts that when St. Paul declared to the Colossians, "Now I rejoice in my sufferings for your sake," his joy came from the discovery of the meaning of suffering.[532] In a very real way, this is the basis for the entire apostolic letter, a work that the pope completed shortly after his recovery from an assassination attempt. Later in the document, perhaps speaking of his own personal experience, St. John Paul II writes: "It is when the salvific meaning of suffering descends to man's level and becomes the individual's personal response that man finds in his suffering interior peace and even spiritual joy."[533]

[532] John Paul II, *Salvifici doloris*, 1, quoting Colossians 1:24.
[533] Ibid., 26.

Nor is St. John Paul II the only one to recognize that understanding the meaning of suffering can relieve it. Simone Weil, writing a half-century earlier, declared that "Only through contemplating Jesus on the cross in affliction and recognizing our solidarity with him in denying ourselves can affliction be relieved."[534] Speaking from a medical perspective, Eric Cassell notes that "Transcendence brings relief to the pain and deprivation—to the suffering itself—by giving it a meaning larger than the person."[535]

The ultimate message of the theology of suffering is one that provides the perspective that God loves us as only the Creator of the Universe could. He made us from dust and sustains us with every breath we take. He knows what is best for us but respects us enough to let us make our own choices. However, He does not leave us unaided or unattended. He sent Jesus to show us how to fulfill our destiny, and He gave us suffering to warn us when we leave the path that leads us to true happiness in His presence. He builds us up as an ecclesial community, providing the grace of the sacraments while calling on us to share our experiences with each other and to act in love to alleviate the suffering of our neighbors, just as the Good Samaritan did in Jesus' parable. In this way, the unity of the Church prefigures our ultimate union with God. The fact that suffering is uncomfortable and relentless when we deviate from the good is a sign of His mercy and love; it needs to be that way to motivate us to turn away from our vices because we are creatures of habit.

Understood properly, suffering gives us hope both for the Beatific Vision and the motivation to attain it. This perspective leads to joy and is consistent with the rest of the Christian

---

[534] Weil, "The Love of God," 464.
[535] Cassell, *The Nature of Suffering,* 44.

message based on the love and mercy of God and is therefore credible. It allows us to dismiss the view of suffering as the wrathful action of a vengeful God as an unfortunate interpretation of the facts based on a perspective limited to the physical world. There can also be joy in the knowledge that those who suffer are not guilty or whiners, as some would suppose, but are messengers of God's glory, called to share what they experience for the edification and salvation of their fellow humans.

There are two important reasons as to why there is joy in finding meaning in suffering. The first, unmentioned by any of the commentators, is to recognize that God wants us to share in His life every bit as much as the father desired to share his life with the Prodigal Son in Jesus' parable.[536] The realization that God has provided humans with the ability to sense whenever they stray from the path He set out for their happiness and fulfillment is a huge cause for joy. There should be great joy in the realization that suffering is God leading us home like a divine beacon, highlighting all obstacles that would keep us from His love, rather than an act of spite as sometimes claimed by society.

As described by St. John Paul II and other commentators, the second reason for joy is that our suffering has purpose when it is united to that of Christ and that it can lead to eternal life in the blissful presence of God, both for the sufferer and the person who aids him. In fact, it is joyful that God the Son deemed us worthy of emptying Himself and coming as the man Jesus to demonstrate how humans can love in a way that leads to eternal life, even dying on the Cross to show the unlimited

[536] Luke 15:11-32.

nature of His love.[537] We should rejoice in our ability to follow His example when we suffer for the benefit of others, and we should most assuredly rejoice when we understand that those who share in His suffering will also share in His glory.[538]

[537] John Paul II, *Salvifici doloris*, 22.
[538] Ibid.

Bibliography

Adams, Marilyn M. "Redemptive Suffering as a Christian Solution to the Problem of Evil." In *The Problem of Evil: Selected Readings*. 2nd ed. Edited by Michael L. Peterson. Notre Dame, IN: Notre Dame Press, 2017.

Adams, Robert. "Must God Create the Best." In *The Problem of Evil*. Edited by Michael L.Peterson. Notre Dame, IN: University of Notre Dame Press, 2017.

Ambrose. "Death as a Good (*De bono mortis*)." In *Seven Exegetical Works*. Edited by Michael P. McHugh. Washington, DC: Catholic University of America Press, 1972.

American Cancer Society. *Cancer Facts & Figures 2019*. Atlanta: American Cancer Society, 2019.

Arendt, Hannah. *Eichmann in Jerusalem: A Report on the Banality of Evil*. New York: Penguin Books, 1994.

Aristotle. *Nicomachean Ethics*. Translated by Robert C. Bartlett and Susan D. Collins. Chicago: University of Chicago Press, 2011.

Augustine. *The City of God against the Pagans*. Edited and translated by R. W. Dyson. New York: Cambridge University Press, 1998.

———. "Epistle 93," *New Advent*, 408. http://www.newadvent.org/fathers/1102093.htm.

Banner, Michael. *The Ethics of Everyday Life: Moral Theology, Social Anthropology and the Imagination of the Human.* New York: Oxford University Press, 2014.

Bendix, Jeffrey. "The Real Reason Docs Burn Out." *Medical Economics* 96, no. 2 (January 16, 2019). https://www.medical economics.com/business/real-reason-docs-burn-out.

Benedict XVI. *Encyclical Letter: Spe salvi.* Vatican City: Libreria Editrice Vaticana, 2007.

Bishop, Jeffrey P. *The Anticipatory Corpse: Medicine, Power, and the Care of the Dying.* Notre Dame, IN: University of Notre Dame, 2011.

Boltanski, Luc and Graham D. Burchell. *Distant Suffering: Morality, Media and Politics.* New York: Cambridge University Press: 1999.

Bonaventure. *The Life of St. Francis of Assisi.* Edited by Cardinal Manning. Rockford, Ill: Tan Books and Publishers, 1988.

Brown, Joanne Carlson and Rebecca Parker. "For God So Loved the World?" In *Christianity, Patriarchy, and Abuse: A Feminist Critique.* Edited by Joanne Carlson Brown and Carole R. Bohn. New York: Pilgrim Press, 1989.

Butt, Leslie. "The Suffering Stranger: Medical Anthropology and International Morality." *Medical Anthropology* 21 (2002): 1-24.

Cahill, Lisa Sowle. *Theological Bioethics: Participation, Justice, Change.* Washington, DC: Georgetown University Press: 2005.

Cassell, Eric J. *The Nature of Suffering and the Goals of Medicine.* 2nd ed. New York: Oxford, 2004.

Catholic Church. *Catechism of the Catholic Church.* 2nd ed. Vatican City: Libreria Editrice Vaticana, 2000.

————. *Compendium: Catechism of the Catholic Church.* Washington: USCCB, 2016.

Cicero, Marcus Tullius. *Tusculan Disputations.* Translated by Andrew P. Peabody. Boston: Little, Brown and Company, 1886.

Commins, Gary. "Is Suffering Redemptive? Historical and Theological Reflections on Martin Luther King Jr." *Sewanee Theological Review* 51, no. 1 (Christmas 2007): 61-80.

Curlin, Farr A. "Hospice and Palliative Medicine's Attempt at an Art of Dying." In *Dying in the Twenty-First Century: Toward a New Ethical Framework for the Art of Dying Well.* Edited by Lydia S. Dugdale. Boston: MIT Press, 2015.

Delkeskamp-Hayes, Corinna. "The Price of Being Conciliatory: Remarks about Mellon's Model for Hospital Chaplaincy Work in Multi-Faith Settings." *Christian Bioethics* 9, no. 1 (2003): 69-78.

Didache. Translated by M. B. Riddle. From *Ante-Nicene Fathers.* Vol. 7. Edited by Alexander Roberts, James Donaldson, and A. Cleveland Coxe. Buffalo, NY: Christian Literature Publishing Co., 1886. Revised and edited for New Advent by Kevin Knight. http://www.newadvent.org/fathers/0714.htm.

Eiesland, Nancy L. *The Disabled God: Toward a Liberatory Theology of Disability.* Nashville, TN: Abingdon Press: 1994.

Elliot, David. "Defining the Relationship Between Health and Well-being in Bioethics." *New Bioethics* 22, no. 1 (2016): 14-16.

Engelhardt, H. Tristram, Jr. "The Dechristianization of Christian Hospital Chaplaincy: Some Bioethics Reflections on Professionalization, Ecumenization, and Secularization." *Christian Bioethics* 9, no. 1 (2003): 139-160.

————. "Generic Chaplaincy: Providing Spiritual Care in a Post-Christian Age." *Christian Bioethics: Non-ecumenical Studies in Medical Morality* 4, no. 3.

Fergusson, David. *The Providence of God: A Polyphonic Approach.* New York: Cambridge University Press, 2018.

Ferngren, Gary B. *Medicine and Health Care in Early Christianity.* Baltimore: Johns Hopkins Press, 2009.

Fisher, Anthony. *Catholic Bioethics for a New Millennium.* Cambridge: Cambridge University Press, 2011.

Francis. "Address to Participants in the Meeting organized by the Pontifical Council for the Promotion of the New Evangelization, 11 October 2017." In *L'Osservatore Romano*, 13 October 2017.

———. *Laudato si': On Care for Our Common Home.* San Francisco: Ignatius Press, 2015.

Frontline. "Merchants of Cool." Produced by Barak Goodman and Rachel Dretzin. PBS, 2001. http://www.pbs.org/wgbh/pages/frontline/shows/cool/view/.

Gandhi, Mahatma. *The Essential Gandhi.* Edited by Louis Fischer. New York: Vintage Spiritual Classics, 2002.

Griffin, David Ray. "Divine Persuasion Rather than Coercion" in *The Problem of Evil: Selected Readings,* 2nd ed. Notre Dame, IN: University of Notre Dame Press, 2017.

Grimes, William. "Nancy Mairs, Who Wrote About Infirmities, Dies at 73." *New York Times,* December 8, 2016, sec. A. https://www.nytimes.com/2016/12/07/books/nancy-mairs-dead-author.html.

Grisez, Germain. *The Way of the Lord Jesus.* Vol. 2. *Living a Christian Life.* Quincy, Ill: Franciscan Press, 1993.

Hauerwas, Stanley. *Suffering Presence: Theological Reflections on Medicine, the Mentally Handicapped, and the Church.* Notre Dame, IN: Notre Dame Press, 1986.

Herdt, Jennifer. *Putting on Virtue: The Legacy of the Splendid Vices.* Chicago: University of Chicago Press, 2008.

Hitchcock, James. *History of the Catholic Church: From the Apostolic Age to the Third Millennium.* San Francisco: Ignatius Press, 2012.

Ignatius. *Saint Ignatius of Loyola: Personal Writings.* Translated with introductions and notes by Joseph A. Munitiz and Philip Endean. New York: Penguin, 1996.

Jerome. "Commentary on Jonah." *Aquinas Study Bible,* chapter 1.11. https://sites.google.com/site/aquinasstudybible/home/jonah/st-jerome-on-jonah/chapter-1.

John Paul II. *Apostolic Letter: Salvifici doloris.* Vatican City: Libreria Editrice Vaticana, 1984, AAS 76: 201-50.

———. *Encyclical Letter, Fides et ratio, of the Supreme Pontiff John Paul II: To the Bishops of the Catholic Church on the Relationship between Faith and Reason.* Vatican City: Libreria Editrice Vaticana 1998.

———. "Homily for the Canonization of Saint Maximilian Maria Kolbe." Vatican (October 10, 1982). https://www.piercedhearts.org/jpii/jpii_homilies/homilies_1982/oct_10_1982_canonization_max_kolbe.htm.

Koenig, Harold and Andrew J. Weaver. *Pastoral Care of Older Adults.* Minneapolis: Fortress Press, 1998.

Konstan, David. "Epicurus." *The Stanford Encyclopedia of Philosophy.* 2014 ed. http://plato.stanford.edu/archives/sum2014/entries/epicurus/.

Kukin, Marrick. "Tay-Sachs and the Abortion Controversy." *Journal of Religion and Health* 20, no. 3 (Fall 1981): 224-242.

Kushner, Harold S. *When Bad Things Happen to Good People.* New York: Avon Books, 1981.

Lactantius. *"De Ira Dei."* Translated by William Fletcher. From *Ante-Nicene Fathers.* Vol. 7. Edited by Alexander Roberts, James Donaldson, and A. Cleveland Coxe. Buffalo, NY: Christian Literature Publishing Co., 1886. Revised and edited

for New Advent by Kevin Knight. http://www.newadvent
.org/fathers/0703.htm.

Leibniz, Gottfried. "Best of All Possible Worlds." In *The Problem of Evil*. Edited by Michael L. Peterson. Notre Dame, IN: University of Notre Dame Press, 2017.

Leo XIII. *Encyclical Letter, Aeterni patris: On the Restoration of Christian Philosophy*. Vatican City: Libreria Editrice Vaticana, 1879.

LisbonLisboaPortugal.com. "The Lisbon Earthquake of 1755." https://lisbonlisboaportugal.com/Lisbon-information/1755-lisbon-earthquake.html.

Lysaught, M. Therese. "Suffering in Communion with Christ." In *Living Well and Dying Faithfully: Christian Practices for End-of-Life Care*. Edited by John Swinton and Richard Payne. Grand Rapids, MI: Eerdmans, 2009.

Mackie, J. L. "Evil and Omnipotence." In *The Problem of Evil: Selected Readings*, 2nd ed. Notre Dame, IN: University of Notre Dame Press: 2017.

McKenny, Gerard. "Bioethics, the Body, and the Legacy of Bacon." In *On Moral Medicine: Theological Perspectives on Medical Ethics*. Edited by M. Therese Lysaught, Joseph J. Kotva, Jr., Stephen E. Lammers and Allen Verhey. Grand Rapids, MI: Eerdmans, 2012.

McLean, Athena. *The Person in Dementia: A study of Nursing Home Care in the US*. Ontario, CA: Broadview Press, 2007.

NIH. "Tay-Sachs Disease Information Page." https://www
.ninds.nih.gov/Disorders/All-Disorders/Tay-Sachs-Disease
-Information-Page.

Norris, Kathleen. "The Gift of a Difficult Life." *The New York Times*, June 13, 1993, sec. 7. https://www.nytimes
.com/1993/06/13/books/the-gift-of-a-difficult-life.html.

Nussbaum, Martha. *The Therapy of Desire: Theory and Practice in Hellenistic Ethics*. Princeton, N.J.: Princeton University Press, 2009.

O'Brien, Barbara. "Who Was the Buddha?" In *Lion's Roar: Buddhist Wisdom for Our Time*, May 29, 2018. https://www.lionsroar.com/who-was-the-buddha/.

Paul VI. *Apostolic Constitution: Sacrament of the Anointing of the Sick*. 1972.

Pauw, Amy Plantinga. "Dying Well." In *Living Well and Dying Faithfully: Christian Practices for End-of-Life Care*. Edited by John Swinton and Richard Payne. Grand Rapids, MI: Eerdmans, 2009.

Pellegrino, Edmund D. and David C. Thomasma. *The Christian Virtues in Medical Practice*. Washington, DC: Georgetown University Press, 1996.

Peterson, Michael L., ed. *The Problem of Evil: Selected Readings*. 2nd ed. Notre Dame, IN: University of Notre Dame Press: 2017.

Pettinger, Tejvan. "Biography of Bernadette Soubirous," Oxford, UK. November 24, 2007. Updated March 21, 2017. www.biographyonline.net.

Pew Research Center. "US Becoming Less Religious." Pew Research Center. November 3, 2015. https://www.pewforum.org/2015/11/03/u-s-public-becoming-less-religious.

———. "In U.S., Decline of Christianity Continues at Rapid Pace: An Update on America's Changing Religious Landscape." October 17, 2019. https://www.pewforum.org/2019/10/17/in-us-decline-of-christianity-continues-at-rapid-pace/.

Pinckaers, Servais. "Aquinas's Pursuit of Beatitude." In *The Pinckaers Reader: Renewing Thomistic Moral Theology*. Edited by

John Berkman and Craig Steven Titus. Washington, DC: Catholic University Press of America, 2005.

————. *Morality: The Catholic View*. Translated by Michael Sherwin. South Bend, IN: St. Augustine's Press, 2003.

Public Health Division, Center for Health Statistics Oregon Health Authority. "Oregon Death with Dignity Act, 2018 Data Summary." Revised April 25, 2019. https://www.oregon .gov/oha/PH/providerpartnerresources/evaluationresearch /deathwithdignityact/Documents/year21.pdf.

Quinn, Mattie. "The Loneliness Epidemic." *Governing* 31 no. 8 (May 2018): 53.

Quinn, Philip. "God, Moral Perfection and Possible Worlds." In *The Problem of Evil*. Edited by Michael L. Peterson. Notre Dame, IN: University of Notre Dame Press, 2017.

Robinson, Paschal. "St. Francis of Assisi." *The Catholic Encyclopedia*. Vol. 6. New York: Robert Appleton Company, 1909. http://www.newadvent.org/cathen/06221a.htm.

Ruse, Michael. "Genetics and the Quality of Life." *Social Indicators Research* 7, no. 1/4 (January 1980): 419-441.

Samuelson, Scott. *Seven Ways of Looking at Pointless Suffering*. Chicago: University of Chicago Press, 2018.

Saunders, John. "God, Evil, and Relational Risk" in *The Problem of Evil: Selected Readings*, 2nd ed. Notre Dame, IN: University of Notre Dame Press, 2017.

Schroeder, H. J. "The Canons of the Fourth Lateran Council, 1215." *Disciplinary Decrees of the General Councils: Text, Translation and Commentary*. St. Louis: B. Herder, 1937.

Söelle, Dorothee. *Suffering*. Philadelphia: Fortress Press, 1975.

Somin, Ilya. "Lessons from a Century of Communism." *The Washington Post*, November 7, 2017. https://www.washington

post.com/news/volokh-conspiracy/wp/2017/11/07/lessons
-from-a- century-of-communism/.

Stump, Eleanor. "The Problem of Evil." *Faith and Philosophy* 2,
no. 4 (October 1985): 392-423.

Swinton, John. *Dementia: Living in the Memories of God*. Grand
Rapids, MI: Eerdmans, 2012.

———. "Why Me, Lord?" In *Living Well and Dying Faithfully:
Christian Practices for End-of-Life Care*. Edited by John Swinton and Richard Payne. Grand Rapids, MI: Eerdmans, 2009.

Swinton, John, and Richard Payne. "Christian Practices and the
Art of Dying Faithfully." In *Living Well and Dying Faithfully:
Christian Practices for End-of-Life Care*. Edited by John Swin-
ton and Richard Payne. Grand Rapids, MI: Eerdmans, 2009.

Swift, Christopher. *Hospital Chaplaincy in the Twenty-first Century*. New York: Taylor and Francis, 2014.

Tertullian "Tertullian Quotes," Brainyquote.com. https://www.
brainyquote.com/authors/tertullian-quotes.

Thomas Aquinas. *Summa Theologica*. Translated by the Fathers of
the English Dominican Province, 1920. New York: Benziger
Bros., 1948.

USCCB. *The Ethical and Religious Directives for Catholic Health
Care Services*. 6th ed. June 2018. http://www.usccb.org/about
/doctrine/ethical-and-religious-directives/.

Vaghi, Peter. "Faith in Focus: Challenge and Opportunity."
America, October 31, 2005.

VandenBerg, Mary. "Redemptive Suffering: Christ's Alone." *Scottish Journal of Theology* 60, no. 4 (November 2007): 394-411.

van Inwagen, Peter. *The Problem of Evil*. New York: Oxford, 2006.

Verhey, Allen. *The Christian Art of Dying: Learning from Jesus*.
Grand Rapids, MI: Eerdmans, 2011.

Wall Street. DVD. Directed by Oliver Stone. 20th Century Fox Home Entertainment, 2000.

Weigel, George. *The Truth of Catholicism: Inside the Essential Teaching and Controversies of the Church Today*. New York: Harper, 2002.

Weil, Simone. "The Love of God and Affliction." In *The Simone Weil Reader*. Edited by George A. Panichas. New York: McKay, 1977.

Williams, Delores. *Sisters in the Wilderness: The Challenge of Womanist God-Talk*. Maryknoll, NY: Orbis Books, 1993.

World Health Organization. *Global Health Estimates 2016: Deaths by Cause, Age, Sex, by Country and by Region, 2000-2016*. Geneva: World Health Organization, 2018.

About the Author

Paul Chaloux was born in Maine in 1960 and grew up in Northern Virginia. After graduating with a chemical engineering degree from the University of Virginia in 1982, he worked for more than thirty years as an engineer, manager, and strategist for IBM in upstate New York. For fifteen years, he served as a catechist at St. Columba Parish in Hopewell Junction, New York.

In 2015, after earning a master's degree in religious education from Fordham University and retiring from IBM, he earned a Ph.D. in moral theology from the Catholic University of America.

Dr. Chaloux currently teaches theology as an adjunct professor at the Catholic University of America and serves as a catechist at St. Agnes Parish in Arlington, Virginia. He has been married for more than thirty years to his wife, Sue, and they have four adult children and two granddaughters.

Sophia Institute

Sophia Institute is a nonprofit institution that seeks to nurture the spiritual, moral, and cultural life of souls and to spread the Gospel of Christ in conformity with the authentic teachings of the Roman Catholic Church.

Sophia Institute Press fulfills this mission by offering translations, reprints, and new publications that afford readers a rich source of the enduring wisdom of mankind.

Sophia Institute also operates the popular online resource CatholicExchange.com. *Catholic Exchange* provides world news from a Catholic perspective as well as daily devotionals and articles that will help readers to grow in holiness and live a life consistent with the teachings of the Church.

In 2013, Sophia Institute launched Sophia Institute for Teachers to renew and rebuild Catholic culture through service to Catholic education. With the goal of nurturing the spiritual, moral, and cultural life of souls, and an abiding respect for the role and work of teachers, we strive to provide materials and programs that are at once enlightening to the mind and ennobling to the heart; faithful and complete, as well as useful and practical.

Sophia Institute gratefully recognizes the Solidarity Association for preserving and encouraging the growth of our apostolate over the course of many years. Without their generous and timely support, this book would not be in your hands.

www.SophiaInstitute.com
www.CatholicExchange.com
www.SophiaInstituteforTeachers.org

Sophia Institute Press® is a registered trademark of Sophia Institute.
Sophia Institute is a tax-exempt institution as defined by the
Internal Revenue Code, Section 501(c)(3). Tax ID 22-2548708.